"ALWAYS BRING A CROWD!"

Dedication

To the Wisconsin Steel workers whose fighting spirit, multiracial unity and endurance have inspired us and set an example for all workers.

"ALWAYS BRING A CROWD!"

The story of
FRANK LUMPKIN
Steelworker

Beatrice Lumpkin

INTERNATIONAL PUBLISHERS, New York

Acknowledgments

This book came into print thanks to the encouragement and expertise of Betty Smith, president of International Publishers. I thank Peggy Lipschutz for the cover design and Jonnie Lumpkin Ellis, Bessie Mae Lumpkin Slifkin, John Woodford, George Meyers, Michael Honey, Fred Gaboury, Larry McGurty, George Edwards, Denise Winebrenner, Oliver Mongomery, Rose and Emil Shaw, Christy Kosary, Bobby Wood, Scott and Corey Marshal, Claudia Zazlavsky and Beth Lehman, who read the manuscript and made valuable suggestions. Soren Schulein, my grandson, provided vital technical support. Any errors are mine alone.

Photographs: Permission to use photographs was kindly granted by the *Chicago Tribune*, the *Chicago Sun-Times*, the Southeast Historical Society, the *Chicago Defender* and the *Daily Southtown*, successor to the *Daily Calumet*. We thank Larry Ruehl, photography director of the *Daily Southtown* for his help, and photographers Warren Lumpkin and Scott Marshall who donated many of their photographs.

Cover credits: Design by Peggy Lipschutz. *Tribune* photo by James Mayo, the *Chicago Tribune*, June 30 1982, front cover. Back cover, photo by Scott Marshall.

Copyright ©1999 Beatrice Lumpkin

First edition, 1999 International Publishers Co., New York

Printed in Canada

Library of Congress Cataloging-in-Publication Data

Lumpkin, Beatrice.
    "Always bring a crowd" : the story of Frank Lumpkin / Beatrice
Lumpkin.
        p.   cm.
    Includes bibliographical references and index.
    ISBN 0-7178-0725-8 (pbk. : alk. paper)
    1. Lumpkin, Frank, 1916-   . 2. Afro-American iron and steel
workers--United States Biography.   I. Title.
HD8039.I52U567   1999
331.6'396073--dc21
[B]   99-35042
                                                              CIP

Contents

List of Photographs

Foreword
Guys like Frank don't come around often.

Maybe, if you're lucky enough, you'll cross paths with someone like him within your own lifetime. Guys like Frank are truly American heroes. His untiring commitment to his family, his strong work ethic, his labor solidarity, political leadership, his devotion to his neighborhood—making it a better place in which to live—are all lessons from which to draw solid examples.

My association with Frank began in the fall of 1987. I was a labor relations specialist in the Personnel Office of the City of Chicago. Mayor Harold Washington had just brought formal collective bargaining to public employees in the City of Chicago. For one hundred years prior, unions operated on "hand shake" agreements with the city, exclusively, with the sitting mayor.

I happened to run into Frank while walking the halls of the 11th floor of City Hall. He had on his trademark hat, a type of fedora reminiscent of the 1930's—you know—labor's finest hour. He wears that hat to this day. I tend to believe that his wife Bea is the only person ever to see him without it on; that is if he's ever had it off. When we met, he had the most remarkable campaign button on his lapel. It was a picture of himself and it said that he was an Independent Progressive candidate for State Representative. It is one of the most cherished buttons in my collection.

Frank didn't know who I was at first. When I introduced myself and asked about the nature of his business that day, Frank said he was "looking for jobs for the people down on the South Side." I told

him my name was Sadlowski[*] and that struck an instant chord. He called me "Little Ed," and that's how I'm still known in the Save Our Jobs Committee. Everyone in Save Our Jobs is known only by a first name or a nickname. Hell, there are guys who worked together in the mill for 30 years, day in and day out, who only know each other by an alias. You know guys like Wagon, or Smiley, or Bubblenose, the Lawyer, or Chubbyboy.

When I met Frank in 1987, we were both very excited about the leadership that Harold Washington brought to the City of Chicago. I told Frank that I had marched with Save Our Jobs on March 28, 1981, on the first anniversary of the closing of the mill. A few hundred Wisconsin Steel workers and their supporters marched from the plant gates at 106th and Torrence, all the way to USWA Local 65

Edward E. Sadlowski campaigning for national president of USWA
Southeast Historical Society Photograph

[*] Edward A. Sadlowski, who was the only paid staff person of the Save Our Jobs Committee under a two-year foundation grant and an unpaid volunteer for four more years. He is the son of Edward E. Sadlowski, a former district director of the United Steel Workers of America AFL-CIO, who made labor history as a rank-and-file candidate for national president of his union.

located at 95th and South Chicago Avenue. I still vividly recall the day that the Wisconsin Steel mill closed, March 28, 1980. Word spread quickly through my high school, which was located less than one mile from the plant gates. Many of my classmates' brothers and fathers were employed there. Many of my own friends and neighbors spent their lives inside those gates. We all thought it was just another cyclical downturn in the industry, similar to the ones that had occurred for decades. It was no big deal, it would open back up within a month or so. Not this time!

In the fall of 1987, Mayor Washington had a massive heart attack and died literally at his desk, four floors directly beneath mine. Within months, the entire progressive coalition, which had been brought to City Hall by the late mayor, had either been fired or had quit. I was desperately seeking to do the latter. The atmosphere at City Hall was like a morgue, at least it was to me! I wanted out of the city service real bad. I wanted to return to my roots and my own family's legacy within the labor movement.

Enter Thomas Geoghegan [pronounced Gay-Gon]. Tom has been a friend of mine and my family for as long back as I can remember. I have been blessed with a lot of constants in my life. I consider Tom one of these. His law office is directly across from City Hall, and we would frequently lunch together while I was working for the city. I was always telling Tom about my yearning to do something more fulfilling, such as working in the labor movement. Then one day it happened. Tom mentioned that Frank and the Save Our Jobs Committee were looking for an executive director. Save Our Jobs had just secured a one-year grant to organize a not-for-profit organization to aid and assist dislocated steel workers and their families. Tens of thousands had been affected by the massive plant closings that cut across all of the steel mills of Chicago's Southeast Side. The grant would pay a staff person to provide services to this population of workers and their families. This was the same work that Frank has done for 17 years in the community on an unpaid basis.

After numerous meetings with the players involved, my wife Emilie and I decided to sit down with Frank and Bea and talk about the specifics concerning my career change. After five minutes at their dinner table, my mind was made up. Emilie, however, thought I was crazy to pass up a guaranteed paycheck with the city to work with a bunch of guys who had been thrown out on the street by their former employer seven years earlier. Save Our Jobs had trouble just paying the rent at the Steel Workers' Union Hall, let alone paying a wage. I knew that I had my work cut out for me.

At the Save Our Jobs office, I was welcomed like a guy who had spent his entire life within the plant gates. No one questioned my motives or my intentions. They were just happy to have a new face around who demonstrated interest in what their struggle was all about. Born in the neighborhood, and knowing hundreds of people who had worked at the Wisconsin Steel facility, I fit right in.

I must admit, looking back on my experience with Frank and the Save Our Jobs Committee, I learned more in the six years that I was actively involved than I learned in hundreds of hours of college courses that I have attended. For two years I was paid from grant money from various foundations. Hell, I should have been paying Frank for the education I was receiving. I got sucked in and wound up sticking around another four years on a volunteer basis.

Even with my limited involvement with the Save Our Jobs Committee, Frank to this day has an uncanny way of making me feel that without my help, the Save Our Jobs Committee would have never made it. This is his perfect strength as a leader and sets him apart from many others. He makes everyone who volunteers or contributes to the cause feel like they truly make all the difference in the world. It makes him a natural organizer.

Frank is real, no hidden agenda. He's uncompromising on positions or issues of principle when it comes to the men and the families of the Save Our Jobs Committee. If people are hungry, Frank makes sure that someone makes a trip to the Greater Chicago Food Depository for a truckload of food. If someone is having problems with a worker's compensation claim from years before, Frank organizes a workshop with free legal counseling. If people have an issue with their pension benefits, Frank calls the Pension Benefits Guarantee Corporation. When another person is cut off of an unemployment claim, Frank calls the local Congressman's office. Once he even organized a picket line in front of the Unemployment Office to help draw attention to the plight of those workers in the South Chicago community who were in need of work and were experiencing problems with their unemployment benefits.

That is Frank Lumpkin. If there is a union on strike anywhere within driving distance, that's where you'll find Frank, with a picket sign in his hand. When I was working with Save Our Jobs, we provided strike assistance to at least a dozen different unions who had hit the bricks.

During the years that I have known and have worked alongside of Frank, he has carried himself in a way that fits his hat, and the period of time that his hat reflects. You know, the 1930s and organized labor's finest hour—a time in which community efforts were focused on bettering the human condition. Much of what we as American workers have today was hard-won during the labor struggles of that period. My grandfather, who was a founding member of the United Steel Workers of America, always referred to the 1930's as "labor's finest hour." The CIO (Committee of Industrial Organizations) organized the unorganized. Their hard-won gains were often made with the supreme sacrifice by rank and file workers.

The efforts of the Steel Workers Organizing Committee (SWOC) to organize Republic Steel in 1937 was met by one of the most vicious attacks on American workers and their supporters. It happened in our neighborhood, on Memorial Day.

Men, women and children, dressed for the holiday, peacefully moved to establish a picket line at the main gate of Republic Steel. Suddenly, hundreds of armed Chicago police charged the picketers. Panic broke out. Unable to defend themselves, the marchers stumbled on top of each other. The police clubbed workers with batons and ax handles. More than 200 shots rang out in just seconds. By the time the smoke had cleared from the open prairie, over 40 marchers had gunshot wounds and ten workers were dead. All of the wounds inflicted on the workers were back or side wounds.

The union martyrs who gave their lives on Memorial Day, 1937, did not die in vain. More than fifty years after the Massacre, their story continues to be told as part of the oral tradition of Chicago's Southeast Side. We have an obligation to those who have gone before and given their lives in the struggle to secure a better way of life and to promote industrial democracy. The Wisconsin Steel workers have lived up to this obligation by engaging in collective struggle for justice for the last 17 years. Many Wisconsin Steel workers also lost their lives in *this* struggle, not through gunshot wounds but the slower death caused by the stress and hardships of unemployment and a closed mill.

Republic Steel Memorial Day Massacre, 1937.
Southeast Historical Society, 81-77-79K

My connection to Frank has been limited since I moved to Madison, Wisconsin with my wife Emilie and my daughters Faith and Evelyn. I now have steady employment in a union staff position. I enjoy working with the Madison Teacher's Union. My experience in working with Frank Lumpkin and the Save Our Jobs Committee has paid big dividends in my own awareness, abilities, work ethic and patience in servicing the needs of those I represent in my union. Whenever I have had the privilege of addressing the Save Our Jobs membership, I have always made it known to the fellows that I have been truly blessed to be able to be a part of what they have accomplished collectively. No matter where my travels have taken me within the labor movement, when people find out who I am and learn that I am a fourth-generation trade unionist from the Southeast Chicago steel community, the conversation immediately turns to Frank Lumpkin and his work with the Save Our Jobs Committee. Frank and the membership of Save Our Jobs have truly left their mark on the labor movement. I, too, will continue to carry on Frank's legacy.

Frank may have trouble remembering someone by name, or he may be completely unable to find what he's looking for in the Save Our Jobs office (no one can find anything they're looking for in that office). However, Frank Lumpkin is still one of the most resourceful human beings that I have ever met. For over 17 years now, on an unpaid basis, Frank has kept regular office hours and has provided complete servicing to members of the Save Our Jobs Committee and others in need who have come to the office. He has held annual dinners commemorating the closing of the mill. Even more impressive, Frank has held regular monthly Save Our Jobs meetings that are attended by a couple of hundred men each month since the closing of the mill that day of March 28, 1980.

Frank confessed to me at Christmas of 1996 that he was 80 years old. I told him that I was 34 years old. That means that when Frank and I crossed paths in 1981, he was 64 and I was 18. He continues to exhibit the vitality of a man half his age. And people keep insisting that I'm too young to be telling the stories that I tell.

Edward A. Sadlowski

"It's according to who writes the book. If the persons with the pen understood ideology, they could make a man or kill a man. Some can make a good story out of very little, pick all the positive points. Or you can get a reporter who picks all the negative points and has nothing. The reader must judge." Frank Lumpkin.

Preface

As Frank Lumpkin's wife and comrade, I witnessed and participated in the long battle to save pensions and benefits of thousands of workers at Chicago's Wisconsin Steel plant. For nearly 17 years they stuck together; they forced their employers to make two settlements. The last checks arrived for Christmas, 1996.

As the years rolled by, we realized that Wisconsin Steel workers were making history. They were proud that they were fighting for all workers, not only for themselves. Their goal was to stop any company from ever again dumping their workers without paying all the severance benefits. The steel workers gathered up a lot of help. Attorney Tom Geoghegan made a key contribution with his brilliant legal work. The United Steel Workers of America, AFL-CIO, and community organizations gave crucial support, including Citizen Action, the Greater Chicago Food Pantry, the Illinois Communist Party, local Catholic churches, the Center for Urban Economic Development of the University of Illinois, and many more.

This book is based on eyewitness accounts, newspaper and magazine articles, and other sources. Wisconsin Steel workers and their wives gladly gave hundreds of interviews for the record. They wanted justice and talked to anyone who would listen. An important source for the legal issues in the Wisconsin Steel workers' case is Tom Geoghegan's book, *Which Side Are You On?—Trying To Be For Labor When It's Flat On Its Back.*[1] Information on the Lumpkin family was supplied by Frank Lumpkin, his sisters Elizabeth (Bay) Rollins, Jonnie (Pat) Ellis and Bessie Mae Slifkin, and his brother Sam (Warren) Lumpkin. We also visited Washington, Georgia and Orlando, Florida for background materials.

Although I am not a poet, no other format could express the pain I felt when I saw hundreds of unemployed steel workers and their children standing in a Save Our Jobs food line. They waited for hours in a pouring, November rain. I tried to put those feelings into this poem.

Food Line

The crops are in; November rain is welcome
Rain readies the earth for the next spring planting.
In the big city, rain washes streets clean
But no one wants rain in South Chicago.

There's something new and terrible in steeltown!
The rain still pours down and the wind still cuts,
People stand in the rain for hours, waiting,
Their babies wrapped in blankets, wet with rain.

At the end of the wait—two bags of food
Handed out by grim-faced men, hearts hurting.
These are their brothers and sisters, all hungry
Years and years of working, and now the bread line.

A hurt anger is growing in the rain
Smoldering coals, wet with rain but still hot
Ready to burst into flame, red-hot flame
Needing only air and a clear direction.

Beatrice Lumpkin, Chicago, 1982

Families waiting in the rain for food (*Daily Calumet* photo, Nov. 16, 1982)

"ALWAYS BRING A CROWD!"

Hattie and Elmo Lumpkin and children, 1958

*"When they closed the plant, Harvester never, **ever** expected to have to pay the Wisconsin Steel workers!"* Tom Geoghegan

1. Introduction: Incredible Victory

It was to be the perfect corporate crime. Of course, directors of the companies* that owned Wisconsin Steel in Chicago thought of it as "good business." After 75 years of making profit on the workers at Wisconsin Steel, Harvester dumped the plant in a phony sale. Two years later, in March 1980, the mill closed without notice and without paying workers' wages or benefits. The in-house union, PSWU (Progressive Steel Workers Union), folded soon after the mill closed. Not one government agency would help the workers win justice. All too often faceless corporations get away with dumping workers, their pensions and their benefits. And they would have got away with it this time had it not been for Frank Lumpkin and the Save Our Jobs Committee.

Harvester had every reason to think they could get away with this crime. Their ace in the hole was a signed contract from PSWU giving up pension rights and plant closing benefits. But that is not what happened! Left leaderless and seemingly helpless, the workers found courage and strength among themselves to fight on, and win. Under the leadership of Frank Lumpkin, they formed a new organization, the Wisconsin Steel Save Our Jobs Committee (SOJ).

Frank Lumpkin did not put on a platform personality. Only his calm and confident manner distinguished him from the other workers in the hall. His confidence in the power of united, organized workers saw him through what turned out to be a 17-year struggle.

* International Harvester, now known as Navistar, owned the Wisconsin Steel mills in Chicago from 1902 to 1977. In 1977, Harvester loaned Envirodyne, a company with less than 20 employees, the money to "buy" Wisconsin Steel, a company with 3,500 employees. Workers charged that the sale was "fraudulent."

1

Seven hundred former Wisconsin Steel workers overflowed the union hall in 1988 but the room was strangely quiet. A packed union hall was a rare sight in South Chicago. Layoffs had thinned steel workers' ranks; union meetings rarely had more than 30 or 40. The hall was full of smoke but nobody objected, not even the former smokers who had given it up since they left the mill. Faces were somber. Instead of rejoicing, there were bitter thoughts about how long it had taken and the hundreds who had died before they could taste the victory.

Wisconsin Steel workers' meeting, March 27, 1980

They did not know that it would take eight years more for the Wisconsin Steel workers to win their second settlement in 1996, the last bit of justice they could win from the courts. The last settlement checks were mailed late in December 1996, almost 17 years after the mill closed in March, 1980.

For eight years the Wisconsin Steel workers had come to monthly Save Our Jobs Committee meetings to hear what Lumpkin had to say and to show support. They wanted to hear again the same optimistic report that they heard at every Save Our Jobs meeting. Lumpkin did not disappoint them.

The year before the big victory it was sub-zero outside. The windows were covered with ice but it was hot in the meeting room. The men's faces were alike, worn from a lifetime of hard physical work and the frustration of unemployment. The air was heavy—with steam, smoke, worry, and hope against hope. They looked up at the man who stood up to talk, unemployed like they were, but not beat. What could he tell them that he had not told them the month before, and the month before that, and almost every day for seven years? Wasn't he tired of saying the same thing, again and again? But in the faces that turned up to hear Lumpkin, there was a silent request. It was almost, "tell us that story again of how we're going to win."

Lumpkin always had something to say: "No, there is no news, but the outlook is good. It is really up to us, the workers, to make things happen. Yes, the lawyers are working, doing something on the case every day. No, they won't get paid until we get paid so you know they're moving as fast as they can. The judge is the boss. But it's really up to us. We can sit and wait while our people are dying every day and won't live to get their money. Or we can take action, remind people we're fighting and we need their support. We can join the unemployed demonstrations to extend unemployment benefits. Let people see that the Wisconsin Steel workers are supporting them. Maybe it won't benefit those of us who are too old to work. But it will benefit other workers. It will benefit our children. We'll carry our signs. The Wisconsin Steel workers Save Our Jobs Committee will be there, fighting for justice!

"We are going to win our case but we don't know how much and we don't know when. We can make it happen sooner by taking action now. People are dying every day for lack of heat. We can picket the gas company to turn the heat back on. The Wisconsin Steel workers care about people freezing without heat. Let's stay out there, where people can see us, and we will win."

Respected labor leaders told Lumpkin that it was hopeless, that he should quit "lying" to people about how they could win. Everything seemed to be against their struggle. Their in-plant union, PSWU, folded soon after plant gates were suddenly padlocked on March 28, 1980. Since the automatic dues check-off ended, no money flowed into the union treasury. PSWU had no reason to exist. Workers were left with nothing—no jobs, no pensions, no health benefits. Even the last paychecks bounced. Local 65 of the United Steel Workers Union AFL-CIO was sympathetic and provided a meeting place. But what else could they do for non-members? The company had pulled a dirty, fraudulent deal, but the workers had no money to go to court. Harvester had every reason to think that they had succeeded in dumping the pensions by "selling" the mill to Envirodyne. They had not reckoned with Frank Lumpkin and the fighting potential of the workers and their families.

The workers' choice was simple, summed up by Lumpkin: "Fight or die!" Thousands of workers followed Lumpkin's lead and decided to fight. Every step of the way was hard and slow. Frank often said, "I'm a very patient man." For over a year after the mill closed, lawyers offered sympathy but not one would touch the Wisconsin Steel workers' case. The case required an expensive, long-term commitment with no chance of recovering costs for many years. And the unemployed workers had no money. At last a young labor lawyer named Tom Geoghegan convinced the head of his law firm, Leon Despres, to let him take the case on a contingency basis. That meant the lawyers would work without pay until, and if, the case was won.

Who Is Frank Lumpkin?

Who is this Frank Lumpkin whose grass roots organization foiled a big company's plans to dump workers' pensions and benefits? He had never been in the limelight before. In his 30 years inside the plant he was known as one of the best workers—never late, never absent, never refusing to work overtime. If anything, he was on the quiet side. His technical skills had won him promotion to the tool room. He had even put in a few years as a foreman, a position he had accepted to encourage promotion of African Americans in the plant.

As the Wisconsin Steel workers' struggle attracted media attention, reporters and authors began to write about Lumpkin and the steel workers. Their descriptions sometimes missed the mark. Bensman and Lynch, in *Rusted Dreams* wrote: "Frank Lumpkin's face is worn and his body stooped."[2] A very different picture of Frank was painted by John F. Wasik in *The Progressive*: "He commands attention with his barrel chested form and anvil nose."[3] The workers thought of Lumpkin as a man not to trifle with—the ex-boxer who stayed in shape.

Frank Lumpkin was born into a strong family that had survived slavery, wars, depressions, and lynchings, and has every intention of surviving capitalism as well. The story begins in Washington-Wilkes County, Georgia.

Part I

Little boy sat on the burning deck
Eating peanuts by the peck.

2. Red Earth and Blue Stone

There is no official record to show that Frank Lumpkin was ever born. The State of Georgia has no record of his birth. The Coast Guard let him risk his life during World War II without a birth certificate. They got him a passport based on an affidavit of birth signed by his mother. There is no other proof that Frank Lumpkin came into this world in Hilliard Station, just outside of Washington-Wilkes County, Georgia on October 13, 1916.

In 1916 "Cotton was King" in central Georgia. Cotton fields no longer surround Hilliard Station but the big mansion house of the Callaway plantation still dominates the landscape. The small church built by the cotton sharecroppers still stands. Behind it is the old cemetery where the Callaway slaves, sharecroppers and their descendants are buried. Some are marked with simple headstones. An unknown number are not marked at all.

There are lots of Lumpkins in Georgia, as well as a town, Lumpkin. In 1784, plantation owners named Lumpkin moved from Virginia to Oglethorpe County, Georgia. They grew rich from the work of enslaved Africans, Cherokees and Creeks. Some Lumpkin descendants became judges and political officeholders, doctors, lawyers, etc.[4] After Emancipation, some families who had worked the Lumpkin plantations adopted the name. However, that was not how Frank became a Lumpkin. After the Civil War, Frank's step-great grandfather adopted the Lumpkin name because it was *not* Callaway, the name of his hated slavemaster.

5

Washington, Georgia

In 1997, a search for his roots led Frank Lumpkin to Washington, Georgia, and the Callaway Plantation. He had to make two trips to Washington, Georgia—the first trip was frustrated by excessive Southern hospitality. Frank had not seen his cousin, Lulamat, for 35 years and was not sure of her state of health. Five blocks away from his cousin's house, Frank phoned to announce his arrival. "We'll be sitting on the porch, waiting for you," Lulamat told him. In a few minutes, Frank saw two elderly people in rocking chairs on their porch. "Come right in," they said.

They did not seem in good physical condition but welcomed him warmly. After a few hours of conversation, Frank thought they were tiring. "It was wonderful to see you," Frank said as he got ready to leave. "Next time you come, stay in our house," the elderly people replied.

On his return to Chicago, Frank visited his sister, Jonnie (Pat). They called Lulamat to thank her for her hospitality and were stunned by her reply. "I cooked for three days," Lulamat said, "and you never showed up! What should I do with all this food?" Frank had to promise a second trip to Georgia to the real Lulamat's house. She lived just a few feet down the road from the people who welcomed him as "family" although they had never seen him before.

The real Lulamat was a very active 83-year old who was proud of her cooking. She spread out a feast of Brunswick stew, smothered chicken, stuffing and gravy, macaroni and cheese, collard greens, biscuits, corn bread and preserves of many kinds. Home-made jams for the biscuits included fig, apple, pear and scubindine, a red fruit larger than a cherry but smaller than a plum. Pecans from the tree in the back yard were on the table. Lulamat's wit was even better than her cooking. They split their sides laughing as Lulamat cracked jokes about Frank's "other house" in town and the false Lulamat who had claimed Frank as kin.

At the Courthouse, a historical marker states that the town was built on land "ceded" by the Creeks and Cherokees. There is no explanation of "ceded," and no claim is made that the Native American Indians got anything in return. Actually, they were cheated and coerced off their land in federally masterminded "legal" robbery.[5] A few feet away from the marker, there is a monument to the Confederate soldiers of Wilkes County.

The book, *Washington, Georgia after 200 years, 1780-1980,*[6] has photographs of the mayor and city council in 1980 (all white), newspaper staff (all white), the WLOV radio staff (all white), County Airport Commission (all white), the Fire Department (all white), and

Frank Lumpkin at historical marker on founding of Wilkes County, 1777

the Street and Sanitation Department (all African American except for the department head, who is white). Three of the sixteen police officers are African Americans. Frank Lumpkin noticed, however, that the operators of heavy earth-moving equipment were African American. "You don't see that in Chicago; up North, the operators would probably be white."

The town boasts seven traffic lights on state roads that skirt the city. Trucks loaded with long red logs roll up and down the highways. Pine trees have replaced cotton as the main crop. "You can't make a living any more by farming," said Mr. Randall, a friend of the Lumpkins. He had never left the area, just moved from a nearby farm to the town of Washington. Randall started working in the sawmills in 1936 at $1.00 a day: "Now the working man can hardly make a living. They won't hire you unless they can make a lot of money off your work. Yes the pay is more now [than in 1936] but everything is so high, it amounts to the same." He added that some people were working in the clothing factories that had opened up there. He didn't know the pay rate but thought it wasn't much.

The Callaway Plantation

The Callaway Plantation is still on highway 78 just west of Washington, Georgia. In 1983, the Callaway Family Association, Inc. included 1,000 descendants. The town of Washington still maintains the big houses of the plantation as a museum and tourist attraction. The town even moved a log cabin to the site to show the "humble" origins of the Callaway "farmers." The same authorities did not see fit to reconstruct any homes of the people who actually chopped and picked the cotton that made the Callaways rich. The contrast between the brick mansion and the poor shacks would contradict the official myth of how the Callaways got their wealth.

"The Callaways were very hard-working farmers, and accumulated 3,000 acres," the plantation museum director said, in a cleaned-up version of the Callaway history. Actually, Aristide Callaway, who lived in the brick mansion, owned an additional 11,000 acres just east of the Callaway Plantation. The mansion was built in 1869 to be a showplace. According to the curator, closets were taxed as rooms in those days.

To keep taxes low, most houses were built with few closets. But Callaway flaunted his wealth with 19 closets and more than 15 rooms. Craftsmen from England carved the woodwork; furniture was imported from France and England. The shipping cost to bring the piano from France, via a sailing ship, was $3,000 over 100 years ago. From the second-story balcony, Callaway could survey thousands and thousands of acres of cotton, all his.

Evidently, the Civil War did not seriously damage the Callaway fortune. Fighting never reached Washington-Wilkes County. Official guidebooks proudly report that the Confederate Cabinet's last meeting was held May 3-5, 1865, in Washington-Wilkes County, a safe refuge for the slavocracy. This sentiment was put into verse:

> Washington?
> Oh, it's a friendly little town
> with beautiful colonial homes;
> thanks to General Sherman
> who never came to town.[7]

When Emancipation came, the former slaves were free to leave the plantation to look for work. They never did receive the promised "40 acres and a mule" [8] Most freedmen could find no work except on the cotton plantations still owned by their former masters. Working for a share of the crop was an improvement over slave conditions, but soon the former slaves were trapped in a web of debt and could not legally leave until the debt was paid.

Life on the Plantation

The Lumpkin family tradition did not paint a pretty picture of life on the Callaway Plantation. The family's oral history reached back into slavery times; force and violence led to the mixed ancestry of the Lumpkins. The story was told, retold and passed on for five generations. It was very different from the official story at the Callaway museum. The curator did admit, when questioned, that some of the land was taken from Cherokee families who were in debt to the Callaways. The Cherokees ceded their land to satisfy the "debt." Yes, there were some slaves and sharecroppers, but "that came later."

The Lumpkin tradition said that Callaway (the first name is not known) owned over 380 slaves, including a beautiful African teenager named Sophie. Callaway raped Sophie when she was only 16, and she became pregnant. When Callaway learned that Sophie was pregnant, he made her "jump the broom" with Si, an African who was also enslaved on the Callaway Plantation. Tradition has it that both Si and Sophie were very unhappy about the forced marriage. Sophie bore Callaway's son in 1862 and named him Frank. Sophie and Si remained together and had four children of their own. Although Frank was never acknowledged by Callaway, he received many favors and was raised somewhat apart from Sophie's other children.

The First Frank Lumpkin

After Emancipation, Si took Lumpkin as his family name. Any name was better than the hated "Callaway." Si's stepson Frank became the first Frank Lumpkin. Si Lumpkin began to rebel openly on the streets of unreconstructed Washington, Georgia. When the plantation boss came to get sharecroppers to do extra labor for him, Si refused. Miraculously he escaped with his life. Perhaps that was why people said that Si was "crazy."

When the first Frank Lumpkin reached the age of 21, he told his former master and biological father that he was now a man. He had decided to get married. On the Callaway Plantation, a beautiful Cherokee woman named Betty had caught his eye.

"That's the woman I want," he told Callaway. However Betty was already married and had four children. Shortly after, Betty's husband met with an unexplained fatal accident on the plantation. Frank was given Betty as his bride and 400 acres to farm. The community assumed that foul play was involved in the convenient death of Betty's first husband. For many, many years, these suspicions remained, and Grandpa Frank, known as the "white man's son," was hated in the African American community.

Betty had another four children in her second marriage. The fourth and last child, Elmo, was born to Betty and Frank in 1890. Elmo's Indian grandfather had long hair. (Little Elmo thought the purpose of the long hair was to keep the ears warm in cold weather.) About 1911, 21-year old Elmo Lumpkin married Hattie Martin, who became the mother of the modern Lumpkin family. The family tradition also places a Native American woman among the Martin ancestors. Although the name of this ancestor is not known, her features clearly show in Hattie's proud eyes and high cheekbones. The other ancestors were believed to be African.

Hattie Martin Lumpkin

Grandpa Frank was also remembered for his wealth. "He was the only one in our community to have a rubber-tired buggy," his niece Mary remembered. He was also the first to get one of those new "horseless carriages," which he didn't know how to drive. Elmo's wife, Hattie, was still a teenager. She didn't know how to drive the car either but she was not afraid to try. She got in and drove off. That's how people learned to drive in those days.

Hattie was the daughter of Bess Hill and Wellburn Martin, a couple with an interesting history. Ma Bess, as she was known in the Lumpkin family, was a very proper woman with a strong sense of her own worth and the right way to do things. At 21, she got a job as a cook in the home of a very wealthy white woman who lived outside of the city. Bess lived in the city. Since Bess was a fine cook and very efficient in the kitchen, her employer wanted to make sure that Bess would come to work regularly and on time. The rich woman had a chauffeur who lived in the city. His granddaughters remember him as "Dapper Dan," always smartly dressed. The chauffeur was instructed to pick up Bess and take her back and forth from home to work every day.

"You can't do that," Bess told the chauffeur.

"Why not?" he asked.

"Because there are some days that I will not feel like going to work. And I don't want anyone telling me which days those will be."

Bess's boss had another idea. "Bess," she said. "I'm going away for a week. I would like you to stay here and look out for things."

"I can't do that," Bess replied.

"Why not?" her boss demanded.

"Because I don't believe that Black people should live in white people's houses. That's like slavery."

Time passed and Bess agreed to date the dapper chauffeur, Wellburn Martin. Some time later they married.

"I want just two children," Bess told Wellburn. He agreed, and just two children were born: Tommie Martin in 1893 and Hattie Martin, 1895. Bess Hill Martin outlived her husband, her children and all of her friends. She died, still in full possession of all of her faculties, at the age of 103. Her grandson, Frank Lumpkin, thinks she died of loneliness because all of her friends were gone. Until her last days, she was busy with her quilt making and needlework. She gave each of her 10 grandchildren one of her quilts. The quilts were a way of passing on family history, with each design commemorating an important feature of the culture.

The union of Elmo Lumpkin and Hattie Martin in 1911 was very fruitful. In 12 years they had 6 children: Wade, Elizabeth (Bay), Frank, Ozzie, Jonnie (Pat), and Elmo Jr. (Kiyer). In Orlando, Florida, they would have four more: Warren (Sam), Bessie Mae, Gladys and Roy. Friends and neighbors often commented on the strong family resemblance among the ten Lumpkin children.

Sharecropping and Lynchings

One of Frank's earliest memories is the lynching of Will Lumpkin, Elmo's half-brother. Will was sharecropping for a white landlord. They got into an argument when Will demanded his proper share of the crop. The landlord claimed he didn't owe Will more money. Then Will called the landlord a liar. Elmo realized that his brother was in danger. He tried to get Will to leave town at once, but

The first Frank Lumpkin and sister

Will wouldn't go. As Elmo worked in the field, he heard a gun shot. He ran to the scene and saw Will hanging dead from a tree. A gun was on the ground. There was no police investigation and no one was ever arrested. Eight little children were left without a father. Will's daughter, Lulamat, credits help from Grandpa Frank for the children's survival after their father was lynched. She still remembers the help they got from her uncle Elmo "in those hard, hard times." He did what he could but that was not a lot.

Elmo and Hattie were sharecropping grandpa's farm and times were hard. Frank Lumpkin remembers that he was always hungry as a child. Sometimes they stole into Grandpa Frank's smoke house and cut a thick slice of meat. But they couldn't do that every day. The share of the crop was not enough to feed the growing family. Cotton was the main crop but peanuts, corn and vegetables were also raised. Elmo told his children a "humorous" story about sharecropping:

> "When the crop was in, a sharecropper brought his cotton, peanuts and corn to be weighed and counted. The plantation boss entered the amounts and figured out how much was to be deducted for food, seed and fertilizer advanced to the sharecropper. He figured and figured. Finally he told the sharecropper, 'OK, that leaves us even. What you brought in just pays for the supplies you borrowed since the last crop.'
>
> " 'What shall I do with the rest of the cotton I have in the barn?' the sharecropper asked.
>
> " 'Damn,' said the boss. 'Now I have to figure everything all over!' "

In the 1920s, some African Americans in Georgia were still forced to work under slave-like conditions. These conditions were exposed in an article by Art Shields in the *Daily Worker* of June 4, 1927. The headline read, "Fight to Free Negroes Held as Peons in South." The article quoted James Felton, the only survivor of six workers who tried to escape forced labor on a Georgia plantation. He reported that, "We ate the same food three times a day; just peas and corn bread. We could not sing, write letters or talk, and when we did not work fast enough we were whipped with a strap." [9] The five other escapees were caught, hit on the head with axes and shot, but Felton got away and made his way through the woods. Felton reported that on this one farm there were 45 men and 25 women who were forced to stay and work in the cotton fields and in the sawmill.

Mule Trek North

In 1918 Elmo and Cousin Clint heard that Proctor and Gamble were hiring in Cincinnati. They hitched a mule to their wagon and set off from Washington, Georgia, a trek of almost 1,000 miles. There they rented a cheap basement room and waited for Proctor & Gamble to call them. Happily they did not wait long and worked all that summer. Winter came early with a heavy snow. That morning, the door froze shut. It would not budge. Feeling trapped, both men put their shoulders to the door, only to find they were snowed in and had to be dug out.

It was so cold up North
The birds could hardly fly
You had to close your eyes
And let winter pass on by

Elmo and Clint were not prepared for the snow and ice. Nor for the layoff notice at the job. They had to go back to Georgia with the mule and wagon. When they finally reached Georgia, Elmo decided that North was the wrong way to go. The next time he headed out of Georgia by mule and wagon, he went south—to Orlando, Florida.

Leaving Georgia

About 1922, when Frank was just six, a rabid dog bit the Lumpkin's dog. Their dog became rabid and bit their pig, their heifer cow, and Frank's older brother, Wade. They shot the dog and they had to shoot the pig and the cow. Wade took 10 rabies shots in 10 days, which saved him. But the family had lost their livestock. About the same time, the boll weevil hit the cotton crop and everything went dead.

"We had two crops," Frank explained, "a money crop—cotton, and an eating crop—potatoes and corn. The sharecropper got a share of the money crop. When the crop failed, the sharecropper family got half of nothing, nothing! The landlord risked nothing."

Frank's family moved in with Ma Bess, Hattie's mother, in the town of Washington. Elmo decided to try his luck elsewhere. Cousins already in Orlando told them there was plenty of work in the orange groves. So Elmo and Hattie sold their few possessions, and got ready to move. Elmo went first, with his brother Oz, Cousin Clint and friends Dover and Harry. They "borrowed" two of Grandpa

Frank's mules, hitched them to a wagon, and set off for Orlando, 400 miles south. On the way the box with Elmo's clothes fell off the wagon, unnoticed. Elmo arrived in Orlando with only the clothes on his back. He started to work in the groves, slept outdoors in a box, and saved his money. After a few months he sent for Hattie, their two daughters, and baby Elmo (Kiyer). Frank, Wade and Ozzie stayed with Ma Bess until Elmo had enough money to send for them. Ma Bess's brother, Steven Hill, set Frank to work, hauling bags of blue stone to spread on the soil. "That stone was heavy," he complained, "heavier than fertilizer, and fertilizer was heavy enough." Thus began Frank's life of hard labor. In time the Lumpkin family was reunited in Orlando, but Frank took some of the Georgia culture with him. He loves peanuts and he still recites a folk rhyme on appropriate occasions:

> Little boy sat on the burning deck
> Eating peanuts by the peck
> His mother called him
> But he would not go
> Because he loved his peanuts so.

Growing up in the Orange Groves

"I was here before TV and all these automated things." Bay Lumpkin Rollins.

Elmo expected to find work in Florida and build a better future for his large family. He met relatives in Orlando and went to work at Simon's Packinghouse in the orange groves in nearby Conway. The packers were glad to hire men with large families. Packers expected the bigger children to work in the groves, at least part time. With the job came a company house in the grove.

When the Lumpkins arrived in the early 1920's, Florida was going through some so-called reforms of the prison system. The state set up a prison farm at Raiford and put prisoners on chain gangs to repair the roads. How could chain gangs be considered a reform? Before that time, the state had no penitentiary buildings. Instead the convicts were leased out to private contractors for phosphate mines and turpentine camps (the ultimate "privatization" of prisons). The NAACP charged that some "convicts" had committed no crimes and were arrested only to supply contract labor. The system of convict leasing, with its lash and sweatbox, did not end in Florida until replaced by prisons in 1923.[10]

Ocoee, FL and the Right to Vote

Nor did the Lumpkins find the orange groves freer of racist violence than the cotton fields of Georgia. If anything, Florida was worse, with the highest rate of lynchings in the country.[11] In 1923 an entire town of African Americans was wiped out at Rosewood near Cedar Keys. Those who were not killed fled as their houses burned. Seventy-four years later, the film *Rosewood* made public the facts about the massacre. Near Orlando itself, an African American community in Ocoee was destroyed and many were murdered. Despite threats by the Ku Klux Klan, an African American named Mose Norman attempted to vote on Election Day, November 2, 1920. He was unpopular with some whites because he was "too prosperous," owning his own home, an automobile and an orange grove worth $10,000. Norman was not allowed to vote and was beaten severely. Two days later, Walter White was sent to investigate for the NAACP and reported in its journal, *The Crisis*:

When Norman left the polls he went to the home of July Perry, another colored man, who likewise was unpopular with the whites in that he was foreman of a large orange grove owned by a white man living in New England—a job which the community felt was too good for a Negro. When the mob attacked the colored community, the colored people fought in self-defense, killing two white men and wounding two, according to news accounts. Citizens of the town told me that eight or ten whites were killed but that they could not allow the information to become known, fearing the effect on the colored population. However, the mob surrounded the settlement, set fire to it, shot down or forced back into the flames colored men, women and children who attempted to flee. The number murdered will probably never be known. The figures generally given varied from thirty-two to thirty-five. One lean, lanky and vicious looking white citizen of Ocoee of whom I asked the number of dead, replied: "I don't know exactly but I know 56 n---- were killed. I killed 17 myself."

Whatever the number, two of those known to have died were a colored mother and her two-weeks old infant. [12]

Lumpkin relatives living in Orlando during the Ocoee massacre remember that white people raided the vegetable gardens belonging to African Americans who fled Ocoee or were murdered by the racist mob. When thieves brought the produce to sell, African Americans refused to buy it because they knew the whole bloody story. In 1920, violent attacks on African Americans trying to vote occurred in the Florida towns of Orange, Gadsden and Suwanee Counties. In Jacksonville, more African American women than white women had registered to vote in the first Florida election since women won the vote. Walter White reported that "frantic stories threatening domination by 'Negro washerwomen and cooks' failed to bring out the white women to register." Thousands turned out to vote despite parades by the Ku Klux Klan and other intimidation. Although many African Americans did succeed in voting, White estimated that over 4,000 qualified African Americans who came to the polls in Jacksonville were denied their right to vote.[13]

Turpentine Stills and Wages in Scrip

There was a turpentine distillery near the orange groves that employed hundreds of African Americans. The Lumpkins never considered working at the still because wages were paid in company scrip instead of cash. The scrip was good only in the company store—another form of bondage. No matter how hard or how long you worked, you were always in debt to the company store. Those who left without paying their "debts" were subject to capture by the law. Sometimes escapees were killed to terrorize the others.[14]

An Orlando relative of the Lumpkins, Hattie King, had married Lord Biggers, a soldier from Beckley, West Virginia. In later years, he heard about the wages paid in scrip at the Florida turpentine mills and told his own story about the West Virginia miners. These miners were also paid in company scrip, well into the '30s. While he was still in high school, about 15 miners were trapped in a mine disaster. They knew they would probably die before rescuers could reach them. So they took pencil and paper and wrote letters to their families. The letters were found with the bodies and published in the newspaper. When Biggers read the letters, he promised himself that he would never go into the mines. True to his promise, he joined the Army after high school and was sent to Orlando. "There," as he said, "I met this lovely lady, and bam! Fell in love." Then the army sent him away to another post. As soon as he could, he returned to marry

Hattie King, and he has been there ever since. Hattie and Lord Biggers still have some of the best Valencia oranges growing in their back yard.

Of the Lumpkin children who survived into the '90s, Bay was the only one old enough to remember the details of their move to Florida:

"I was here before TV and all these automated things. I was 8 years old when we left Washington, Georgia, with Jonnie (6 years younger); and Kiyer, just a baby. It was better in Orlando because we didn't need fire in wintertime and we could go barefoot all year around. But things have changed. They've cut so many trees down that I hear the weather has gotten colder. It was summer all year when we were there. We lived in a worker's house from Simon's Packing, right there in the grove. It was 3 rooms up off the ground. We used to like to play under the house.

"When I was in sixth grade, Hattie said to me, 'Bay, I have a good job coming. I would like to work for the Stone family. If you would take care of the children, I could work and be able to send the other children to school.' So I left school and I was glad of it. There were no buses and no convenient way to get to school. We lived in Conway and I had to pass two white schools to get to the colored school. My shoes would be turned and it hurt my feet."

After a few years in Orlando, Hattie gave birth to another boy and a girl, Warren (Sam) and Bessie Mae. When Bessie Mae grew up, she realized that her mother had given all the Lumpkin children a good start in developing their minds. Hattie wanted her children to learn different things so she took them everyplace. She kept their minds as active as their bodies. One of the advantages in being year-round grove employees was the children could go to school. During the height of the citrus seasons, the permanent grove employees made a lot less money than the migrant pickers, who worked piecework. But migrant pickers' children did *not* go to school during the harvests. They had to move with their families from grove to grove. Early and mid-season orange picking rose in November and December and peaked in January and February. March saw substantial picking and April through June was the Valencia-orange picking season.[15] That did not leave much time for pickers to go "home" or for their children to go to school.

Child Labor

For the Lumpkin boys, school did not free them from work in the groves. The school day ended early, leaving many daylight hours for work. "America Still Home of Child Labor," headlined a *Daily Worker* article on May 8, 1927. The article exposed the child labor laws in Florida that permitted boys and girls under the age of 16 to work up to 54 hours a week. Even that was better than the Georgia law, which did not limit hours per day and allowed children to work 60 hours a week. In North Carolina, children were allowed to work up to 11 hours a day but no more than 60 hours a week. Children under 14 could not legally work in factories. Still 20% of the 13-year olds were not in school in North Carolina mill towns. [16]

Employers who profited from child labor lobbied successfully against any law to end child labor. In 1918, the Supreme Court declared the recently passed Child Labor Act unconstitutional. The Act banned child labor in the manufacture of goods produced for interstate trade. In *Hammer vs Daggenhart*, the Supreme Court limited the power of Congress, finding that "power to regulate commerce did not extend to the production of goods."[17] During the early New Deal period, the Court continued to use *Hammer vs Daggenhart* to throw out any social legislation. Public opinion mounted against the Supreme Court. Only after FDR (Franklin Delano Roosevelt) threatened to "pack" the court by appointing additional judges did the Supreme Court allow New Deal social legislation to stand.[18] A ban on work by children under 16 was finally included in the Fair Labor Standards Act of 1938.[19]

Playing in the Groves

The move to Orlando brought some improvement in the Lumpkins' living conditions. The climate was kinder. Good shirts could be made from sugar sacks that were dumped outside the liquor distilleries in the woods. The Lumpkins raised chickens and had milk for the small children. There was plenty of room for children to play in the groves. Frank put it in rhyme:

> Up the hickory, down the pine
> Tore my britches down behind
> Asked my mother good and kind
> "Sew my britches up behind."

There were also many dangers. The Power Company did not trim the trees that grew under the bare electric wires. When Frank was 13, playing in a tree, he took a dare and put both hands on a bare, high-voltage line. He had heard that high voltage wires were safe as long as you grabbed them with both hands. He could see that birds perched on the line without burning. He didn't realize that the tree connected his bare feet to the ground, making a complete circuit. It was a near fatal lesson in science. The heat of the current cut off joints of three fingers, including his index (trigger) finger. The huge surge of electricity passed through his body and bent up the toe where the current exited. Frank fell out of the tree to the ground, unconscious. People heard a neighbor screaming in horror and ran to the scene. The screams brought the local scoutmaster who lived down the road. He immediately applied artificial respiration.

When Frank began to breathe, the onlookers cheered. They sent for the doctor but he could only apply some antiseptic. Frank's hands would remain disfigured. Miraculously, or so it seemed, the asthma that had troubled him never returned. But it was a cure at a great cost. In later years, the army wouldn't take him without a trigger finger. The auto plants wouldn't hire him because he was "handicapped." Still, fellow millwrights in the tool room at Wisconsin Steel believed Frank could do more delicate work with his remaining fingers than most people could do with intact hands. And when he balled his hand to make a mighty fist, he was anything but handicapped.

Sixty-three years later (1992) his crooked toe was repaired so he could wear a shoe without discomfort. The repair was a gift from the podiatrist husband of Toni, Frank's niece and Bessie Mae's daughter. It was a gift because Humana HMO, a for-profit managed-care insurance company, refused to pay for the surgery. The accident, as often happens when the victim survives, gave rise to some humor over the years. Frank's son Paul, as a Cub Scout, liked to tell friends the story of how the scoutmaster had saved Frank's life, using artificial "perspiration." Frank's sister Jonnie laughed as she described Frank acting the part of an Indian Scout in a school play.

When he pointed to the direction of travel, he had to use his middle finger for lack of an index finger. Laughing when he felt like crying was a trick Frank learned very young. It proved to be useful in his years as a fighter. Frank's opponent could not tell when Frank was hurt, because he laughed.

In time most of the extended Lumpkin family relocated to Florida. There was always work to do on the citrus plantations, whatever the season—plowing, weeding, pruning and fertilizing. Frank plowed

Frank Lumpkin and father, c. 1941

with a mule. "The mules were slow to go out at 4 a.m., but they were always fast when it was time to go home." Plowing behind a mule "was nice, especially if the earth was soft. You could walk behind a mule barefoot—just step in the places the plow turned over. Just follow the mule; the mule knows where to go."

Racism Is Unnatural

Down the road from the Lumpkin house lived the Harveys, a white family with two boys about Frank's age, Roy and Frank. They became good friends. The family had a tool shed and the boys were allowed to use the tools. That began Frank's love affair with tools and machinery. But when it came time to go to school, the boys parted ways. Roy and Frank Harvey went to the white school, not that far away. The Lumpkin children had to walk past the white school and hike four more miles to the "colored" school, one of the early experiences that convinced Frank "racism is unnatural."[20]

Elementary school for the African American children was held in the one-room schoolhouse attached to the Conway Baptist Church. Upper grade children went to Jones Town School. When it was time for high school, all African American students in the Orlando area went to Jones High School. The high school has since been relocated but the facade was left in place as a historic monument.

When Frank was 14 years old, he was still barefoot most of the time. He had one pair of overalls that he could call his own. One day his brother Ozzie wore the only shirt they had between them to go to a ball game. Frank went to the game and removed the shirt from Ozzie by force. When Elmo came home, Hattie had ordered a whipping. For the first time in his life, Frank did not submit. Still he did not want to directly challenge his father. So he ran away and slept in the outhouse, afraid to come in. During the night, Elmo woke him up and told him roughly, "Come into the house." There was an unspoken agreement between them—Frank was too old to whip.

That incident spurred Frank to make a hard decision. He decided to leave school although he was a good student. The only way he could get some clothes was to work full time and earn some money. He quit school at 15 and went to work full time on the citrus plantations. The young Lumpkin men continued to share their dress clothing but with Frank's wages, there was more to share. When Frank later left the Lumpkin house to marry, he had little besides the clothes on his back. Everything else had been shared.

When Frank quit school, Hattie and Elmo had eight children. Two more were born in the next four years. Elmo worked hard, and Hattie worked, too. There was no question that everybody had to work. Together, husband and wife didn't earn a living wage, yet they made do for the whole family of ten. When Gladys and Roy were born, somehow they raised them, too. Bay was in charge while the parents worked.

The citrus plantation where the Lumpkins lived and worked was owned by "old man Sims." His son owned a large share of the Palmolive Soap company. The older Sims took a liking to young Frank and let him drive the tractor at 16. That was a special treat. "You're spoiling that boy," Frank's grandfather Wellburn warned Sims. Wellburn and Bess Martin, Hattie's parents, also lived in the groves. "Ma Bess," as she was called, had been a cook in white families' homes. Wellburn, the chauffeur, sometimes worked in the groves. Their daughter Hattie, known simply as "Ma" in the family, took in washing and did other work to add to the family income. Workers in the grove were mostly men. Women earned what they could by doing domestic labor for white families, or other service jobs.[21]

Hattie Lumpkin, c. 1942

As a teenager, Frank used his wits to make his work easier. One of his jobs was weeding rows of orange trees. Frank looked the rows over at night, finding those that took a lot of work and those that were almost clean. He planned to race ahead in one row in order to take the next "easy" row. In the easy rows he could take a rest. One day grandfather Wellburn saw Frank sitting comfortably in the shade of a tree, his rows all clean. "While you're resting, sharpen your hoe" his grandfather told him, in a disapproving tone of voice—advice that Frank never forgot and never followed. He laughs when he tells the story. Frank preferred to work hard and finish fast so he could have time to relax and think.

Collective Action

Frank began to work full-time in 1931, the bottom of the Great Depression. He does not remember a special "Depression" period because they could not remember any better times. The fact is that the whole state of Florida was in deep depression by 1932. After the election of Franklin D. Roosevelt, the WPA provided jobs for many of the unemployed. Some citrus workers had developed their own form of collective action, encouraged by the start of the federal WPA (Works Progress Administration). These public works jobs began to raise the local economy from its extremely depressed condition. Among the federal agencies that supplied jobs for the unemployed were the CCC (Civilian Conservation Corps) employing 40,000 young men in the State of Florida and the WPA with 40,000 public works jobs.[22] The boost to the economy would have been greater if African Americans had received these jobs in their proportion of Florida's population, about 30% in 1933. WPA jobs paid workers $12 a week, a living wage in 1935. Elmo made only $7.50 a week for working long hours in the groves. The WPA wage scale was one of the factors that inspired many workers to fight for a higher wage.[23]

As a teenager, Frank experienced the power that workers could exert when they united. Sometimes he got away from Simon's groves for a day to earn extra money as a picker at another grove. During harvest time, grove-owners' trucks came through the African American communities around Orlando to recruit pickers. One of the pickers, nicknamed Livewire, was trusted by the workers to negotiate the right rate for the job. It was piece work and the rate depended on the height of the trees and other factors. Frank has remembered the lessons that Livewire taught him:

"I'll never forget Livewire. At an orange grove 20 miles from town, the company offered us 5 cents a box. Livewire looked the trees over and said we had to have 6 cents. The boss said 5 cents, no more. Livewire refused to give the signal to start picking. 'We can't work for that rate,' he told the boss.

"'Then you can walk home,' the owner told us. Livewire began to walk and we all followed. About an hour later the truck came after us. 'Get in,' the driver said. 'You can have your 6 cents.'"

Elsewhere in Florida, some union organizing drives had begun, but this news had not reached the orange grove workers in Conway. In 1920, the Brotherhood of Sleeping Car Porters was organizing the train porters in Jacksonville, Florida. Their organizer, Ben Smith, was fired from his job and told by the police to leave town. He refused. That organizing drive eventually succeeded. By 1940, 20% of Florida's "permanent" workers were unionized.[24]

Of the Lumpkins, Jonnie was the only one who had ever met a union organizer in Florida. She was very busy working as a bartender in a white bar. The New Year weekend in 1940 was at the height of the orange-picking season. Jonnie got a call from a man who said he had been given her name and would like to talk to her. She told him to come over. When he showed up she saw that he was white. He talked to her about organizing the orange pickers and said that he would be back. The next day, Mr. Buchanan, Chief of Police, came in with another policeman and asked Jonnie if she knew the man.

"Where is he?" Jonnie asked.

"We just want to know if he talked to you," Buchanan replied.

"Where is he?" Jonnie demanded.

"He was talking to the orange pickers, so we arrested him."

"Where is he now?" Jonnie persisted.

"We took him to the county line and told him to get out of Orlando County. He had some papers we don't allow."

"Where are the papers?"

"We burned them," the policemen answered.

Tampa and the Cigar Workers

Orlando is only 80 miles from Tampa and its suburb, Ybor City. In the '30s, Tampa was a center for the revolutionary-minded cigar workers. The Depression also cut into luxury industries such as cigar manufacturing. Thousands of cigar makers joined the Communist-led Tobacco Workers Industrial Union, affiliated to the Trade Union Unity League (TUUL). Robert P. Ingalls, in *Urban Vigilantes in the New South*, wrote that Communists "campaigned for unemployment relief, led protests against evictions, held rallies, and staged plays with titles like 'Downfall of the Classes.' " On October 31, 1931, one thousand workers gathered peacefully to protest an eviction. Three Communists were arrested, charged with vagrancy and inciting a riot. Four days later, a rally protested the arrests. One of the rally organizers was kidnapped by five men, taken to a deserted spot and flogged. This terror did not slow the pace of organizing in Tampa and Ybor City.[25]

In 1935, Joseph Shoemaker, an ex-Socialist Party member in Tampa, organized the Modern Democrats, an independent, grass-roots political organization. Without a warrant, the police raided a home where Modern Democrats were meeting and arrested six men. One of the six was a police spy and was released. The others were kept for "questioning." They were asked if they were Communists or believers in racial equality. A union organizer who had come to Tampa to organize longshoremen was also brought in to witness the "interrogation." Then those arrested were released, one at a time. Three of them were forced into waiting cars and taken to a deserted area. All three were brutally beaten. Joseph Shoemaker died of his wounds. A national outcry forced Tampa authorities to take some kind of action. Many thought that the outcry was so great because the victim of this lynching was white. In 1937 eleven were tried for this crime, including three Orlando men. All eleven had ties to the Tampa Police. Civil liberties groups around the country hailed the arrests. However, all eleven were acquitted and set free. No one was punished for the murder.[26]

In 1936 Earl Browder, the Communist candidate for President, attempted to speak in Tampa but the hall was locked. He returned and spoke to over 400 workers who rallied in an empty lot. The Ku Klux Klan had threatened violence to stop the Communist meeting. Local police officers led an attack on the rally, wounding several people. Browder was forced to flee.[27] Perhaps it was the mass response to the Communist program that led Mayor Way of Orlando, in 1938, to put out his appeal: "Negroes of Orlando, Do not join the 'Communist International Organization.' "[28] However, the Lumpkins lived out in the country. News of these historic labor struggles never reached them.

Chauffeur

At the age of 18, Frank was asked to chauffeur for the plantation owner's father. Frank shared in the national love affair with the automobile and had taught himself to drive at 14. All you needed to know was how to start and stop. Without a real road, the car ran in two deep tracks. "You could hardly get out of the tracks," Frank said. One day as he neared the railroad tracks he saw red lights flashing. He didn't know what the flashing lights meant and continued to drive across the tracks. Just as he crossed, a fast steam engine came around the bend, pulling a lot of cars. A few seconds later, and the train would have hit him. After that he knew what flashing red lights meant.

Driving for Mr. Sims expanded Frank's horizons. He could walk into the best hotel in Orlando with his chauffeur's cap on, and be greeted warmly. "Mr. Sims is right in there," they would say. In the South, a chauffeur's cap allowed him to go any place, and he did. When his boss went out of town for a few weeks, Frank did not allow the Grimm Supercharger to sit idle for a moment. His boss returned to a gas bill of $100. "I just have one question," his boss said. "Where did you go?" At that time, gas sold for about 12 cents a gallon. Frank could not explain how he had driven about 8,000 miles without taking any long trips away from Orlando.

Frank lost his chauffeur's job for a while but they called him back to take care of old man Sims. Sims had fallen ill and was being waited on, hand and foot. Frank said, "OK, I'll take care of him but I'm not going to empty any bed pans. I'll get him up and make him walk to the bathroom." When the old man heard that threat, he demanded that they hire Frank to make him get up. Frank made Sims get up, making a friend of the old man.

In 1937 Elmo found a job in the city that paid a little more than his work in the groves. It was very hard labor, shoveling by hand to make holes big enough for gas station gasoline tanks. Because their house in Conway belonged to the orange grove owner, the Lumpkins had to move. The Lumpkins moved to 920 Carter St. in Orlando, a four-room frame house less than 24 x 24 feet. Warren said, "Don't know how we did it. Five brothers slept on the back porch, three sisters in one bedroom, and ma and pa slept in the other bedroom. By that time Ma Bess was a widow and moved in with them. Nobody remembered where Ma Bess slept. Jonnie thought that Ma Bess had moved in with Bay, who had married at the age of 18.

Close behind the Lumpkin house on Carter St. was another house just like it so the Lumpkins had no back yard. But there were vacant lots across the street, and it was near the city dump from which one could get a free view of the boxing matches. You could see everything, but couldn't hear what was going on.

Feeding and Clothing 10 Children

For much of the time, the Lumpkin children went barefoot. With ten children to clothe, nothing was thrown away. Good parts of worn-out clothing could be salvaged to help dress some of the smaller children. In later years, Frank often thought about the problem of clothing ten children. It reminded Frank of one of the poems he loved:

> "Little boy, little boy
> Who made your britches?
> Daddy cut them out
> And mama sewed the stitches."

Hattie used to send Warren to the store with a dime to get food for 13 people. He got a free soup bone, 5 cents worth of rice, and a nickel can of tomatoes. They used the green tops of wild onions for seasoning. That was a meal for 13 people. Or cook up white potatoes with some salt pork. The potatoes would turn into a tasty sauce. Warren was always selling something to get a little money. He made and sold his own root beer and sold well-known brands of face cream and shaving lotion. Frank also tried selling face cream but that kind of selling was not to his liking. He would rather do hard physical work than talk people into buying something they did not really need.

Although none of the Lumpkin children starved, neither did they get enough to eat. Frank was always hungry, but fruit kept him going. You could always find something to eat in Florida, on the vines or in the trees. There were mangoes, a stray orange that happened to fall off a tree (with a slight tug), or a watermelon that a hungry child thought a farmer wouldn't miss. Frank felt bad about eating a whole orange he found, when he knew his brothers and sisters were hungry. But he ate it anyway because there was no sense trying to divide an orange 10 ways.

Sometimes they were lucky enough to shoot a rabbit to add to dinner. One day Frank saw a partridge sitting on a clutch of what looked like 20 eggs. The eggs and the bird would be a feast. Frank ran home to get a shotgun. By the time he returned, the bird was gone and a big rattlesnake was gulping down the eggs. In Florida, Frank learned to be careful where he stepped. In addition to rattlesnakes and water moccasins, there were the even more poisonous coral snakes.

It is a great tribute to Hattie and Elmo that all ten children survived to become strong, productive adults. As parents they provided more than just food, clothing and shelter. They instilled self-confidence. This was a family trait that Frank shared with all of his sisters and brothers.

Frank was never heard to say, "I can't." In later years, Frank worked to inspire a feeling of self-confidence and power in the workers that he led. The Lumpkin children grew up with the feeling that the family was important and that each one of them was important. It was a trait that could be traced back to "Ma Bess" Martin.

"Ma Bess," c. 1970

Frank and Warren Lumpkin at 920 Carter St, Orlando, 1995

"I saw these fighters wake up the next day with eyes swollen and head hurting. They'd have just enough money to buy a bottle of wine and some food." Warren Lumpkin.

3. Fight Your Way Up

Working people know that the odds are against them. Many dream of escaping from poverty. Many in Florida hoped to win in bolito, a numbers game then popular. Frank once won $10, more than a week's pay. That win inspired hope of one day hitting it big. But often he did not have even 5 cents to play. He had heard that clues to the winning number could be found in a *Pittsburgh Courier* newspaper column written by "Sonny Boy," if you read it backwards or upside down. "It was up to you to figure it out," Frank recalled.

Then as now, professional sports appeared as a way out of poverty for a handful of stars. Each one of thousands of young people hoped to make it big. Frank really loved baseball. He could have been a good professional player. But major-league baseball was closed to African Americans until Jackie Robinson broke through the ban in the mid '40s.[29] It was also a few years before Joe Louis would become heavyweight champion in 1937. Still a few African Americans were making money in the ring. So the Lumpkin boys all decided to become boxers. Wade, the eldest, led the way. He was the first to begin and the last to quit.

At times Wade's boxing ability helped Frank survive. When Frank was 14, a white man who lived nearby fell out drunk near the Lumpkin house. Wade and Frank saw him, got him to his feet and led him to his house. The next day the police came, picked up Wade and accused him of stealing the drunk's money. About 1 a.m. the police returned to take Frank to the Orlando jail. Frank was very upset because the police didn't give him time to find some shoes. They threw him into the police car and dragged him to jail barefoot. When Frank arrived the police put Wade and Frank in the bullpen. A big, rough and tough prisoner dominated the bullpen. It was expected that every new arrival would get a beating. So Wade instructed Frank in a loud voice, "You grab him. I'll duck him [knock him down]." The brothers weren't bothered after that. Wade's, "You grab him. I'll duck him," lived on as a family joke, telling a mouse to bell the cat. After a few hours the police told Frank he could go. They kept Wade for another day. The cops took Frank to jail in a car but he had to get back home as best he could. It was a long trip. He walked many miles through city streets, barefoot. He still remembers the pain and humiliation. "I was afraid that I would meet someone I knew and they would see me in town, barefoot."

Before Frank left school at age 15, he made 25 cents in his first paid fight, but he tore his pants beyond repair. That fight was called a "battle royale," a group fight open to all. Luther Yates, later to become Frank's manager, had rounded up a truckload of young contenders. The fight went on until all but one was knocked out or quit. It was a way for young unknowns to get into the game.

"My first fight was a battle royale ," Frank recalled. "They didn't let us in until the last two rounds. All I picked up was 25 cents. People throw money in the ring. You can't pick up money with boxing gloves on. So 25 cents was all that was left." His ruined pants cost more than that.

Warren remembered *his* first fight. It was the only time that several Lumpkin sons fought on the same night. Hattie and Elmo usually didn't care to watch but they decided to come. It proved to be Warren's undoing.

"Ma and pa came in so I turned to look at them. I got hit in the head and saw stars. That's why I got only a draw and didn't win. Four of us were in that fight, Frank, Ozzie, Kiyer and me. It was a tough fight that night for Frank, too. He went eight rounds with a fighter named Slaten before he won."

Warren tells how the fighters were exploited. "I saw these fighters wake up the next day with eyes swollen and head hurting. They'd have just enough money to buy a bottle of wine and some food."

Frank and Wade were having some success, gaining in fame and making a little money. But Frank's $15 or $20 per fight was still not enough to support him. He could not afford to quit his job in the groves. Training and sparring was done after a long day of farm work. What kept the fighters going was the hope of a big fight, getting into the big money.

Frank earned the unofficial title, "heavyweight champ of the South." When Johnny Paycheck (who fought Joe Louis) trained in Orlando, Frank was his sparring partner. Frank had faster legs. With his speed and a good jab, Frank beat Paycheck in the gym. On March 29, 1940, when Paycheck fell to Louis in two short rounds, Frank heard that Paycheck was paid $50,000. Frank got $20 a fight. When all the Lumpkins fought the same night, Warren got 50 cents. Kiyer, Oz, and Frank got $1 each.

At age 20, Frank had become known as Frank "KO" Lumpkin. He was booked for a big fight worth hundreds of dollars. In the days before the fight, Frank worked in the groves. Somehow, he injured his arm but he did not know the bone was broken. He got into the ring with a fractured arm. By the fourth round he had to quit. The Boxing Board was about to disqualify him but ordered an X-ray of the arm. Frank had fought three rounds with a broken arm!

Frank found something to laugh at even in that disappointment. His boss in the groves read the Boxing Board's decision in the newspaper. "You just can't believe what you read in the papers," he told Frank, "they say you have a broken arm!" He could not believe that Frank had a broken arm because Frank continued to work, losing no time on the job.

Frank's manager, Luther Yates, owned a barbershop. Yates was proud of "his" gladiator. For decades after Frank left Orlando, Yates displayed a pair of Frank's boxing gloves on the wall of his barbershop. It was said that Yates belonged to the Ku Klux Klan (KKK). Frank thought most businessmen in Orlando were KKK members at that time. When the Klan met, most of the shops closed. Luther drove Frank to a fight in Atlanta. When they stopped overnight at a motel, they knew the rules. Frank had to sleep outside in the car. During the night Yates brought out a blanket to keep his fighter from catching cold. Next morning the motel owner told him that he knew about the blanket. Luther had to pay for the blanket because it "had to be burned."

Frank continued to work in the groves by day; training and fighting at night and on weekends. To get some idea of the effort involved, try skipping in place three minutes, holding your arms at shoulder height. Then think of doing an intense workout for three hours, after a full day's work in the orange groves.

Actually, the training was the part that Frank liked best. There were also significant rewards for the endless cycle of work. Fighting

Frank "KO" Lumpkin c. 1936 (photo partially retouched by Justin Jordan)

earned extra pay, even though small. There were lots of admirers, especially female. Frank then believed the myth that sexual activity detracted from a gladiator's strength. As a disciplined athlete, he put his fighting career first even if it meant no cigarettes, no alcohol, and severe limitations on sex.

At 20, Frank married Lorraine, a woman of striking beauty. The young couple went to work for a wealthy white family. Lorraine was the maid and cook, Frank the butler and chauffeur. Throughout his life, Frank has never considered dust to be sinful; he took care only of spots that his boss would check, such as under the edge of the table and high on the molding above the door. Frank kept those areas clean and smooth. He didn't worry about the rest of the house.

One day, Frank answered a guest room bell and found a most unwelcome sight. She was lying on her bed, quite naked. "You rang?" he said coldly.

"Oh, I didn't know you'd come so fast," she said, as she pulled the covers over her body. If there was anything Frank did not do, it was to respond quickly when the butler's cord was pulled. He was keenly aware of the danger posed by a white woman trying to use him, especially in the South. One lying word from a white woman could cost the life of an African American man.

In later years, Hattie heard about the fight to save the life of Willie McGee. McGee was sentenced to death in Mississippi on a charge of rape of a white woman. Civil rights groups were convinced that McGee was framed. Hattie told about a similar case in Florida. A mother traveled throughout the state in a mule-drawn wagon, trying to raise money to save her son from execution. She did not succeed in saving her son. And progressives did not stop the execution of Willie McGee, although large protests were organized in many cities. Still the fight to save these lives bore fruit in the years that followed. The protests reduced the number of legal lynchings and eventually led to anti-lynch legislation.

Frank could take time off from his butler-chauffeur's job when he had a boxing match. Boxing took him to many cities: Miami, Tampa, Birmingham, Atlanta and also Columbus, Georgia. One match took him to Memphis, the farthest north he had been. From his hotel window near Beale Street, he saw an African American man and a white man fighting. The African American had the best of the fight and beat up the white man. Then both men went away. That was something Frank had never seen before. Frank did not leave his hotel room that night, expecting the KKK to come and terrorize the neighborhood. But the Klan did not come. Frank thought, "This is certainly different from Orlando."

On his job, Frank had his first experience with a northern white liberal. Some wealthy guests were visiting from the North. Frank was instructed to take the man out in a rowboat so the guest could fish in the lake. Frank hoped for a good tip. He rowed very diligently while the guest trolled for bass. After an hour, the visitor gave Frank the rod-and-reel and took over the oars. "Now you fish and I'll row," he said. "There goes my tip," Frank thought in disgust.

Other guests would have been more generous with their tips, had they not been restrained. One guest tried to give Frank a $5 tip. "That's too much," Frank's boss warned the guest. "The gentlemen have agreed that we will not give more than a $1 tip."

"No kin of mine will have to sleep in the street." Hattie Lumpkin

4. Flight to the North

By 1940, war orders demanded more labor at northern factories. Many workers were leaving the South for better jobs in the North. Wade was already in Buffalo, New York—working, boxing, and sending home glowing tales of high pay. Hattie visited Wade and decided to move the Lumpkin family to Buffalo. She returned to Orlando and began to move her family north—if necessary, one by one. Brother Ozzie visited Wade, found work at a steel mill and stayed in Buffalo. Then the family sent Frank to join his two brothers. His wife Lorraine soon followed.

Black-white relations in Buffalo were different from Orlando. There were no signs on the washrooms saying "white" or "colored" and Frank did not have to sit in the back of the bus. Still Buffalo did not prove to be the "promised land." Instead of the $30 a week pay that had encouraged Frank to move north, all he could find in 1940 was a janitor's job in a Neisner's 5 and 10 cents store at $9 a week The steel mill would not hire him because of his lost fingers. Steel mills and auto assembly plants gave complete physical examinations that included a finger check.

Frank stayed at Neisner's until he could raise the money to buy a union card in the Hod Carriers Union. With the card he worked as a laborer at 75 cents an hour ($30 for 40 hours). He helped build Bell Aircraft and Curtiss Wright Aircraft in Tonawanda, New York. Construction work was highly segregated, Frank remembers:

> "All the Black workers were hod carriers only and were not allowed to touch a trowel. I had to go to Niagara Falls to join the union. The Buffalo local did not admit Negroes. It was union but it was discriminatory. It was like the Masons [African American Prince-Hall Masons]. The white Masons were discriminatory, but they recognized each other [African American and white Masons]."

36

The week before Christmas, 1941, Frank and Ozzie drove to Orlando. They returned to Buffalo with Jonnie. The Japanese had attacked Pearl Harbor (December 7, 1941). The United States was at

Frank Lumpkin in Buffalo, c 1940

war. "Remember Pearl Harbor!" was the slogan used to drum up the war spirit. The slogan did not take root in the Black community, as Jonnie Lumpkin remembers it. "Remember Pearl Who?" she laughed. "Pearl was probably some white woman—that was not the business of African Americans." And there were too many things to worry about right at home.

Casualty of the War at Home

Bay's husband, Taft Rollins, was among the millions who joined the army. He was also among those who died. But he fell victim to the war at home. The last time Bay saw her husband alive was at the train station in Orlando, as he left for Fort Bragg, North Carolina, at the end of a leave. They did not know that an anti-African American race riot was raging at the army base. This is the story:

"In 1933 I got married to Taft Earl Rollins from Tallahassee. I hated to leave my one-year old baby sister, Gladys. I met Taft in the Conway Baptist congregation. We Georgiamans [people from Georgia] used to stay together but in the school and the church we mixed with the Floridians. Between Taft's mother and me, he joined the army in 1939 [to get away from home]. He was at Fort Bragg, North Carolina. He told me the whites had guns to practice with but they gave the African Americans sticks for their practice.

"One day the government sent Taft back to me in a box. Sergeant Rogers Lee came to tell me my husband was dead. When I asked the Sergeant what had happened, he told me, 'It is not your business.' It was after Pearl Harbor. Lee said that when one soldier did something to another soldier, the government would do nothing about it because they needed all the soldiers for the war. He told me that Taft had been an honorable soldier and had a pass for leave in town. Something happened at a bus stop but it was not my business to know."

Sergeant Lee told the family that his orders were not to let anyone open the coffin. Bay's sister Jonnie went to the funeral home and opened the box. The top of Taft's head had been knocked off. Jonnie decided to leave the coffin open for the funeral so everyone could see what had happened. The murder of Taft Rollins was not reported in any newspaper. Along with millions of others killed in the "Black Holocaust,"* it made a mark that will never be erased from the collective memory of a family and a people. Bay went on with her life and lived with the pain.

Near-fatal Accident

Back in Buffalo, on a day that was almost his last, Frank was working with a demolition crew. They were tearing down a brick brewery with crowbars (before the use of big wrecking balls). The demolition crew was eight stories up, at the top of a huge brewery vat. Frank lost his grip and began to slide down the inside of the curved vat. With his hands he tried desperately to slow his fall. His mind raced, thinking about the big hole at the bottom of the vat. Anyone who fell through at the hole would drop another 30 feet. He had slid only a few feet when a large hand reached out to grab him and stopped his fall. Frank laughed as he told the story, "Always bought that man a drink whenever I saw him on William Street."

* A term widely used to describe the disastrous depopulation of Africa and whole-sale destruction of cultures caused by the kidnapping of tens of millions of Africans for enslavement in the Americas.

Lumpkin reported the incident to the demolition office. The fore-man immediately sent Frank up again to the top of the vat, to make sure that fear of heights would not set in. Frank went up again that day and the next day too. But some days later, he thought it over and quit. He never went back to demolition work.

Frank moved on to a job at Bell Aircraft, a factory he had helped to build when he was a construction worker. Aircraft plants needed labor and were ready to overlook Frank's missing fingers. Despite his mechanical skills, Frank worked as a janitor, the only type of work for African Americans at Bell Aircraft. Some time after Frank left Bell Aircraft, Jonnie led a successful fight at the plant for the right to work on production jobs.

Frank Becomes a Steel worker

One day Frank took his brother-in-law to look for work at Bethlehem Steel in Lackawanna, just south of Buffalo. The man doing the hiring asked Frank if he was looking for a job. Frank said, "I'll seek a chance."

"Well we need chippers," the man said.

"Good," Frank answered, "I'm a chipper."

Chippers use air hammers with a cutting edge to cut out surface defects in steel billets. Chippers made a lot more money than janitors, but Bethlehem wanted only "experienced" chippers. Frank became an "experienced" chipper.

"I learned how to chip on a Sunday. In that time they didn't have the picture ID's. All you had to do was hold a pass in your hand and follow a friend into the mill. I learned how to chip in one day. So I started chipping for Bethlehem Steel in 1942. And I've been working for a steel mill ever since, except for five years in the Merchant Marine."

Pa Comes to Buffalo

In February 1942, the worst part of winter, Elmo gave in to his children's pleas and came to Buffalo. He left his job in Orlando reluctantly, and arrived in Buffalo wearing lightweight Florida clothes. Thick snow flakes were piling up in six-foot drifts. The snow seemed so light but it came down in tons until everything stopped. Buses went as far as they could; then everyone had to get out and walk home the rest of the way. Motorists were forced to abandon their cars in the middle of the highway. It was one of those years that gave rise to a local joke: "There are two seasons in Buffalo — Fourth of July and winter."

Nor did Elmo have much to cheer about as far as work went. From $9 a week in Orlando, he went to $10 a week in Buffalo and all the snow you cared to shovel. He had agreed to move north partly because he was angry with Mr. Gore, his boss in Florida. When he told Mr. Gore that his children wanted him to move to Buffalo, Gore said, "Don't go. If you stay here I'll pay you more."

"Can you do that?" Elmo asked Gore. "Sure," Gore replied. Elmo thought about all those years that Gore had exploited him, paying him less than he should have paid. He never went back to that job.

Dressed for Florida weather, Elmo looked out at the snow dropping down without end. Finally he asked his children, "Is this what you got me to leave Orlando for?" Some months later, he got a better-paying job in construction. His spirits really picked up when he got a job at Chevrolet that paid a living wage. Elmo stayed at Chevrolet for the rest of his working life. He did not retire until he was 68, when the company forced him to.

A few weeks after Elmo arrived in Buffalo, Hattie drove back to Orlando to get the rest of the family. She loaded them in her car: Kiyer, Bess, Gladys, Roy, and grand-nephew "Bro." The next year Bay and Ma Bess came to Buffalo on the bus. Only Warren was left behind to finish school. It was a long way from the orange groves of Orlando to the steel mills around Buffalo. Despite the distance, family ties were never broken.

Watson Street - Always Room for One More

With the first few paychecks, Hattie put a down payment of $300 on a two-flat, 11-room house at 263 Watson Street. Soon it was full. Hattie, Elmo, the ten children, their spouses, Ma Bess, and after a while, the grandchildren lived there. When cousins came and had nowhere to stay, Hattie made room for them. People criticized her for overcrowding her house but she said, "No kin of mine will have to sleep in the street. The house became the physical and spiritual center of the extended Lumpkin family and for years to come no one strayed too far. At 263 Watson Street the culture that had developed over the generations in Georgia and Florida grew and flourished. It was their life.

The Lumpkin brothers, l. to r., Wade, Frank, Ozzie, Elmo , Warren and Roy
The Lumpkin sisters, l. to r., Gladys, Bessie Mae, Jonnie (Pat), and Bay

In 1997, Bay's large family; Ozzie's family which included six grandchildren; Kiyer's three daughters; Gladys's son John Henry; and cousin Mary were still living in Buffalo. Mary's only child, "Sonny," had been killed in an accident at Bethlehem Steel a few years earlier. Parts of Buffalo looked like a ghost town in 1997, devastated by the closing of the mills and factories. Bay still remembers her first impression of the thriving, cold, industrial city.

"Finally I met big bad Buffalo. The preacher said, when you first see Buffalo, it looks good. But after a while it becomes rough. Move out while you have the chance. It was different then. All the stores on Williams Street had meats and vegetables out. When the war [World War II] was over, they couldn't leave those little things out.

"I remember a cute little girl who came from New York City. She would go out with Hattie to visit the neighbors. When they saw anyone put out of their house, they struggled to put them back. She spent a lot of time with Hattie. One day this little girl came to Hattie and me to say she was getting married. She said she didn't have any people in Buffalo. We went with her to City Hall and she put a white gardenia on Hattie and me."

By 1948, that "cute little girl" was divorced and met Frank, also recently divorced. They would fall in love, marry and stay together the rest of their long lives. [But that's getting ahead of the story.]

Hattie's move to Buffalo shifted the family's center of gravity from Orlando to Buffalo. She was a strong woman, intelligent, quick, tall, and large-boned. Called by all simply "Ma," she looked and acted like a tower of strength for her family and community. Her younger children still required a great deal of care, yet Hattie found the time and strength to continue to work outside the home. For a number of summers she went to Cape Cod to cook for wealthy families.

In Buffalo, Elmo continued to work and have the final say about anything affecting the family. The strength of the family was based on love, mutual respect and the understanding that ma and pa had the ultimate authority to make all important decisions. Wade, Ozzie, and Jonnie married but still stayed close, just a couple of blocks away. Frank and his wife Lorraine also found a place close to Watson Street. Except for military service, even married members of the

Lumpkin family lived close enough so they could "smell what was on the stove for dinner and drop in for a taste."

KO Lumpkin

In between his shifts at Bethlehem Steel, Frank continued to box as "KO Lumpkin." He explained, "I won those knockouts by counter-punching. You watch your opponent's fists. He's coming at you in front. You have to get him off balance, disrupt his attack, come at him from the side. Joe Louis was an aggressive fighter. Schmeling won his first fight against Joe Louis because he was a very good counter-puncher."

Frank's fighting weight was at the low end of the heavyweight class. Perhaps his relatively light weight explained his fighting style. He could not get his weight down to the light-heavyweight class, so he always fought under a big weight disadvantage. Still he continued to fight and win. By fighting in Pennsylvania as well as in New York State, Frank was able to fight sanctioned purse rounds twice a month. One night he came up against a left-hander, unusual in the fight game. Then it was Frank's turn to get knocked out. It was Frank's first bruising defeat, also his last. He decided it was time to quit the ring. Frank nursed his broken nose through two difficult operations. He never went back to the gym, not even to collect his gear.

Thirty years later, Frank's former manager kept the legend of KO Lumpkin alive. In 1973, a feature story in the Orlando *Sentinel Star*, about Luther Yates's Dollar Barber Shop, reported that Yates almost went into another career —Boxing Manager.

When he was a barber in downtown Orlando, he had this little shoe shine boy with big eyes. The kid wanted to be a fighter. 'You're too small,' Yates told him. But the kid was determined. Yates turned to a friend, champion boxer Gene Tunney, for advice. 'Coach him yourself,' advised Tunney.

Yates figures his protégé, Frank (KO) Lumpkin, could have been a champion, if only he didn't have that bad break.

The yellowed photographs of Lumpkin, which Yates often shows customers, picture a formidable-looking man wearing dark trunks, in a crouched position. He looks alert, ready to jab. The caption says the man is Lumpkin, "184 pounds, undisputed black heavyweight champ of the south."

Lumpkin was getting ready to meet the contenders when he had his accident one October night in the Orlando American Legion Hall. It was an exhibition match. Free. People wanted to see Lumpkin, this boxer they had heard so much about. During the fight, Lumpkin hit his opponent with his best punch: a strong left jab. He struck the man so hard, it broke his arm in several places. Yates still has the X-rays. The accident that ended Lumpkin's career was such a freak, he says, that Ripley used it in *Believe It Or Not*. After his broken arm, Lumpkin went to New York City [sic], became a factory worker. Yates went back to barbering full time, buying his present shop 20 years ago. [30]

Some details in this story are not accurate. Frank was never a shoeshine boy but a farm worker. He went to Buffalo, not New York City. Still it is remarkable that the legend of "KO Lumpkin" was kept alive in Orlando for so many years. Also, X-rays showed that Frank's arm was broken *before* he entered the ring; new bone had already started to form around the break. The complete story, that Frank fought three rounds with a broken arm, truly deserved a place in Ripley's *Believe It Or Not*.

"The struggle around Robeson profoundly changed my life."
Frank Lumpkin

5. War Abroad and At Home

World War II was changing the lives of all of the Lumpkins. Ozzie and Kiyer were drafted into the Army. Every day Hattie worried about her sons in the Army. Would she ever see them again? The situation of the anti-fascist Allies was grave. The Nazis controlled most of continental Europe. Their army had occupied the Ukraine and was threatening Moscow. The U.S. Congress was talking about lowering the draft age to 18. Then Warren Lumpkin would have to go, too. Hattie did not see that she had any stake in the war other than to get her sons back as soon as possible. So she was very angry when Jonnie campaigned to lower the draft age to help win the war. Jonnie came home one night to find that Hattie had locked her out of the house.

Jonnie Discovers the Communist Party

Hattie could not understand why Jonnie wanted to lower the draft age. Didn't Jonnie know that would put Warren in danger? But a lot had changed in Jonnie's life. She had discovered the Communist Party while working as a housekeeper. An employment agency had sent her to the home of two trade union organizers. At the end of two months of work, they referred her to baby-sit for a family of militant transit-worker unionists and members of the Communist Party. The lynching of Taft Rollins while in army uniform still burned in her heart. Her mind was wide open for revolutionary ideas. She was already convinced that capitalism was an evil system and found the Communist program of socialism very attractive. She wanted to replace capitalism with a system of production to satisfy the needs of people, instead of production for corporate profits. Jonnie moved rapidly into a leadership position in the Young Communist League (YCL). When asked how she rose to leadership so quickly, she said,

"Just give a hungry man a steak. Even if he's never seen one before, you don't have to explain much to him."

Jonnie agreed with the famous statement made by Joe Louis that there were many problems in the United States, but Hitler would not fix any of them. She became a staunch supporter of the war against fascism and everything that would speed up a victory against Hitler. This included opening a Second Front in Europe. Of the Allied Forces, the Soviet army was fighting the bulk of the Nazi army, concentrated on the Eastern Front. A Second Front in Western Europe would split the German army and quickly bring the war to an end. Lowering the draft age would make the army large enough to win. Meanwhile she was locked out of her house. So she told Hattie that God had told her to support the draft for 18-year olds. It was a winning argument; the door opened for Jonnie.

Jonnie Lumpkin and nieces Linda and Patricia

Through Jonnie the whole family was introduced to the ideas of Marx, Engels and Lenin. Soon Hattie joined the Communist Party and became a leading activist. When she saw an eviction on her block, she called out the neighbors to return the evicted tenants to their apartment and to put their furniture back. The family always had confidence in their "own people." They began to broaden their idea of their "own people" to include people of other races. They began to think in terms of class and to see racism as an attempt to weaken and divide the working class. A united working class could end capitalist oppression, just as earlier generations overthrew slavery. Socialism became the goal of most of the Lumpkins. But first they had to defeat Hitler and the Nazi Empire that stood for slavery and genocide, the murder of whole peoples.

When the draft age was lowered to 18, Warren became the third Lumpkin son drafted into the army but he was never shipped out of Florida. Kiyer and Ozzie were sent to Europe as part of the massive force that opened a Second Front. Their companies hit the beach at Normandy and fought their way across Europe to Berlin. They were caught in the Battle of the Bulge. In this battle, American troops were trapped by an unexpected Nazi offensive. However, the greatest danger that Ozzie faced during the war was racism. Racism almost cost Ozzie his life in Paris. A German woman pointed Ozzie out and claimed that he had raped her. African American soldiers were being hung every day on that kind of charge, according to Jonnie. The only thing that saved Ozzie was that his company commander came forward and said that Ozzie had not left the company at any time.

The two brothers went on to Berlin but they never saw each other. Nor did they meet Henry Ellis, their future brother-in-law, who was also in the infantry in the same campaign. Ellis was worried about what he would find in Berlin. When his company reached Berlin, they found the Soviets already there, celebrating their victory over fascism. Some Russian soldiers offered to teach the American soldiers how to ice skate. Later Kiyer was sent to the Pacific but his ship turned around when word came that the war was over.

With full employment during the war, a previously unknown prosperity was spreading in Buffalo. It was a time in Buffalo when all job seekers, including the disabled, could find work. A friend told Jonnie about a sad incident at Colonial Radio-Sylvania. A worker said, "I hope the war lasts long enough so I can pay off my home." The other women moved away from her in horror and disgust. Most had friends and relatives risking their lives in combat. When Frank heard the story he said it was a rotten system that needed a war to provide jobs.

Fair Employment

In many northern cities, factory doors that had been closed to African Americans and women were gradually forced open during the war. Discriminatory hiring practices yielded slowly to pressure of organized workers and to a Fair Employment Practices Commission (FEPC) order by President Roosevelt. Roosevelt is justly remembered for social legislation and leadership in the war against fascism. What the books leave out is that he was responding to the pressure of working people. The Lumpkins were part of that pressure. Jonnie became a leader in the fight to open up the factories to people of color.

Armed with two references from her jobs as a housekeeper, Jonnie got a job at Bell Aircraft. Bell Aircraft put her to work sweeping. The white women hired at the same time were given assembly jobs in production. Jonnie noticed that all of the African Americans at the plant were doing janitorial work. So she went to the United Auto Workers officers and told them, "Put me on production!" The chief steward told her, "Well put on this steward's button, sign up members in the union, and give me their $1 initiation fee. Here's a contract. If a member has a complaint, write up their grievance and we'll fight it."

As Jonnie tells it, "Black folks were eating outside at the railroad tracks. White folks ate inside at the lunchroom. One day the national anthem was played in the lunchroom and all the whites stood up. The Blacks outside did not stand. So they called me in to ask why we didn't stand. I told them, 'That's not my flag. The government's never done anything for Black people.' "

A week later Jonnie heard her name over the loudspeaker. "Jonnie Lumpkin, you're wanted in the front office." A government man started to talk to her, asking what she thought about the government. She told him, "Show me your shoes." He put out his foot. Jonnie said, "If I didn't know better, I'd say you're a f--- flatfoot." He warned her that she would get into trouble, talking like that. But she told him, "I have a [union] button, and it says that I have rights."

Jonnie turned to the Young Communist League for advice on how to fight racial discrimination at Bell Aircraft. Years later she reminisced, using the terms Negroes and Blacks that were common in the 1940s:

> "We agreed that we should organize a fight to put Negroes on production. We went to the Urban League, of which I was a member, and they said to get some more cases and send letters to the FEPC. The NAACP thought it was a good issue, too. We wrote to Claudia Jones of the Young Communist League (YCL) and she agreed that it was a good

issue to fight on. The FEPC, NAACP, YCL and Urban League agreed to send speakers to a meeting at the Urban League headquarters on Walnut Street. Letha Cloare, a director of FEPC, came but we didn't know that she was Black. [Cloare had a light complexion.]

"So we set up a conference with the company about the segregated dining room and the failure to put Blacks on production jobs. The company denied everything, but Letha Cloare stopped them. She knocked them dead, saying, 'I'm as Black as Jonnie. I've seen what's going on.' The next day 140 Black workers were upgraded to production jobs. They put me in the gun room, me and seven southern whites."

Jonnie saw no contradiction between the fight to win the war against fascism and the fight against racism. She followed the lead of the African American Communist Benjamin J. Davis, twice elected to the New York City Council. In a letter to the *New York Age*, Davis replied to their editorial, which claimed that Communist support of the War implied shelving the fight for equality.[31]

The *Daily Worker*, the Communist Party and other clear-headed win-the-war forces, are fighting for full Negro equality now as before and we consider it even more necessary now in order to secure our country's victory over Hitler. . . .

For some time, there has been a whispering campaign under way among the Negro people with reference to the *Daily Worker* and the Communist Party. This campaign claims falsely and fantastically that since the Communist Party supports the war they believe "now's the time to keep silent about Negro rights. . ."

The Negro people cannot be true to their own best interests without supporting the war.

The slaveowner's Fuehrer, Jeff Davis of 1861, is today reincarnated in Berlin. His name is Adolf Hitler. The lynchers, Ku-Kluxers, the Rankins, the jim-crow poll-taxers, the defeatists and fifth columnists . . . are serving Hitler today as the Copperheads served Jeff Davis against Lincoln in 1861. The Negro people will fight the Jeff Davises of Berlin today as they fought the Jeff Davises of Montgomery, Alabama in 1861.

Jeff Davis' slave-market stench in 1861 extended into the North and poisoned the Union forces with a brutal attitude toward the Negro, a hatred of Abolitionists that seriously impeded the war. In order that the people could be united to crush the "Adolf Hitler" of 1861, it was necessary to combat these brutalities and weaknesses in the northern forces. But the war had to go on, even while the injustices still continued in the North. Also now the stench of Hitlerism must be removed from our American life in order to strengthen national unity for victory over Hitler—and this is not in contradiction to our demand that the war must go on. No enemy voice must side-track us from that necessity.

There are those who say this is a "white man's war," as many of the followers of Garrison said of the Civil War. In reply, permit us to quote Frederick Douglass, the noblest Negro leader and the one who saw clearer and further than any other man—even Lincoln—and who proved himself to be one of the greatest statesmen of our country's history:

There are weak and cowardly men in all nations. We have them amongst us. They tell you that this is a "white man's war," that you will be no better off after than before the war; that the getting of you into the army is to "sacrifice you on the first opportunity." Believe them not; cowards themselves, they do not wish to have their cowardice shamed by your brave example. Leave them to their timidity or to whatever motive may hold them back.[32]

Bessie Mae Lumpkin, Secretary

Only one of the ten Lumpkin children broke into white-collar ranks—Bessie Mae, the third youngest. After her first year at Hutchinson Central High School in Buffalo, she went to New York City to become a secretary. Her way was paved by the progressive movement's network, starting with a summer job at Briehl's farm.[33] Among the guests at the resort were families, including some theater people, who had invited her to stay with them. These families were friends of Hattie, all progressives. Only 14, Bessie Mae enrolled in the Washington Business Institute in New York City, where she finished high school.

It took a lot of courage for Bessie Mae to leave 263 Watson Street and move so far away from Ma and Pa. But from the age of 6 or 7, she was her own person. With Hattie's encouragement, Bess took control of the house at 263 Watson Street. There she inflicted her tyranny of order and cleanliness on the entire family. She was more than ready for the big city. Bess wrote about Hattie for this book:

"I have always loved my mother more than anyone can imagine. She was very protective of me because I was sickly and skinny. She always worked and therefore was not my idea of a good mother, not being home and all. So when I was about six years old I decided I would show her how to take care of a house, making beds, sweep, dust, put things away—not realizing that she did that ALL DAY at the 'white folks house.' In my earlier years (8-10) I adopted Gladys and Roy [younger siblings], taking care they were properly dressed for school, bathed, fed and so on. In Buffalo Ma became extremely active politically and I resented it very much because the people we associated with cooked dinner, took their children to school and didn't seem as responsible in the progressive movement as my mom. (Of course mom cooked, too.) I even took Gladys and Roy to church, movies, and saw that they were well cared for when she was busy. "It wasn't until I went to work for Dworkins Dress Shop that I began to really see who she was. They [the Dworkins] were so respectful of her and talked about how great she was all the time. I was about 14 then. So I took another look and found she was the matriarch I wanted to be. She did take care of the house, children and family, and worked and was a leader as well. When I went to Briehl's farm and later went to school in New York I found out the whole world loved and respected her. I have truly appreciated EVERYTHING about my mother for 55 years, to this day! I have never regretted that she was not a housewife and felt sorry for those friends whose mothers were. I could discuss ANYTHING with my mother. I could go on for days about how much love she had for all of us and treated her ten children as individuals, knowing each of their weaknesses and strengths."[34]

"To become a secretary!" What else could be the goal of a young, Black, working-class woman in the 1940s? Housewife, entertainer or secretary—otherwise there was only domestic labor—or during the war—factory labor. College was not an option for most African American teenagers in Harlem then. While still a student in New York City, Bessie Mae lived next to Miriam Dweck who later married Clem Balanoff, noted steel labor activist in South Chicago. Miriam Balanoff became an attorney, a State Representative, and later a Circuit Court Judge in Chicago. After Wisconsin Steel closed, Miriam Balanoff, unaware that Frank was Bessie Mae's brother, provided the first office for the Save Our Jobs Committee. A small world!

Bessie Mae never again lived in Buffalo. She was part of the people's movement in New York City, married, moved to the Peekskill, N.Y. area and then to Mesa, Arizona. In Arizona she hoped to escape the asthma that plagued her. Her office skills helped organizations such as the Committee to Protect the Foreign Born and the Communist Party. The family remained closely knit. Bess stayed in touch, paying big telephone bills and frequent trips to Buffalo.

Bethlehem Steel

Frank learned a lot about unionism while working as a chipper at Bethlehem Steel. He also saw the need for political action that went beyond "bread and butter" unionism. At a mass meeting of the Young Communist League on Buffalo's West Side, Frank was one of two hundred young workers who joined. He understood the importance of winning the war against fascism. But victory was being delayed by anti-communism. This was his analysis:

"When I was working in Bethlehem Steel, the big issue was opening up a Second Front to win World War II. The Soviets had the First Front in Europe against the Nazi army. With the U.S. taking the lead to open a Second Front to attack the Nazi army from the West, the war could soon be ended. But Churchill and Roosevelt were holding back. The first concerns of the United Kingdom and United States governments seemed to be class considerations. Not win the war as soon as possible, but win the war in a way that would leave the socialist Soviet Union as weak as possible. Cold War considerations were delaying victory against Hitler.

"True anti-fascists in the United States were pressing for a Second Front. Charlie Chaplin became identified with this movement and was hounded out of the country as a result. The issue was decided with the Soviet victory at Stalingrad and the march of the Red Army towards Berlin. Then the Western allies rushed to open a Second Front. They wanted to reach Germany before the Red Army had liberated all of Germany without them."

Frank had learned from others and his own experience. When Jonnie joined the Young Communist League in 1942, she was asked to recruit other members of her family. "There's one person *you* have to get," she told her fellow Communists, "my brother Frank." Frank was always "teaching." When people said they would not work at such low-paid jobs, Frank told them, "Take the job. Then fight for more." Frank was not easy to convince, but once convinced of the justice of a struggle, he stayed with it to the end.

The Merchant Marine

With three brothers in the army, Frank wanted to do more to help win the war. While the army wouldn't take him with a missing trigger finger, the Merchant Marine would. So he signed up in the Merchant Marine. Ships in his convoy were torpedoed but his ship did not stop to help the survivors. There were corvettes in the convoy whose job it was to do that. Although they were often in combat zones and suffered heavy casualties, merchant seamen were considered civilians. It took 40 years, after the war, for merchant seamen to receive recognition for military service. They never did get veteran's benefits.

As "civilians," seamen could belong to a union. East Coast and Great Lakes seamen joined the National Maritime Union (NMU). Before the union, working on ships had been a very hard job with bad living conditions, poor food and low pay. By the time Frank joined, the union had won decent food aboard ship and a better wage. As soon as the ship returned to the United States, Frank sent his paychecks home to Buffalo to help pay for the Lumpkin house at 263 Watson Street. In the port of Baltimore, he planned to visit friends for a couple of days before flying to Buffalo. He had his ticket and just a little spending money, with enough for a cab to the airport. Or so he thought. As the taxi meter began to rise quickly, Frank told the cab driver, "I have just $10 in my pocket. When the fare gets to $10,

Frank Lumpkin in the Merchant Marine, 1943

stop and let me out." Perhaps the cab driver had some influence on the meter because the $10 didn't run out until they reached the airport.

On most voyages, there was not enough time in port to visit Buffalo. In port the engine crew worked eight hours on and 16 hours off. Frank could visit the town as long as he returned in time for his shift. In New Orleans, Lumpkin and friends from the engine crew got on a bus. Frank took a seat behind the "colored" sign, just as he had done in Orlando. His buddies, who were white, came back to sit with him. The bus driver stopped the bus and made Lumpkin's friends get up and move to the front of the bus. That was just about the only difference between southern and northern cities, Frank concluded. Northern cities were segregated too. They just didn't put up any signs.

As a seaman, Frank was no saint. Aboard a new ship, he would size up the crew and figure out his strategy. Often there would be a chief bully aboard ship, perhaps the largest man. He really didn't like to fight, but if the bully provoked a fight, Frank would take care of him. Sometimes his ship carried troops, and boxing matches would be set up to help pass the time on the long transatlantic voyages. Frank gave tips to the young fighters. His boxing skills were known and respected.

One trip carried African American troops to Liverpool. (The U.S. Army was segregated during World War II.) The merchant seamen laughed as they watched the soldiers having a "ball," playing cards and listening to music. The soldiers seemed unaware that ships were being sunk everyday on the North Atlantic. Docking at Liverpool was rough because ships could not enter until high tide. On Frank's first trip there, his ship was waiting with many others when German bombs began to fall. Some ships went down. Later, the German army sent over V-2 missiles and Liverpool was devastated.

One day Frank got into a touchy situation.

"I was a professional and didn't want to fight the young, amateur boxers. But the bo'sun asked me to 'help out' and go three rounds in an exhibition match. The bo'sun wasn't even my boss. The chief engineer was.

"No one is supposed to be hurt in an exhibition match. You wear 16-ounce gloves—they're almost like pillows—instead of the regular 6-ounce, and head gear to protect your eyes and nose.

"Most of my friends had to work during the match. You worked 4 hours on and 8 hours off, seven days a week. The soldier I was fighting had a lot of buddies among the troops. The soldiers began to bet. There was nothing else to do so there was a lot of gambling on the ship. It was supposed to be an exhibition match; you know, show the advantage of the rules—jab, jab, don't hit below the belt.

When the match began, my opponent tried to hurt me. So I got mad and knocked him out. After that fight there were a lot of angry soldiers who had lost a lot of money. Things were tense. The captain and I agreed that I would not fight on the ship any more. That didn't stop the captain from asking me to show him how to box."

In the ship's engine room Frank had plenty of chances to work with the machinery he loved. He rose from wiper, to oiler, water tender, fireman, deck engineer, and finally, junior engineer. He worked on the auxiliary shaft, main shaft, oil pumps and water pumps. He got the chance to work on the engine too, a big, reciprocating steam engine with large pistons going up and down. Most of his work was maintenance, greasing and oiling the engines. If they broke down it was usually on some other shift, not his.

Off duty, Frank often played cards. "A ship is a bad place to gamble. It was a prison kind of thing. You couldn't go nowhere. You couldn't spend money. So I sent my money home."

While at sea, Frank began a lifetime habit of serious reading. He read to learn, to try to find answers to the questions that swarmed in his mind. Even when he worked at Wisconsin Steel, he would get up two hours earlier to get some serious reading in before he went to work.

The bombs and torpedoes were not the only dangers the seamen faced. To meet the war's shipping crisis, the United States began to mass-produce "Liberty Ships." Safety standards were set aside, and sometimes the hulls split apart in the cold North Atlantic. In the engine room, there was plenty of asbestos insulation around the steam pipes. Frank paid no attention to the asbestos fibers that were inhaled because then asbestos was thought to be harmless. Some 45 years later, seamen filed a class action suit against the shipping companies, but the harm had already been done. Frank was among thousands of ex-seamen who got a token settlement of $1,200 (after lawyers' fees) for years of exposure to asbestos. Fortunately, to date he has escaped arthritis that affects many who work out in the cold.

August 6, 1945 - the Atom Bomb

The bombed-out European cities were sad. Saddest of all were the children. If you gave them a candy bar, they never ate it. Instead they took it home to be sold or exchanged for food for their family. Frank was in Belgium on August 6, 1945, after the war had ended in Europe. On that day an atom bomb was dropped on Hiroshima. The first mate had been on shore and came back to the ship with the news. "They dropped a bomb in Japan," he said. "It melted everything until the sand ran like water." Frank did not believe that report. "How could sand melt and run like water?" Just three days later, another atom bomb was dropped on the city of Nagasaki. On August 14, Japan surrendered unconditionally and the war was over.

At that time Frank thought that dropping the bomb was a terrible act. But he believed the bombing was needed to end the war. Some Americans did ask why it was necessary to use the atom bomb a second time, in the city of Nagasaki. The destructive power of the nuclear bomb had already been demonstrated in Hiroshima. Few Americans ever learned that the Japanese government had sent peace feelers to the United States eight months before the bomb was dropped. Little by little, some Americans began to question the motives for dropping the atomic bombs. Robert R. Young claimed that the motive for the bombing was to put pressure on the Soviet Union. He was Chairperson of the Board of the Chesapeake & Ohio Railroad when he wrote this analysis:

> We are kidding ourselves if we believe the atomic bomb was dropped [only] on Japan. There is evidence that fully eight months earlier Japan was ready to capitulate. If the purpose of the bomb was to save American lives, then a fair warning before Okinawa would have saved more. . . . No, the atomic bomb was dropped not militarily but diplomatically upon Russia.[35]

After the war ended, Frank continued to work as a junior engineer. By that time he had adapted to a seaman's life. In foreign ports, Frank did pretty much what most of the other seamen did. He headed for the nearest bar to drink and find a woman. In Marseilles he met a woman who wanted to marry him. His marriage with Lorraine had broken up, but Frank never returned to Marseilles. Sometimes he liked to take a long walk and explore. In a German port after the war, he noticed that a little boy had followed him for many blocks. The child looked as though he wanted to talk to Frank. Finally, the boy got up his courage and asked Frank, "Are you a n---?" Frank was angry and hurt. "What could I do? I could not hit a child. It was grownups who taught the child to use that word." During the war, the unions observed a no-strike pledge; the shippers made billions of dollars of guaranteed profits. With the war over, seamen were no longer willing to work 56-hour weeks at sea for low wages. The unions tried to negotiate but the shipping companies would not budge. Ship and dock workers were split along craft lines into more than six different unions, each negotiating on its own. Some of the maritime unions had strong progressive traditions and worked to form a united front of maritime workers.

National Maritime Strike

On May 6, 1946, seven maritime unions joined to form the CMU, Committee for Maritime Unity. Six were affiliated to the Congress of Industrial Organizations (CIO) and one was independent. The co-chairs were Harry Bridges of the International Longshoremen's Union who was also director of the California CIO, and Joe Curran of the National Maritime Union (NMU). Although rank and file members of the American Federation of Labor (AFL) supported maritime unity, the AFL did not join the Unity Committee. This was about twenty years before the CIO and the AFL merged into the AFL-CIO. The CMU set a strike date deadline of June 15, 1946, unless an agreement was reached. The strike would affect 156,000 workers, with another 49,000 workers under contracts serving as a reserve. Only troop ships and relief vessels would be allowed to sail. On May 27, strike preparations were strengthened when NMU seamen voted to reject a raise of $12.50 a month. The seven unions had agreed not to settle individually so many were angry that Curran had even put the company proposition to a vote.[36]

On May 30, President Truman threatened to use the Navy to keep merchant ships sailing if workers struck on June 15.[37] Angry union leaders charged that Truman had "fired a torpedo" into the wage negotiations. The CMU statement, quoted in the June 1, 1946 *Daily Worker*, said "President Truman has turned his back on his and the Democratic Party's pledge to American seamen to support their struggle for a reduction of their work week from 56-63 hours to 40 hours." The union leaders also referred to Truman's action to break the railroad workers' strike and asked the President to take "a cooling off period in between breaking strikes."

During all of this excitement in the port cities, Frank was working at sea. He was a good union man on the ship and served as a steward for the NMU. He was also a great admirer of Caribbean-born Ferdinand Smith, a founder and national secretary of the NMU. This was the highest elected post held by an African American in any union in the country. To many unionists, Ferdinand Smith symbolized the leading role played by African American workers in the organization of the CIO. In contrast, the AFL had excluded African American seamen. [38] The deportation of Ferdinand Smith during the Cold War was a setback to labor unity and militancy.

Frank spent his time between trips in Buffalo, far from the maritime union centers. Already a member of the Young Communist League, he joined the Communist Party, as he put it, because "Communist seamen were so solid; they were always fighting discrimination. The top and bottom of the ship were mostly white, on deck and in the engine room. Blacks were mostly in the middle, in the mess room. The Communists were fighting to change that." Frank was aware that Communists had played a vital role in organizing the NMU as well as many other CIO unions.

When the union crisis of 1946 came to a head, Lumpkin was at sea, near Portland, Maine. On June 14, 1946, the CMU almost had a national agreement granting their main demands. At the last minute, the West Coast Waterfront Employers Association refused to sign the agreement. The strike was on! Lumpkin's ship pulled into Portland the night before the strike and all the power was turned off. The crew packed up all of their personal possessions and left the ship to join the strike.

Once off the ship, the crew had to find a place to sleep. Frank and two white engine room workers tried to get a hotel room. The hotel management said they were full. The next hotel was also full. And the next, and the next. Finally, Frank told his friends, "Look, I know what's going on. You go and get a room and I'll find one in the colored part of town." It was the Southern white who refused to split up. He said he'd expect that in the South but was surprised to find such racism in Maine. So they persevered, and before the night was up they finally found a hotel where they could sleep.

For the seamen who came from all parts of the country, the National Maritime Union was a good school for interracial solidarity. Every union victory helped the fight against racism, and vice versa. The NMU had won a rotary hiring hall to replace the degrading "shape-up," where seamen lined up and the company agent picked out the crew he wanted. With the rotary hiring hall, seamen were hired in the order that they registered after they came off their last ship. Racial discrimination in hiring ended. Seamen of all races benefited from the union hiring hall, which restored the seamen's dignity.

Frank and his buddies spent only two nights in the Portland hotel. The strike was so effective that the workers won almost all of their demands within 24 hours. The seamen, firemen, oilers, water tenders, cooks and stewards won a 40-hour work week while in port, and reduction from 56-63 hours a week at sea to 48 hours. They won a raise of $17.50 a month; the seamen's solidarity paid off. The seamen had turned down a separate offer of $12.50, which would have broken the CMU united front. Radio operators, engineers and West Coast longshoremen won substantial improvements in pay and hours. The West Coast longshoremen retained their rotating hiring hall run by the union. Meanwhile the East Coast longshoremen, controlled by the AFL union, continued to be hired under the humiliating shape-up.

The CMU held together for a few months after the great victory but then the separate unions began to drift apart. Cold War attacks on the maritime unions created further divisions. For two more years Lumpkin sailed and enjoyed the fruits of the victory. The CMU lesson of unity stayed with him for life and was reflected in his political style of work.

Who Won the War?

In 1945, the Nazis and their allies were defeated. The war was over. But Frank did not go back to work in steel right after the war. He was never one to quit a job. Besides, he liked the life of a skilled seaman. But Grace Lines sold his ship from under him in a Greek port in 1948. The company handed the seamen airline tickets back to the United States. In Frank's last action as a union seaman, he and his fellow-workers refused to take the airline tickets. "We sailed here, and we're sailing back," they insisted. They were not in a hurry to go back. The seamen knew that they would stay on the payroll until they reached the United States. After that, they didn't know where their next paycheck would come from.

When soldiers, sailors and seamen returned home to the United States, they found a country going through many changes. The unions were stronger than they had ever been. The fascists had been defeated and people could live in peace. Or so it seemed. But after the war, millions lost their factory jobs and the decent wages that the unions had won. Women workers and workers of color were first to be laid off when war plants closed down. In Buffalo, the auto workers' union contracts had separate seniority lists for men and women. No man lost his job until every woman who did that kind of work was laid off. At plants still open, returning soldiers were supposed to get their jobs back, and everybody understood that. But if everyone was needed to win the war, Frank asked, why wasn't everyone needed to keep the country going after the war?

Post-war Strikes and Unemployment

After VE day (Victory in Europe) in August 1945, Bell Aircraft laid Jonnie off. Then she got a job as a "bumper" at the Curtiss Wright aircraft plant. The bumper held the part in place at the receiving end of the riveting process. That job lasted a few months, and in 1946 Jonnie was laid off again. After that, she could find only low-paying jobs.

The workers had sacrificed a lot to win the war. At Jonnie's plant, for example, the UAW had agreed to a no-strike clause and no increase in pay until the end of war. Winning the war against fascism had been labor's number one concern. Naturally, with the war won, unions were ready to play catch-up. In contrast, the companies' main concern was making more profit. A clash between workers and the big companies seemed inevitable.

At least the Lumpkin family was united again. Warren had returned from Florida with Frances, his strikingly beautiful, young bride. Frances never let her beauty interfere with her brains. From the Lumpkin family in Buffalo, she gained new hope and new interest in political matters. She said that, "My grandmother and mother were resigned to conditions facing African Americans in Florida. They said, 'It's always been like this and it always will be.' But when I saw a chance to change things, I grabbed it."

The war over, the labor movement was poised to make some big gains. A record number of strikers, 3,500,000 in 1945 and 4,600,000 in 1946, showed that workers were in a militant mood.[39] Community organizations were also planning to make big advances. As soon as a

Frances Lumpkin

victory in the war was in sight, the NAACP and the Urban League were among those who raised the slogan of a Double V: Victory against fascism abroad, and Victory against racism at home. A new phase of people's struggles was beginning. The only thing that could stop workers from advancing was disunity, workers fighting among themselves.

Anti-communism and Racism

Those who wanted to divide organized labor had two big guns in their arsenal: anti-communism and racism. They used both. When the Cold War began right after World War II, an anti-Communist hysteria was created during which the Taft-Hartley law and other anti-labor legislation was passed. Cold War pressures took a suicidal form within the CIO. Twelve unions with millions of members were charged as "Communist" and subjected to raids by other CIO unions. In 1949 the CIO expelled the targeted unions. Many labor activists date the loss of union strength in the United States to 1949 and the CIO split.[40]

This mess was brewing when Frank Lumpkin returned to civilian life. Cold War warrior Harry Truman had been re-elected President. Truman had been openly anti-labor in the coal strike and the railroad strike, as well as in the maritime strike. Truman broke the railroad strike of 1946 by threatening to draft the strikers into the army.[41] Truman's foreign policy made a break with FDR's policy of a stable peace based on the tripartite alliance of the United States, Soviet Union and Great Britain. Instead, Truman adopted the World War II goal of the fascist powers—the destruction of the Soviet Union.

Henry A. Wallace, FDR's third-term vice-president, decided to run against Truman for president in 1948 as a third party candidate on the Progressive Party ticket. Wallace's program called for a return to the policies of the New Deal, to defend the gains made by working people and people of color in the '30s and '40s. In foreign policy, the Progressive Party program advocated world peace instead of Cold War and nuclear threats.

Paul Robeson and Henry Wallace
The whole Lumpkin family in Buffalo joined the Wallace campaign. So did Paul Robeson, star of the screen and stage. Robeson was touring the country, speaking for Wallace and the Progressive Party. In Buffalo, the African American community and progressives generally were excited about Robeson's coming visit. But the Cold War had heated up. Media attacks on Wallace and the Progressive Party became more and more vicious. Security was needed for Progressive Party rallies in Buffalo. African Americans were determined to protect their beloved Paul Robeson who spoke for the oppressed all over the world. The five grown Lumpkin brothers were a security detail almost by themselves. They felt honored to be assigned to guard the great man. When Robeson arrived at the hall, he had to run a gauntlet of police. But the Lumpkin brothers stood at either side of Paul. He would be safe.

"You should have let me know and I would have come prepared," Robeson commented on the intimidating show of police force at the peaceful rally. He told of riding in a truck with striking iron miners

Hattie Lumpkin with "Labor for Henry Wallace" (Wallace left front)

**Bottom, Robeson with Western Electric workers in Buffalo, 1948
Beatrice Shapiro stands at Robeson's left.**

in the Mesabi Range, with company police guns pointed at them along the entire route. Paul Robeson's words inspired courage and determination to fight for the people's dignity, for the children's future. People were proud to stand at his side. "The tallest tree in our forest," they called him.[42]

When the campaign was over, and the votes counted, Henry A. Wallace had 1,150,000 votes. At the last moment, many voters threw their votes to Harry Truman because they feared the election of the Republican candidate, Thomas Dewey. A *Daily Worker* analysis said, in part, "The two-party objective was to avoid a debate on the foreign policy issue. The formation of the Progressive Party and the nomination of Henry A. Wallace (former vice-president) as its presidential candidate shattered this maneuver. Peace became the central issue in the campaign." The *Daily Worker* article said further, "Truman won the election by a hypocritical copying of the speeches of Franklin Roosevelt and by imitating as much as he dared the ... [program] of the Progressive Party and Henry Wallace."[43]

For the Lumpkins, the campaign was a school for independent politics. During the campaign, Frank met his wife-to-be at a fund raiser for Henry Wallace. It was the first of hundreds of fund raisers for progressive organizations that they would attend together.

Police Beat and Arrest Frank
In the summer of 1949, the Buffalo Communist Party learned that African American men had been denied entry to the *SS Canadiana*, a cruise boat that featured a dance band. Single white men, single women and couples of all races could buy tickets, but single African American men were barred. The Communist Party initiated a protest action on July 31, 1949. About 50 people went down to the boat to make a test case and to protest the discrimination. Three African American steel workers were not allowed to board the boat although they had bought cruise tickets. Demonstrators objected and the police were called. A policeman, named Frank K. Dougherty, arrested a young, white demonstrator and was roughly dragging him away. Lumpkin protested the rough handling of the student. The cop lost interest in the student, let him go and brought his club down on Lumpkin's head. The club cracked the forehead and split the flesh.

As the blood spurted, Frank's chief concern was that the blood was staining his only suit.

Jonnie spotted another cop who pulled out his pistol and aimed it at Frank. Although nine months pregnant, she threw her arms around her brother's neck and began to scream, "Don't hurt him. That's my brother!" Her seemingly hysterical conduct was coolly calculated. She probably saved Frank's life. But now it was Frank who was under arrest, and the young white demonstrator had disappeared in the confusion.

After a ride in a police van to the emergency room where it took five stitches to sew up his forehead, Frank was locked up. The charge was "interfering with a police officer making an arrest." In record time Elmo Lumpkin, Sr. reached the police station. Twenty policemen were lined up in front of the police desk, all with guns drawn. They must have thought that the revolution had come. Except for the live guns, they looked like the Keystone Cops.

"Are you holding Frank Lumpkin?" Elmo asked. "Let him out. Here's the deed to my house."

Frank's father had brought the deed to 263 Watson St. as bail. Elmo Sr. was putting the Lumpkin house, home to at least 15 people, on the line to gain Frank's freedom. That was "Pa's" function in the family—to work, bring home his pay, and come through for them in emergencies. The police put their guns away and Frank was out on bail. Even that tense scene had something that Jonnie found amusing in later years. Warren and his camera were on the scene. "Stand there. Hold still," Warren told the line of police so he could get better pictures.

Fortunately, Frank's skull was not fractured. The stitches healed, but the hardest time was ahead. Although "interfering with an officer making an arrest" was only a misdemeanor, a sentence of up to six months in jail was possible. A defense had to be mounted; the discrimination at the cruise boat had to be ended.

Hattie did not sit around idly while waiting for her son's trial. As chairperson of the Ellicott District of the Buffalo Communist Party, she quickly organized a labor-community coalition. The coalition demanded that the *SS Canadiana* stop discriminating. Fifty clergymen asked the State Attorney to drop the charges against Frank.

Before Lumpkin's trial began, the coalition won a victory. The *SS Canadiana* company caved in to community pressure and promised to end racial discrimination on their boats. USWA local 2603 announced that they would continue to monitor the situation. The three workers who had been refused entry to the boat were members of that local. The Buffalo ALP (American Labor Party) also denounced the police assault. James Annacone, then ALP candidate for mayor, stated: "Frank Lumpkin's blood-stained shirt is a warning that jim-crow must always be upheld by the nightstick and the lynch rope. This unprovoked attack on a Negro worker is pure fascism." [44] Lumpkin's defense committee found a very competent civil rights lawyer, Thomas L. Newton. Newton came out of retirement to take the case on a pro bono (without fee) basis. After several postponements, the trial was set for September 22.

On September 22, the defense asked for a jury trial. The student who had disappeared after Dougherty manhandled him came forward voluntarily. He disregarded the risk of being arrested and appeared as a defense witness. The student testified that "the sound of the club striking Lumpkin's head reverberated across the dock."

Community pressure was in Frank's favor. The police officer who clubbed Lumpkin was already being sued for beating two African American women. Still the State wanted a conviction in the Lumpkin case. The State of New York even brought in an African American prosecutor. That was the first time in anyone's memory that an African American had served as a prosecutor in a Buffalo court.

Jury Trial

The jury was all white. Some jurors were store owners and professionals who could not be counted on to be sympathetic to workers. It looked bad. Then, as Frank feared, he was questioned about his professional boxing status. In New York, a boxer's fists had been ruled "lethal weapons." Joe North, the renowned reporter, had already written his story for the *Worker* assuming that the all-white jury would convict Frank. But he gladly tore up that story and wrote another one. The jury took only 15 minutes to reach a unanimous verdict, "Not guilty!" There was a lot of cheering and hugging in the courtroom, including by some jurors. Frank was greatly relieved. His belief in Black-white unity was reinforced.

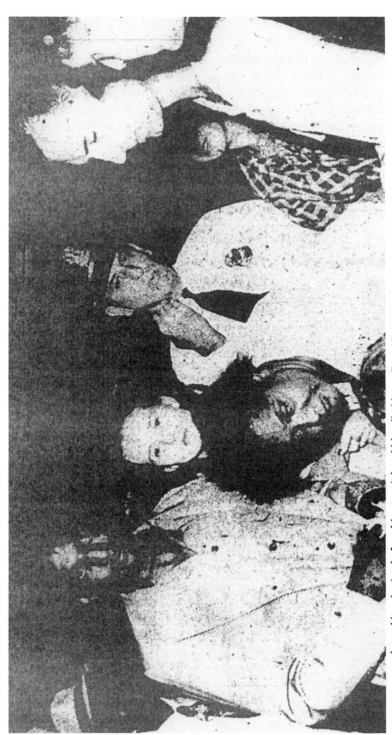

Lumpkin minutes before his arrest, head bloodied by police. His sister Jonnie is on his left, brother Elmo on right.

The Worker, Upstate, August 7, 1949

Robeson Attacked at Peekskill

The stitches in Lumpkin's head had barely healed when he got some upsetting news. On August 27, 1949, a racist mob had stopped Paul Robeson from singing at a concert in Peekskill, New York. The mob attacked the concertgoers, chopped the stage to pieces and burned the sheet music. It was said that the mob was organized by right-wing organizations with the cooperation of the local police. The stage had been set for the violence by a national media attack against Robeson. The concerted media attack focused on Robeson's anti-war statements. At a Peace Conference in Paris, Robeson had stated, "It is unthinkable that American Negroes would go to war in behalf of those who had oppressed us for generations . . . against a country [the Soviet Union] which in one generation has raised our people to full human dignity."[45]

A week later Robeson's supporters organized another Robeson concert in Peekskill. This time they were nearly 30,000 strong. Frank and some of his Buffalo comrades decided to go to the Peekskill concert-rally. The atmosphere of lynch-mob terror in Peekskill was described by an eyewitness.

Paul Robeson stood on a little platform, guarded by a small number of Black and white union men and veterans, endangered, it was said by at least one sniper in the woods. The loudspeaker brought Robeson's voice loud and clear to all those thousands, drowning out the band and the police helicopter circling over us. No description can reflect the enthusiasm after each song. . . . Then the concert ended, perfectly organized and perfectly peaceful. But while the private cars drove off, we discovered that we had no bus drivers. During the concert, obviously by prearrangement, they had gone to the next town and not returned. Before long, each bus found one passenger able to drive it and we moved off. We elected one Black man as our bus leader.

As we drove away, we saw cops hitting one of the Blacks hard over the head with nightsticks. He was a highly decorated war veteran, I learned later. Some men wanted to help him, others insisted that we could do nothing. Since many families were on the bus, the best thing was to get away. At the exit, state police directed all vehicles away from the main road and on to a local road through the woods. . . . All along the road, every fifty yards, groups of men pelted each bus or car with large rocks taken from big piles at their feet.

Our group leader asked us to keep calm, told the children to lie down in the center aisle and the men to hold their jackets to the windows to keep out flying glass. Nearly everyone was hit in our bus, none seriously, although two-thirds of the windows were smashed, including the windshield. But our amateur driver kept the bus moving through the howling mob. After about twenty minutes we left the rock-throwing gauntlet and thought our troubles were over. But now the state cops stopped the buses, "to check drivers' licenses." . . . We had to leave the bus and walk through the dark streets of a small town to the station. . . . Back in New York we heard the excited news reports: Robeson and his Communist backers had been responsible for all the violence.[46]

Thirty years later, a fascinated audience in Chicago's Third Unitarian Church heard Frank Lumpkin tell how a small group of Buffalo steel workers stood with Robeson when he returned to Peekskill. The group included Rufus Frazier, who was later elected chairperson of the Buffalo NAACP and Luther Graves, who became an organizer for the Mine, Mill and Smelter Workers Union.

"The struggle around Paul Robeson profoundly changed my life. I was there on September 4, 1949, the second time Paul Robeson led a rally in Peekskill. This time the people came to guarantee that the racists and the reactionaries would not break up the concert. We lived in Buffalo, New York, 400 miles from Peekskill. The night before I told Walter, 'You know Paul Robeson is going back to Peekskill.' Walter said, 'Is he crazy? They almost killed him the first time.' So I answered, 'But this time we'll be there.'

" 'Who? Just you and me?' 'No. Joe Green, Rufus Frazier and Luther Graves. Five steel workers from Buffalo.

" 'But that's 400 miles!' 'Yes, we'll have to get up very early.'

"We had no problem getting up because we didn't sleep that night. Five Black steel workers from Buffalo went to Peekskill and looked for Paul's camp. But first we had to pass through the enemy camp. We were late and they were prepared. We had no plan but we were determined to see Paul and be counted with him at all costs. Paul was over there singing. But between Paul and us was a mob.

"Five steel workers from Buffalo had come 400 miles to see Paul and could not see him. How could we explain that to people in Buffalo? Went 400 miles to see Paul and the mob would not allow us to see him. Who could sell that story to the steel workers in Buffalo? We came up with this plan. We would walk down to the enemy line and they would run us back. And that's what we would tell the steel workers in Buffalo. Good!

"So we started toward the mob, which had police and state troopers around. Having experience with that kind of action I had my hat on because that hat cushioned many a blow for me. As we walked toward the entrance, the mob got ready and we were ready. We thought the police would tell us to get the hell out of there and with a few bumps we would be on our way home with a clear conscience. We did what we could, and that was it.

"But that was not it. The police did not run us back. They had other plans. They parted the crowd with their sticks and said come on in, but you will never get out. As we walked through the mob, spit hit my face and ran down my suit. Poor Rufus, he was always so neat. He tried to flick the spit off his suit. But we were not provoked. We remembered why we were there. Inside the stadium we met another kind of uniformed guard. They were World War II veterans with baseball bats who came to protect Paul. The mob did not dare to try to break through the people's defense line.

"The rest is history. Like the cowards they were, the mob waited until people left and they could attack them one at a time. Many people were severely wounded and cars destroyed as they took the road back to New York City. But this country was never the same and I was never the same."

When Frank and his Buffalo comrades got to their car, they decided to make a stop in Brooklyn to visit Bessie Mae. They had not slept the night before and hoped to get some rest before the long drive home. When they reached Brooklyn, they were shocked to learn that the mob had injured many concertgoers and had wrecked their cars on the road back to New York City. Frank had used a different route and did not see the violent attacks on the Robeson supporters.

Relaxed in the safety of Bessie Mae's apartment, the Buffalo steel workers helped themselves to some liquor she had in her closet. After what they had been through, they felt they deserved it. Before they knew it, the bottles were empty. They didn't know it at the time, but they had changed Bessie Mae's life forever.

The liquor belonged to Joe Slifkin's Communist Party club and he had to return it. He barely knew Bessie Mae except that a fund-raising party had been held at her apartment. She told Slifkin what had happened. Still somebody had to replace the missing liquor. One thing led to another and they got married. Two children, three grandchildren and one great-grandchild later, they are still together and still fighting racism. And Bess still has not paid Joe for the $8.00 worth of liquor that was consumed.

In June 1950, the Cold War broke out into a hot war in Korea. One month later, Julius Rosenberg was arrested on the charge of conspiring to commit espionage. A few weeks later, Ethel Rosenberg and Morton Sobell were also arrested and the three charged with giving the atom bomb "secret" to agents of the Soviet Union. The Lumpkins believed that the Rosenbergs and Sobell were being framed. The case was used as an excuse to persecute Communists and other labor activists.

The Smith Act, since declared unconstitutional, was used to create a deadly, national hysteria of red-baiting. Twelve national Communist leaders were indicted under the Smith Act and many arrests followed. The Justice Department unleashed a deportation drive against immigrant activists. Of 135 non-citizens arrested, 41 were trade unionists. Most were deported.

World War II was barely over but peace had not come. Tens of thousands of soldiers sent to Korea came back to the U. S. in body bags. In the United States, the Cold War against Communism spread. Any movement that defended the interests of workers, farmers and people of color was subject to persecution as a "Communist" organization. Some people began to wonder, "Who won the war?"

Gladys Lumpkin (right) collecting signatures to ban nuclear weapons

Part II

6. Chicago and Wisconsin Steel

In 1949 Frank married Beatrice (Bea) Shapiro, an electronics worker and divorced mother of two young children. The movement that brought them together has kept them together for many eventful years. Frank and Bea moved to Chicago where they thought there were more jobs than in Buffalo. It was said, "If you can't find work in Chicago, you can't find work anyplace." But Frank did not find work immediately so he returned to Buffalo to finish packing.

Frank Lumpkin and Beatrice Shapiro Lumpkin, 1950 (Photo by Jo Banks)

The year 1949 was a hard time to be unemployed. The post World War II depression created 5 million jobless. Labor economists stated that the real rate of unemployment was 9.12%, double the official rate of the Bureau of Labor statistics.[47] The Korean War had not yet started. Anyway, the Korean War did not create many jobs.

Every day Frank looked for work, checking construction gangs, factory gates, everywhere. The rejections were very hard to take. One day he used his carfare to go to a movie to pick up his spirits. His carfare gone, he walked the 10 miles home.

Sometimes women could find jobs (at low pay) when men couldn't find anything. In Chicago, Bea worked at Spiegel as a typist until she was fired for being pregnant. She found another job on the Motorola assembly line but by this time it was harder to hide the pregnancy, even under a loose smock. So she was fired again. Until labor and the women's movement won some job rights for pregnant women in the 1970s, non-union employers could get rid of pregnant women at will.

At least the Lumpkins had a place to live. Apartments were very scarce in 1949, almost impossible to find without the help of friends. Some friends who were leaving Chicago allowed the Lumpkins to share their Lake Park Avenue apartment before they moved out. Once the Lumpkins were in the apartment, the real estate company agreed to accept them as tenants. By the time the landlords learned that Frank was African American, they could not legally evict them.

Paul Lumpkin was born in March 1950. There was so little money in the house that a friend on welfare bought them groceries with money earned by selling her breast milk. Another friend loaned them a bed for the other two children. Ten dollars sent by a Western Electric co-unionist from Buffalo kept them eating for another two weeks. They were so poor that the housekeeper, provided free by the Salvation Army for a few days after Paul's birth, brought her own brown-bag lunch. The Lumpkins could not get on welfare because they did not meet Chicago residence requirements then in effect.

Chippers wanted

Two weeks after Paul was born, Frank saw a Wisconsin Steel ad for chippers. He showed up and was given a simple test. The air hammer and chipping chisel were put in his hand. "Let me see you chip this bar," the foreman said. Frank took the hammer and made it talk, as he removed a surface crack in the bar. "That was good steel,"

Frank remembered. The chips curled away, as though in a lathe, leaving the surface smooth. The foreman patted Frank on the back and said, "You've got a job." He had never seen better chipping. That was all the reference that Frank needed.

At last Frank had a job. He never doubted that he would pass the chipping test. He was worried about the physical examination and his missing fingers. Fortunately, there wasn't much of a physical examination. The company needed chippers but did not plan to keep them. When Frank asked for a locker, he was told he didn't need one. They said he would not be there that long, perhaps 30 days. But new orders kept coming in and the 30 days stretched to 30 years. Five years after he was hired, he reported a small cut on his hand to the company's medical office. That was the first record that Wisconsin Steel made of his missing finger joints.

From that day of March 20, 1950, until the sudden plant closing on March 28, 1980, Frank rarely missed a day. He loved to work. He liked his job and he loved his fellow workers. Sometimes he expressed his joy with a down-home poem:

"All I want in this creation
Is a pretty little wife and a big plantation.
All I need to make me happy
Is four little kids to call me pappy."

Four Little Kids
The "fourth little kid" was born on July, 28, 1951, and was named "John" after his aunt Jonnie Lumpkin Ellis. As a child, John never could understand how he was named after his aunt when his aunt's name was "Pat."

In 1950, Jonnie and her husband, Henry, made a huge sacrifice. They gave up their jobs in Buffalo and moved to Harlem to help maintain the Communist Party organization. They were needed in Harlem because eleven Communist leaders had been arrested and were being prosecuted. The arrested leaders were charged with conspiracy to teach and advocate the overthrow of the United States Government by force and violence, under the 1940 Smith Act. Later, the Supreme Court declared the Smith Act unconstitutional, but not until many Communist leaders suffered many years in federal prisons.[48] In Harlem, Jonnie and Henry were known as "Pat" and "Al" to avoid harassment by the FBI. The names stuck for the rest of their lives. During this period of unconstitutional persecution of the

Communist Party, other members of the family, and many others, made even greater sacrifices to keep the workers' struggle alive. But that is a story only they can tell.

Rotating Shift work

"Wisconsin Steel was a turning point in my life," Frank often said. "Not just because it was a job I needed. I don't know what I would have done without it. There were no jobs in March 1950. I'd been there and looked and found none. It was so depressing." Of course all of Frank and Bea's money problems did not end with the new job, but the emergency was over. There was an income again.

He liked his job and he enjoyed the company of the other steel workers. The hours were 6 a.m. to 2 p.m. one week, followed by a week of 2 p.m. to 10 p.m. The third week was 10 p.m. to 6 a.m., known as the "graveyard shift." Shift work didn't bother him. Work aboard ship had been shift work, as had Bethlehem Steel before that. Young and strong, Frank seemed to need very little sleep. Nor did he require a bed to get a good rest. Any chair or hard bench would do. However his family found it hard to adjust to the changing shifts.

In fact it was almost impossible to plan family activities. Unlike most of the Wisconsin Steel worker families, Frank had a working spouse. Planning family activities was very complicated. Days off were not known in advance because the mill schedule was not posted until a couple of days before the new shift began. Traditional family feast days like Thanksgiving or Christmas were sometimes celebrated in his absence, while he was pulling a double (shift) in the mill. It was not rare for him to work 16 hours, sleep for a few minutes, then get a call from the mill, "Do you want to come out?" He always said, "Yes."

When Frank became a millwright, his mechanical skill kept him in great demand. The large hydraulic grinding machine clogged up from time to time. Trying to find the cause of the problem, Frank found a small orifice that had clogged. Nobody else knew about the orifice. It did not even show on the blueprint. So Frank kept the information to himself. Whenever the machine clogged up they had to call Frank. This went on for a good while. Finally, he told the machine operators about the orifice. But not before he had collected a lot of overtime.

Just as Frank did not recognize limits to his physical strength, he never acknowledged that time was limited. He never said "no" to a friend, or a commitment. Whoever got him first, had him, and when 24 hours passed, then he had done as much as he could and the day was over. This did not make for an ideal family life, but shift work made that impossible anyway. Frank was like the mythological heroes who got their strength from contact with the earth. He drew his strength from people, especially his fellow workers. He never had a problem with alcohol, but if his friends were drinking, Frank would drink. He didn't particularly like coffee, but if they were drinking coffee, he drank cup after cup.

He drew the line at drugs. An Egyptian fellow seaman during the war hated to see his shipmates come back from shore leave hungover, sick from alcohol. He thought he had something better. So he offered Frank a sample of his supply and Frank refused, saying he didn't touch drugs. "This is not a drug," his friend swore. Frank would try anything once. Whatever was in his friend's potion, the effect was immediate. "When I stepped over a curb," Frank remembered, "my feet never touched ground. I flew." Amazed at his strange state, Frank visited a rifle range as an experiment. A bull's eye every time! Or at least, so it seemed. The next day, on ship, he was back to normal. "No, thank you," he told his friend. "I don't want that stuff."

Friends at Wisconsin Steel

The only thing Frank demanded of his friends was honesty. He didn't waste time with phonies, people who thought they were better than other people. Sometimes at work he'd notice a worker being very friendly to him, and Frank would think, "That man wants to loan me some money." Then he'd go up to the friend and say, "Can you loan me $5?" Frank didn't actually want a loan and quickly returned the $5 the next day. He saw it as a way to bond a friendship.

In some ways the workforce at Wisconsin Steel was especially tightly knit. Around the "salamander" at break time, there were deep political and philosophical discussions. Salamanders are metal containers holding blazing coals, ideal to warm hands in the winter and to reheat tacos for lunch or supper. One day Frank needed a book on Egypt to prove a point for a discussion around a salamander. Another time it might be a book on auto mechanics. Frank came home with questions or unfinished arguments. Then he would do more reading to get ammunition for the next day's discussion.

The closeness among the workers was cemented by the company practice of hiring workers' relatives. Whole families worked there. Some were third generation Wisconsin Steel workers. When the plant closed, the practice of hiring sons, brothers, cousins and a few daughters and sisters added to the tragedy. Relatives all lost their jobs at the same time and could not help each other. The plant tradition was that young people would start working after graduation from high school, or even earlier. Then if they remained healthy and escaped serious injury on the job, they'd work in the mill their entire working life. At 65 they would retire and soon after they would die. That expectation began to change in the early '70s. Some newly hired workers were amazed to find that most workers had been there for many years. A young worker asked Frank,

"How long have you worked here?"

"Twenty-five years."

"Twenty-five years! I'll never be here that long!" And he was right.

Frank ended up spending most of his life in or around Wisconsin Steel. It was a plant with a century-long history—ending with the unannounced closing in 1980—and a post-closing struggle that lasted 17 years. Wisconsin Steel was originally named for Joseph H. Brown. On July 5, 1875, the cornerstone for Brown's Iron and Steel Company was set in the middle of swampland, at what is now 109th Street and the west bank of the Calumet River. It was the first steel mill built in the Calumet area. The Calumet name comes from "Calliminink," a Pottawatamie word for "pipe of peace." The following account of conditions in and around the early mill is based on the official company history of Wisconsin Steel. [49]

Brown's Iron and Steel Mill

About 2,000 men came to work at Brown's mill. They were immigrants from Ireland, Germany, Sweden and Wales. The official history admits, "Conditions were hard," with a work shift of 14 hours in the day and 10 at night. Most lived in boarding houses where they paid $4 to $8 a week for bed and board. Some managed to save the fare to bring over their wives or sweethearts but most could not. Sewage ran in open ditches. Boardwalks were built across the swamps to allow the men to walk from the boarding houses to the mill. The stench in the summer was awful and in winter the wind cut through and through. The official history gives this graphic description:

> C.G. Steele, a roller in the Mill in 1878, reports that during winter months men would often come home from work with their clothes damp from perspiration. Sometimes when they reached their boarding house, they would go to bed fully dressed instead of waiting their turn to dry off

around the crowded iron heating stove. When they got up about 5:30 the next morning their clothes would be stiff. Then they would hurry back to the mill, longingly eat their breakfast (which would be brought to them in dinner pails) and would gradually thaw out again as they resumed work.[50]

Perhaps Brown made an equal sacrifice, saving his money and "doing without" to accumulate capital to build the mill? On the contrary. Like Envirodyne, which took over Wisconsin Steel in 1977, Brown started steelmaking with not one cent of his own money. The official International Harvester history describes how Brown acquired a Youngstown, Ohio mill in 1855 on the "installment plan" without paying a single dollar down.

> Brown flatly told them: "We haven't a cent but we want the mill. We know we can make good iron." . . . They started on such a shoestring that they couldn't even afford to pay money to their employees. Instead the workmen were given notes which Youngstown merchants discounted against the firm for goods and merchandise.[51]

With the substantial profits gained from the unpaid labor of Youngstown workers, Joseph H. Brown founded Brown's Iron and Steel Mill at the present site of Wisconsin Steel. The United States government spent a large sum for that time, $235,000, to build a pier for the mill, and $10,000 for a lighthouse. From the very beginning, the steel mills were on the federal government's corporate welfare rolls. On November 21, 1875, the first ore boat to arrive in the Calumet area delivered 250 tons of iron ore and 250 tons of pig iron to Brown's mill. That was also the first time a big boat proved that the Calumet River was navigable.

International Harvester renames Brown's mill

In 1902, International Harvester bought Brown's Mill and renamed it "Wisconsin Steel." The mill was incorporated in Wisconsin in 1905 to take advantage of more lenient regulations for corporations. However, the steel company's iron and coal mines were given the International Harvester name. For 78 years, Harvester used the mill to supply steel for its farm equipment and truck plants.

Workers hoped for some improvement in conditions under the new Harvester ownership. The hoped-for changes did not come. The long work day continued with the 24-hour day divided into two shifts. Living conditions in Irondale (now called South Deering) remained very poor. Drinking water came from often-contaminated wells and sewage continued to run in open ditches. There was no gas service or electricity. Harvester did promise to pipe gas from the mill to Irondale, and to supply electricity to St. Kevin's Catholic Church and the South Deering Methodist Church. That started the paternalistic tradition that stamped Harvester's relations with the Wisconsin Steel workers and with the company town of Irondale. The myth of paternalism persisted until March 28, 1980, when Harvester closed the mill without an hour's warning.

The company did start a pension plan in 1908, but not until 1910 were any washrooms provided. Before 1910 no bathrooms or outhouses were supplied for the thousands who worked at the mill. The only "sanitary" facility, a sort of makeshift toilet seat, was a 2-by-4 board, suspended over the ground. Day shift remained 14 hours, night shift 10 hours. On Sundays, when shifts changed, workers worked a full 24 hours without relief. Little wonder that the eight-hour day without reduction in pay became the workers' main demand.

The Great Steel Strike, 1919

In 1919, union sentiment was sweeping steel mills nationwide. Harvester tried to head off the organizing drive at Wisconsin Steel by forming "The Harvester Industrial Council," a company union. Fully 712 Wisconsin Steel workers voted against the Council but it passed with 1151 votes. The company union was installed March 12, 1919, just a few months before the start of the Great Steel Strike led by William Z. Foster. Foster had recently spearheaded the successful packinghouse workers organizing drive and later became the Chair of the Communist Party USA. At the first meeting of the Harvester Industrial Council, a worker named Studnik called for an eight-hour day for 11 hours pay. The Council went into executive session to get the motion withdrawn. The official company story is that Studnik resigned. Harvester realized that some concessions were needed to head off strike sentiment.

The Great Steel Strike began September 22, 1919. A few days earlier, Harvester's president had come to Wisconsin Steel. He granted the maintenance men the eight-hour day with a small increase in wages. Still management was afraid to test its strength in face of the rising tide of strike support. The official history states that the company asked the Harvester Industrial Council to vote to close Wisconsin Steel when the national strike began. Some of the screaming headlines from *The Chicago Tribune* give the flavor of the employer hysteria:

[October 1, 1919] **FEAR CONTROL BY UNSKILLED**;
[October 4, 1919] **LIFE OF NATION HINGES ON OPEN SHOP, GARY SAYS.**
[October 5, 1919] **SCENES IN GARY STRIKE RIOT WHICH BROUGHT CALL FOR TROOPS** [photograph shows a peaceful assembly of strikers].
[October 7, 1919] **U.S. REGULARS RULE GARY—MARTIAL LAW.**

The strike lasted until January 8, 1920, bringing out 367,000 workers. It ended without immediate victory, but was the most important factor in winning the eight-hour work day in 1923. Could defeat have been avoided? In reply William Z. Foster wrote:

> The heroism of the steel workers could not avail against all this hostile force [steel companies, all branches of government including city and state police, anti-union hysteria of the media, and sabotage by the AFL's Gompers and craft union leadership]. Twenty-two were killed, hundreds were slugged and shot, several thousands were arrested, and over a million and a half men, women and children struggled and starved. But the great strike, although it eventually abolished the 12-hour day and caused many other improvements, did not win its major objective of unionization.[52]

At Wisconsin Steel, the mill was reopened just three weeks after the strike began. Then the Industrial Council reviewed all the workers, one by one, to decide who should be fired for supporting the strike. In 1921 the company asked for a 20% wage cut. Worker representatives on the council voted 15 to 3 for a wage cut of only 15%. Company representatives on the council outvoted the workers. Since the cut of 20% was being imposed anyway, the worker representatives decided to make it unanimous.[53]

Racist Hiring Practices at Wisconsin Steel

Most of the early Wisconsin Steel workers were European immigrants. In 1926, the company began to hire Mexican workers. Many had worked on the railroad and moved north with the road, settling in Chicago, the end of the line. During World War II, the U.S. Fair Employment Practices Commission (FEPC) forced Harvester to begin to hire African American workers. Harvester's racist exclusion of African American steel workers at Wisconsin

Steel contrasted with general industry practice. By 1920, 16% of the national steel work force was African American, and the percentage rose in later years.

A myth still circulating in 1996 claimed that Wisconsin Steel did not hire African Americans because McCormick was angry that his daughter "had run off with a Black man." This was obviously false because other Harvester plants had hired African Americans. The truth is that Harvester discriminated at Wisconsin Steel as part of its pattern of controlling the steel workers through racial division. It had nothing to do with "McCormick's daughter."

The Great Depression

During the mass hunger of the '30s, Harvester paternalistically allowed 2,000 Wisconsin steel workers to grow food on 1/4 acre plots of company land. The company even provided the seed. It was a cheap way to keep a labor force available until orders picked up. Few Mexican workers were included in Harvester's "charity." Thousands of Mexican workers who lived in South Chicago were "removed" to Mexico, many against their will. Trucks rolled through South Chicago streets, broadcasting false promises of land in Mexico to induce workers to leave.[54] Back in Mexico, workers found conditions that were even worse than in Chicago.

Increased union organizing efforts in 1935 coincided with a slight economic upturn. Workers' mass protests had pressured FDR and Congress to create a "New Deal." The New Deal included the NLRA (National Labor Relations Act), guaranteeing the right to join a union. Making use of the legal right to organize, millions joined the new industrial unions of the CIO. Over the next 10-year period, the CIO Steel Workers Organizing Committee (SWOC) succeeded in organizing the U.S. steelmaking industry.

Key to the CIO success was the development of interracial labor unity and an appeal to unskilled and skilled workers alike. Communists in Pittsburgh, Chicago, Gary, Youngstown and other steel towns actively worked to unite the two great movements, the labor movement and the movement for racial equality. They were continuing the tradition of William Z. Foster, leader of the 1919 steel strike. In Warren, Ohio, CIO steel organizer Gus Hall followed in Foster's footsteps. Hall became general secretary of the CPUSA in 1959. Frank called him "the big man" and looked up to his leadership.

Lumpkin with Gus Hall

Wisconsin Steel Works Council Out - PSWU in

In 1937, the NLRB ruled that the Harvester Works Council in Fort Wayne and similar councils at other plants were company-dominated unions. Forewarned by the Fort Wayne example, the Wisconsin Steel Works Council dissolved on March 18, 1937. Another in-house union, the PSWU, was quickly formed. SWOC-CIO had already signed up many Wisconsin Steel workers. The company quickly recognized the in-house union even though no election had been held. Harvester claimed PSWU had more signed cards than the CIO.

PSWU never honored the national strikes in steel .[55] On January 1, 1946, CIO steel workers called a national strike to catch up on wages frozen during five years of war. PSWU continued to work full blast. They expected that the grateful company would give them the same gains won by the CIO. That's how it seemed to work for many years.

Red-baiting Keeps a Real Union Out

In 1949 the CIO became a victim of the Cold War. The Taft-Hartley law was used to aid the employers' Cold War offensive against the unions. Taft-Hartley required union officers to sign affidavits that they were not and never had been members of the Communist Party. In the name of anti-communism, top union officials shot labor in the heart. They suicidally expelled over 1,000,000 members in left-led unions. The United Electrical Radio & Machine Workers (UE) left the CIO to protest union raiding, but the effect was the same as being expelled.[56] Others forced out of the CIO included the Farm Equipment Workers Union affiliated to UE.

FE-UE had contracts at Harvester's farm equipment plants, the main customers of Wisconsin Steel. After the expulsions, UE did not collapse but fought even harder to get better contracts. They thought all Harvester workers should belong to the same union and decided to organize Wisconsin Steel. Just a few weeks after Frank started working at Wisconsin Steel, FE-UE asked Frank to help them organize the mill. It was a matter of principle for Lumpkin to try to bring a real union to Wisconsin Steel. He decided to help although he knew he would run the risk of being fired. He describes his first months at Wisconsin Steel:

Republic Steel workers picket in national steel strike, 1946
(Reprinted with permission of the Southeast Historical Society)

"By 1949-50, Communist workers were being hounded out of the factories and beaten up by the Cold War warriors. That was the atmosphere when I started working at Wisconsin Steel. The war drums were beating for the U.S. to invade Korea. But we were painting peace slogans on the sidewalk. When I joined the Young Communist League during World War II, it was no secret. Things changed in '49 and '50.

"It used to be 30 days was the probation period for a new hire. Then it was changed to 90 days. I didn't have my 90 days in when FE-UE came in to organize. They had contracts at the other Harvester plants that made farm equipment. The FE-UE contract was much better than the PSWU contract. We needed 2,800 signatures to get an election. I helped, although I knew that I would be fired if I were caught organizing for another union. But after the signatures were filed for an election, USWA [United Steel Workers of America] came in and split the vote. Some of their organizers were worse Red-baiters than PSWU. The end could have been predicted: over 1,100 votes for PSWU, 800 for FE-UE and 300 for USWA. There wasn't even a runoff. After that, USWA made some attempts to organize again. I helped them but nothing came of it."

As soon as Lumpkin's 90 days were in, he tried to join PSWU, but they didn't want him. Aleman, his department union delegate, did want his help to get re-elected as delegate. So they made a deal and Frank became a member of the PSWU. He always believed that any union was better than no union. A few years later, Lumpkin was elected delegate but the PSWU did not let him take his elected position. A worker came up to him after the election and asked,

"Your name Lumpkin? I voted for you. What happened in that election?"

"Ask Scrubby [the general manager]. Ask Joe Weil [president of PSWU]."

Isolation Is Death

The PSWU's excuse was, "Lumpkin—he's a nice guy, but he won't sign Taft Hartley." Under the Taft-Hartley Law, local *officers* were required to sign non-Communist affidavits.[57] Stewards and delegates did not need to sign but PSWU required their signatures for their own purposes. Frank refused to sign, but he remained a force in the union. He said, "My whole struggle was to prevent isolation. If I had been isolated, I'd be dead. I'd be long gone from that plant. Isolation is death."

After a few years, Frank became a scarfer. Scarfers and chippers did the same work but chippers used an air hammer and scarfers used a torch. As a skillful worker in the scarfing dock, Frank was in a good position to organize. The scarfing dock was a large department and one that could tie up the mill. Before bars could be rolled or go through other processing, scarfers and chippers had to remove the surface defects. If the scarfers and chippers slowed down or walked out, the rest of the mill would grind to a standstill.

Cooperation and working together were absolutely necessary in the scarfing dock. Workers were on a departmental bonus. The bonus was based on tonnage put out above the department quota and was shared among the workers in the department. Frank used to say that the company needed few foremen because workers did not look kindly on those who did not do their share of the work. There was also a good side to the department bonus. Frank said, "We took care of each other. Sometimes a worker would come in so drunk that he could not stand up. We would take care of him. We would put him in the locker room and do his work. For someone who would not cooperate it was different. If they broke their neck, we'd say, 'Well, that's life.' "

As jobs go in production, Wisconsin Steel was considered a good place to work. One recently retired worker came back every day. He greeted the men in the locker room and took his shower. That was the only life he knew. Finally, the company stopped him at the plant gate. Their excuse was that insurance regulations barred retirees from the mill. The expectation in South Chicago was that once retired, you wouldn't live long enough to collect much pension.

Injury and Death at Wisconsin Steel

"Yes, it's hot and it's dirty and it's dangerous. But other than that it's a good job." Herman Caldwell

The most obvious thing about integrated steel mills, where steel is made and processed, is that they are very big and spread over many acres. Wisconsin Steel itself covered over 260 acres. You have to be a good walker to work in the mills. It takes a long time to walk from the mill gate to your place of work. In recent years there have been vast changes in the technology of making steel but the following 1910 description still captures the giant scale and the power of an integrated steel-melting mill:

There is a glamour about the making of steel. The very size of things—the immensity of the tools, the scale of production—grips the mind with an overwhelming sense of power. Blast furnaces, eighty, ninety, one hundred feet tall, gaunt and insatiable, are continually gaping to admit ton after ton of ore, fuel, and stone. Bessemer converters dazzle the eye with their leaping flames. Steel ingots at white heat, weighing thousands of pounds, are carried from place to place and tossed about like toys. Electric cranes pick up steel rails or fifty-foot girders as jauntily as if their tons were ounces. These are the things that cast a spell over the visitor in these workshops of Vulcan [Roman god of fire].[58]

Most steel mills are on the shores of large lakes or rivers so that the ore and coal can be shipped in cheaply and the heavy steel products shipped out. Large quantities of water are also used in the steel processes. Mill owners were allowed to dump the polluted water back. The big mills own their own mines and ships. Mountains of iron ore and coal line the shore. Part of the drama of making steel results from the very high temperatures needed to separate iron from the iron oxide ore—$3,000^0$ F (1650^0 C). At these high temperatures, carbon and desired metals are added to the iron to make the steel alloy. The carbon comes from coke made from coal that is precision-baked in coke ovens. When the steel is ready to be worked into various shapes and thicknesses, it must be reheated again. So a steel mill is not the place for anyone who can't stand heat, dirt and grease; or noise, for that matter.

A Hard Place to Work

Steel mills have always been a hard place to work. Before the union, labor was hired from the "shape-up." The foremen picked men out, "You, you and you," depending on how muscular they were and whether they looked tough enough to take the punishment of steel mill work. Russ Depasquale, a long-time Buffalo steel worker, gave a vivid description of how hard steel jobs were before the CIO organized steel. Depasquale was an exceptionally strong person, and only 19. Yet at the end of the day, he did not have the strength to walk across the street to his car. First he had to sit on the curb to regain some of his strength. At the door of his house, he would collapse again and call for his sister to help him up the stairs. When he was fired for union organizing in the '30s, the company had to call him back. They couldn't find anyone else strong enough to do his job. After a union contract was won, three men were put on the job he had worked alone.

Not only was the work hard, it was dangerous. Everyone in the mills knew someone who had lost his life working in steel. Lumpkin's cousin "Sonny" was killed in the Bethlehem Steel mill near Buffalo, NY. Cornelio Ramirez, leader of the "Dead Steelmill" band that dedicated a cassette to Frank, lost his young brother to an accident at U.S. Steel's Southworks. Wisconsin Steel was one of the worst for industrial accidents.

In the two years before Wisconsin Steel closed, poisonous fumes killed four workers in the No. 2 blast furnace; six others were hospitalized. During periods of layoffs, skilled workers were often knocked down to "labor" and could be sent anyplace in the plant. Accidents were more likely when workers were moved to unfamiliar jobs. That's how Emmett Paul, Lumpkin's friend and comrade, lost his thumb. Paul was bumped off his regular job in 3-mill and sent to labor in another department. He was not familiar with the hazardous machinery that sliced off his thumb.

Narrow Escapes
Frank never forgot one close call. During a slow-down, he had been "bumped" back into unskilled labor and was sent to the coke plant. Blinding clouds of steam rolled over the tracks as Frank bent over to pick up pieces of coke that had frozen to the ground. It was so noisy that you couldn't hear yourself think. The thundering noise of coke dumping into the cars combined with the sound of hissing steam as cold quenching water hit the hot coke. It was like a void in time, where you could not see or hear and only the work was real.

Suddenly the shape of a train loaded with coke appeared through the fog. The train was coming straight at him. Frank knew he could not outrun the train. There was no use shouting because the trains were unmanned, remotely controlled by workers in the tower who couldn't see him through the fog. On either side of the narrow passageway were the coke walls. He wasn't sure how much clearance there would be between the train and the wall but he didn't have a choice. A leap took Frank up to the wall just as the train passed by. "It didn't touch me. But it was close."

After years at Wisconsin Steel, Frank's elbows began to swell from some mysterious cause. Or so it seemed to his family. Despite the doctor's opinion that surgery was needed, the swelling eventually went down by itself.

Only years later did Frank admit the truth about an unusual effort that had caused his elbows to swell. He had climbed up to a slippery catwalk, 30 feet above some railroad tracks. The catwalk led to a crane that he wanted to inspect. As he walked on a steel plate on the catwalk, the plate slipped out and fell to the ground. Frank grabbed the rail and swung himself hand over hand until he reached a part of the catwalk that had a floor. With all of his strength, he pulled himself back to safety. It was just another miraculous escape from death that was never reported.

Under ordinary circumstances, chipping and scarfing were dangerous jobs. There was no way to stop the fiery pieces of scrap that flew into your clothing and burned the skin wherever they landed.[59] Especially above the belt line, every chipper had a collection of scars on the skin.

Small billets might have a 4" x 4" cross section and weigh about 200 pounds. Large billets could have an 8 ½" x 10" cross section, a length up to 12 feet and weigh many tons. Typically, the billets that Frank worked on weighed about two tons and had to be turned three times so that all four surfaces could be chipped or scarfed. When a billet had to be turned for finishing, the worker grabbed the billet with a special wrench with a handle about 5-foot long. The billet was on a bed raised above the floor.

After the billet was turned, the bottom jaw of the wrench dropped open to allow the billet to roll around without taking the worker with it. Sometimes the billet would not turn completely and would roll back the wrong way to its original position. When the billet rolled the wrong way, it could throw the worker several feet across the yard. Some scarfers had suffered that type of accident and were painfully bruised. Luckily, Frank never had an accident with a billet wrench.

Lumpkin's Luck Runs Out

Lumpkin's luck ran out in the winter of 1979. At 1 a.m. on the graveyard shift, he was chaining up a half-ton bar. The cable broke, spilling the half-ton of steel on his right foot. Had he not been wearing safety shoes with steel toes and steel shank, the foot would have been smashed to a pulp. The foot was still recognizable, a good advertisement for safety shoes. Still it hurt like hell.

"No breaks," the company doctor said after he looked at the X-ray film, "just some bruises. Use this cane and come back in a week." It was 30 miles back to his home in Broadview. Frank didn't ask for help and none was offered. With his injured right foot on the gas pedal, Frank drove the 30 miles home.

A few days passed but still the foot was no better. His son, young Dr. John Lumpkin, gave Frank some crutches and showed him how to use them.

"Who gave you those crutches?" shouted the company doctor, when Frank went back to see him a week later. The company doctor tried to avoid issuing crutches, perhaps to keep the company's insurance rates down. Since Frank insisted that his foot was no better, the company sent him to an orthopedic specialist. There he got the bad news: "Your foot's broken in two places," the specialist said. The good news was that the foot could be encased in a walking cast to allow Frank to walk.

Robert Thompson holds sign, "Injured at Wisconsin Steel" at election rally

Workers believed that the accident record at Wisconsin Steel was among the worst. Ernie Syrek, a loader in the billet dock, described his experience:

"Years ago, Wisconsin Steel was as bad as working in a coal mine. Dangerous and they cared less. Just money-making, no safety devices. But in the last 10 years or so they were improving. Working outside as a chainman, hooking up the steel, I remember when I started. A couple of years later I got married, talked to the wife, and I inquired about insurance, Prudential. Say 1955.

"So the agent came over, said, 'Hold it. Your job is a chainman?' I said, 'Yes.' He said, 'You have what we call a bad-risk job. We cannot give you insurance unless it's under a bad-risk condition. And I have to put an OK on it. But a policeman or fireman, I'll sign him up today.' And they tell me that a policeman and fireman are bad jobs!

"Maybe a month later, he came over the house and said, 'OK, I got it, and it's so much premium. You're going to have to pay the high rate'. So I took the insurance. Several years later, when I got a marker's job, I called him up. He had told me if I ever changed jobs to let him know. My premiums dropped 50% from a chainman's. A chainman piled steel in the billet dock. We supplied the rolling mill with the steel. We stored the steel and then they rolled it.

"Not too long before the plant closed, four-five people were killed in Wisconsin Steel. That was in the blast furnace. The gas leaked there. That was just an error, somebody opening the wrong valve. It's hazardous work. Human error, the way I understand. But that was a bad area to work in, too. There are certain jobs that are hazardous. But they had safety programs and men suggesting, putting their ideas into effect, which helped. The unions are actually the ones who protest all the unsafe policies of the company. And the unions actually got the safety program started, which is a beautiful idea, asking the men for their own ideas. If you work in an area, they say, 'Why don't we put a guard here, or put a red light, blinking light or Mars light?' A blinking light will draw your attention more than a steady light."

Herman Caldwell worked in 6-Mill, the most modern part of the plant. His attitude towards the job hazards is typical for many steel workers:

"I started as labor and I moved up to different jobs. When the mill shut down, my job was 5-by-5 shear operator. Then I was able to move up to higher jobs like a roll builder, assembling bearings, working on changing of rolls, whatever. Yes, it's hot and it's dirty and it's dangerous. But other than that it's a good job. At first I had to do a lot of lifting and stuff like that. But now they have cranes, and you don't have to do that much lifting. The mill I was working in was supposed to be one of the greatest mills they got in the country. They brought it from Germany, I understand. I hope it opens and I can go back in."

Safety was always the workers' first demand, as Higinio Lopez from 6-Mill explains:

"I came here from Mexico, like anyone else, trying to improve the standard of life for my family. So I had many different jobs. In 1950, one of the great corporations to work for was the steel mill, so I decided to work for Wisconsin Steel in 1954. In 1980, they closed down, leaving us on the street with no pay, no vacation, no severance pay. I was a first loader, assistant roller, craneman. In 26 years you learn the whole mill.

"It was a hard job but it was a good paying job. You had your self-respect, could educate your children. I stayed for 26 years hoping that after 30 years I could retire and live with a good income. But I never trusted it much. Nothing lasts forever.

"We had a lot of problems with safety standards. The machinery was too old, breaking down. The crane went down three-four times while I was working there. Good thing nobody was hurt that time. One crane fell down. Good thing it was near the ground. It cut one fellow worker on the leg. We had to wait for the millwright. We had to wait for the electrician. Finally we picked up some steel bars to get the guy out.

"One time the crane fell on top of me with steel. Well, I saw it coming, and I see the operator can't control it. I was loading steel inside the train car. So I dive out of the train car and go under. I wasn't even thinking. I had to protect myself from the billets weighing 2,000 or 1,500 pounds. I was lucky. The steel bars fell in the place where I had been standing. Ha ha ha ha.

"Some were not so lucky. A lot of people were hurt by negligence of the company. We tried to tell them it wasn't safe to work in those places. But management, they do what they want. A lot of times I refused to work under those conditions. I've seen a lot of people get hurt. I warned them, don't go in there. But they went in there and got hurt, some of my best friends in the blooming mill. Of course, soon as you get in the steel mill, it's dangerous. Something falls down or falls from the crane. Especially they got old machinery. They don't have maintenance.

"I warned the management to fix those cranes. I wouldn't go in there because of safety. The scrap shear on top of the ingot cuts all the scrap on the end. The door opened. When you cut that steel it's red-hot. It bounced out of the bucket where people were working on the ground. It got one of my buddies. A good thing it hit him on top of his head, his safety hat. But it went down on his body, his arm and his leg. Cut them open. So they had to take him out to the hospital. It didn't kill him, but it hurt him bad, believe me. But you can get hurt crossing the street, too. On the job you have to look four ways, up and down, too."

If you're white, all right/ If you're brown, stick around/ But baby, if you're Black/ Get back, get back, get back. Folk rhyme sung by Big Bill Broomsey

7. Fighting Racism and Sexism

Wisconsin Steel sits squarely in the 10th Ward of Chicago's East Side. From 1983 to 1988, 10th Ward Alderman Edward Vrdolyak headed the white racist opposition to Harold Washington, Chicago's first African American mayor. But long before Vrdolyak's time, the steel companies and banks consciously created racial divisions in Southeast Chicago. The steel companies bear much of the blame for making Chicago one of the most racially segregated industrial cities in the country.

Of all the big steelmaking companies in the Chicago-Northwest Indiana area, Wisconsin Steel was last to hire African Americans. From the beginning, all the steel companies had played off workers of different European nationalities against each other. It was said that companies deliberately placed together workers who spoke different languages to make it harder for them to organize.

During the Great Steel Strike of 1919, U.S. Steel brought trainloads of African American workers to its Calumet area mills. When they found that the mill was on strike, some refused to enter but most were far from home and had no alternative. William Z. Foster, national leader of the strike, refuted the argument of those who tried to blame the loss of the strike on these workers:

It is estimated that 30,000 Negroes were brought in as strikebreakers during the great steel strike that began in September 1919. This was a heavy blow, but it was not, as has been said, the main cause for the loss of this vital strike. The decisive reason was the treacherous refusal of the Gompersite [AFL] craft union leaders to support the broad industrial strike, a betrayal which caused a large-scale return to work by the white skilled workers.[60]

By the 1920s, African American workers made up 16% of the steel force nationally. But in the 1930s, the superintendent of Wisconsin Steel still said, "I will not have Negroes in the plant." [61]

Mexican workers hired

In 1926, Wisconsin Steel began to hire Mexican workers. Mr. Martinez was one of the first to settle in the area after moving north with his railroad job. The family lived in Irondale at a time when African Americans could not even enter that area. Mexicans who lived in Irondale faced racial prejudice every day.

One of Mr. Martinez's daughters, interviewed by the South Chicago Historical Project, said Mexican children could not play in the streets for fear of being beaten. The Martinez daughters told about the Depression days of the '30s in their steel worker community when thousands were removed to Mexico.[62] Their father refused to go. He said Serbians weren't asked to go back, so why should he. He never became a citizen because there was a rumor that he'd have to step on the Mexican flag to become a U.S. citizen. Mr. Martinez said he never could do that.[63]

African Americans hired during World War II

When the federal government ordered fair employment practices during World War II, Harvester had to hire African Americans at Wisconsin Steel. Some were transferred from other Harvester plants. These plants did not have the company-town background or ban on hiring African Americans that Wisconsin Steel did in Chicago's South Deering neighborhood. When Frank was hired at Wisconsin Steel in March 1950, other African American workers had already blazed a trail for him. "They must have been some tough people," Lumpkin said in admiration. "When they had to wait for steel, they sat down and made themselves comfortable. Other workers told them, 'You're not allowed to sit.' 'Oh, yeah? Just watch us!' "

After the African American workers broke the ban on sitting while waiting for steel, the company put in benches. It was another example of affirmative action benefiting all workers. However, racist practices of the company continued to deny African Americans the chance to move up to skilled jobs at higher pay. Racist violence in Chicago posed a danger to steel workers, who had to pass through racist mobs on their way to work. More than once, the Lumpkins faced dangerous racist mobs near their own community.

Racial Violence in Chicago

About three weeks before their son Paul was born, Frank's wife Beatrice had a close encounter with a racist mob in Chicago. A call came from Communist Party friends that help was needed outside the home of an International Longshore Workers Union (ILWU) organizer. The organizer lived in Bridgeport near Mayor Richard Daley's home. Union committees had met in the organizer's house. Attendance at the union meetings was mixed, African American and white. A rumor had gone out that the house was being sold to an African American family. A small mob was forming and some were throwing rocks at the windows. It was hoped that the mob could be dispersed if a few rational white people urged people to go home.

By the time Beatrice and her comrades reached the scene, the crowd had lit fires in the street and was shouting racist threats. For a while it seemed that the progressives would be successful in defusing the situation. Some of the women in the crowd seemed to be ready to leave. They were responding to, "Let's go home. We don't want any trouble." Then, mysteriously, everything changed. An unseen hand seemed to be structuring a mob where before there were just some confused, angry individuals. The mob turned on those who had been counseling restraint. Anti-Semitism was added to the racism. The union organizer and some of the progressives were Jewish. Shouts of, "Hitler didn't kill enough of them" broke out. Shouts of, "Rosie, go back to the University of Chicago," were hurled at some young progressives. It was time to retreat, not to the University of Chicago with whom the anti-racists had no connection, but to the South Side where they would be safe. The police were conveniently absent. Fortunately, no one was hurt. But shortly afterwards, the union organizer moved out.

The Lumpkins and their comrades against the mob

Frank and Beatrice were involved in another confrontation with a racist mob in the same Bridgeport neighborhood. About 16 civil rights activists went to test reports of discrimination at the movie house just west of Wentworth Avenue. Wentworth Avenue was a "Mason-Dixon" line that the real estate companies had drawn between Black and white communities. The Lumpkins believed that the purpose of the "line" was to keep rents artificially high in the overcrowded African American neighborhoods. Wentworth Avenue was a boundary that African Americans were warned not to cross.

Movie tickets were sold to the racially mixed test group, and they entered the theater. News of the test traveled quickly. A mob gathered outside the theater. Despite the mob, an incredibly brave African American Communist named Chuck drove his loudspeaker-equipped car up and down the streets of Bridgeport. He called on his "white working class brothers" to come out and stop the mob. They came out all right, but it was to join the mob, not stop it. Every window in Chuck's car was smashed, but he refused to quit or be intimidated. The test group inside the movie house became very apprehensive because the rest of the moviegoers got the word to leave. The theater began to empty and only the protest group was left inside the theater. But Frank wasn't worried. He was enjoying the movie and not worried about the mob.

By this time the mob outside numbered about 500. Finally, the police came, but not to disperse the mob. Instead, they took the interracial group out of the theater through a back door and into a waiting police wagon. In front of the theater the scene grew very nasty. An African American plainclothes cop assigned to the scene had to draw his service revolver to protect himself from the mob. Silently watching the whole ugly affair, a group of African Americans stood on the other side of Wentworth Avenue. Years later, Wentworth was no longer the "Mason-Dixon" line dividing Black from white Chicago. There was still a "line," but it had been moved a little further west.

Trumbull Park

In 1953, four African American families moved into the relatively new and desirable low-rise public housing in Trumbull Park. The Trumbull Park Housing Project was located in South Deering (Irondale), just a few blocks from Wisconsin Steel. The project was also close to Jeffery Manor, site of a recent race riot triggered by a rumor that an African American family was buying a home in the neighborhood. Well-funded racist groups, such as the White Citizens Council, threatened violence in an attempt to force the African American families out of Trumbull Park. They formed a menacing mob around the Trumbull Park apartments when the new tenants came home from work.

The police response was limited to escorting the tenants to their apartments. Once inside, the tenants could not leave because their police escorts were gone. The police never tried to disperse the mob.

Almost every night bombs were exploded outside the new tenants' apartments. This scene went on for months during 1953. The African American tenants stood their ground heroically. One of them, Frank London Brown, wrote a very moving novel about his experiences, *Trumbull Park*.[64] The violence was kept going with aid from right-wing organizations. These organizations, based outside of Chicago, poured money and people into the area to make sure that the anti-Black violence continued.

The racist attacks against the brave African American families aroused anger throughout the large African American community of the South Side. Some called for protest marches from the South Side to Trumbull Park to defend the Trumbull Park families. Community sentiment was building for militant action, including self-defense against racist violence. However, the marches did not take place at that time. Perhaps leaders remembered the bloody Chicago riots of 1919, which took the lives of 38 people and injured 520. Although African American casualties during the 1919 riot outnumbered white casualties almost 2 to 1, the police arrested twice as many African Americans as whites.[65] Thirteen years after the Trumbull Park riots, the people's movement became strong enough to march into a neighborhood threatened by racist violence. The Rev. Martin Luther King Jr. led that historic march in 1966.

The racist violence at Trumbull Park spilled out into the streets around Wisconsin Steel. During these riots, African American steel workers had to drive through a barrage of stones to get to work. Those not lucky enough to have a car were sometimes beaten as they waited at bus transfer points near the plant. The tallest man in the scarfing dock, who was known simply as Owens, had stopped at a red light at 106th Street and Torrence Avenue, one block from Wisconsin Steel's main gate. Racists shouted curses and one man reached through the open window and struck Owens in the face. Secure in his husky 6 foot-4 inch frame, Owens got out of the car to confront the mob. Policemen rushed up and said, "Get the hell back in your car." They said nothing to anyone in the mob. Owens drove into the mill lot and stormed into work, furious and hurt that the police had been on the side of the mob.

Two nearby taverns that served African American Wisconsin Steel workers were bombed.[66] The mill itself was a safe haven. Some Mexican and white workers apologized to African American workers for the violence they faced in the streets near the mill. Even those white workers who belonged to racist organizations in their own communities were angry that fellow workers were attacked on the way to work. All steel workers in South Chicago were upset by the Trumbull Park mob scenes so close to the steel mills.

Lumpkin said that when the company had a meeting, no foremen were there. They were all over at the White Citizens Council meeting. In contrast to the foremen's attitudes, some of Lumpkin's Mexican fellow workers invited him to visit them in their homes, located in South Deering. Lumpkin thanked them, but declined. He did not want them to risk having their garages torched after his visit. Lumpkin's position was always to work for maximum unity among the workers. His position for unity and against racial divisions was well received by many Latino as well as African American workers. After the plant closed, many of European descent also understood the need for unity of all workers against racism.

Lumpkin's gut feeling always favored strong, militant action, rather than gradualism. To those who claimed it would take generations of education to overcome racism, he replied with a practical example that everyone could understand. "Education can be overnight," he said. "That backward Southern white worker who gets on the train in the South has been using the "n" word all his life. In 24 hours he's in Chicago and instantly learns not to walk around saying that word."

Skilled Jobs for White Only

The racist attitude of the Wisconsin Steel owners and management was not new to Lumpkin and he did not let it intimidate him. In 1950, he was denied promotion at Wisconsin Steel on the grounds of race. He had applied for a job as an operating engineer, a trade he had practiced in the Merchant Marine. "The steam generating plant is only for whites," he was told. Years later, the Wisconsin Steel Company had to retreat somewhat from this openly racist stand, but management continued to discriminate against African American office workers.

In the 1960s, Ronald Scott, an African American Wisconsin Steel worker, wanted to become a diesel mechanic. He tells his story:

> "I took a cut in pay to get a job that allowed me to go to diesel mechanics school. When I finished, I had to file a grievance to get into the tractor shop at Wisconsin Steel. Every day there was some kind of

racist slur. A white diesel mechanic told me he wouldn't have stuck it out. But I was determined."

When the plant closed, Scott realized that it pays to fight. Thanks to his diesel engine training, he was one of the few to get a skilled job when the mill closed. But he had to start all over again to earn pension benefits.

Some African Americans Promoted

The Civil Rights upsurge of the 1960s and early 1970s had its impact on the company. They began to promote some African American workers to foremen. Frank was offered an assistant foreman's job. It was a hard decision. On the one hand, foremen were out of the union, although they retained the right to go back to union status. On the other hand, the civil rights movement had fought for the promotion of African Americans to foremen. With the door open to return to union status, Frank decided to try it.

Frank wanted to learn the production process from every angle. And he did learn a lot. He was able to run his department in a way that made life easier for the workers. If management complained that some worker was sleeping while waiting for steel, Frank would go up to the worker and shake him roughly. "Are you sleeping?"

"No, I'm not sleeping."

"See," Frank told the manager, "he's not sleeping."

Frank's department had a good production record, but the superintendent didn't like Frank's methods. Without warning, he demanded that Frank show him his hands. They were full of grease because Frank couldn't keep his hands off the machinery. "You're paid to run the department, not to work," the superintendent warned Frank.

One day Frank was the foreman in charge. It was time to take out the sling of steel from the pickling vat. The acid in the vat had removed the surface scale and the steel was ready for scarfing. Any longer stay in the acid would pit the steel. Then it would not be fit for scarfing and would have to be sent out for expensive reprocessing. The steel could not wait but the picklers and crane operators were someplace else. They were riveted to the radio with excitement. The Yankees had just hit a home run in the World Series game with the Dodgers.

Frank decided to climb up into the crane and move the steel himself. Everything went well. He lifted the steel out of the pickling vat and lowered it into the water bath. After the bath, all he had to do was pull it out of the water and place the steel on the racks. Then it happened. The crane moved forward too far until the bumper hit the wall. The crane recoiled and one of the crane cables jumped off the track. The fun was over. Frank would have to admit that he goofed. The superintendent was angry but decided to overlook the damage in view of Frank's many years of competent work. Frank's popularity with the men probably influenced his decision.

In that period, Frank said, "Some Black guys got a chance to show what they knew. There were suggestion boxes all around the plant. The company tried to take advantage of what the workers knew. That's how some of the Black guys became foremen." He added, "The guy that produced the most was the guy who relaxed the most. I don't mean goofing off. You inspect it, roll it out, turn it over, inspect it. The worker that marks it as he rolls it out don't do the same thing 4-5 times. What counts is getting the most production, not working the hardest. When we wanted to protest by slowing down, we worked very hard. Roll it out, mark it. Turn it, roll it out; Mark it, turn it. . . . We worked harder than usual but nothing got done."

Frank discussed the problems involved in planning production. The lessons he learned were useful in his organizing work. As he put it, "During the plan, the discovery was ten times the plan. There never was a plan that was carried out exactly by the plan. How do you evaluate a plan?" Frank thought, "Progress has to be measured through investigation of the past. Not that something new just sprang up from nowhere. Progress is in bits and pieces."

In 1978 Frank gave up his foreman status and returned to work in the tool room as a millwright. During his last years at the plant, he enjoyed the luxury of working straight days. He made the move just in time. Shortly after, the rules were changed. Foremen were frozen into their positions without the right to return to production work. When Wisconsin Steel closed in 1980, foremen, as well as workers were left high and dry. But foremen had no union contract protection and could not become part of the Save Our Jobs court case.

Lumpkin's attitude toward racism was summed up in an interview by the progressive historian and radio personality, Studs Terkel. Terkel used his unerring ear to select, as the theme for the interview, Frank's profound observation, "I'm Saying Racism Is Unnatural."[67] Frank's whole life proved that. In the Save Our Jobs Committee, the racial divisions that had been fostered by the company were largely overcome under Frank's leadership. Most workers realized that they were now all in the same boat. Latino, African American and white workers were without a job or health insurance or severance pay and other union benefits. As an African American, Lumpkin could not have led the fight without solid support from Latino and white workers, as well as African Americans.

Lumpkin's study of Marxism helped him understand the economic basis of racism. These excerpts, adapted from the Terkel interview, are examples of Lumpkin's combination of theory and practical experience:

> Race is only used when it's to somebody's advantage, and I don't mean the workingman's advantage. It's never to our advantage. It's always an advantage to the man that's making the money, who's using these guys to use this thing to divide them. It's not an advantage to the white *or* the Black [workers] in the final analysis.
>
> Racism is a business. When they were organizing the packinghouses, they brought in these Black guys from the South on boats to break the strikes. What happens? Some of these Black guys become the main organizers of the union. The backbone—it's Black and white.
>
> My observation is that racism is dying. But as things die, sometimes they intensify. It's like clinging on to whatever it can grab. I don't mean it's not dangerous, it's intensified. They do everything they can to try to stop the changes.

Wisconsin Steel Women

Except during World War II, women had been excluded from most steel mill jobs. At the end of the war, almost all of them were laid off. By the 1970s, the women's movement was spurred by the victories of the civil rights movement. African American and women workers sued the steel companies and won consent decrees that required the hiring of women and opening up apprenticeships to women and to workers of color. Lumpkin reported on the impact of the consent decree on women workers at Wisconsin Steel:

> "The government ordered Wisconsin Steel to hire 500 women and give them two years of seniority credit from day one. That was because the company had refused to hire women, just like they refused to hire Blacks until World War II. But there was nothing in that order that said the company had to *keep* the women.
>
> "I watched one woman down at Number 4 grinding machine, trying to clean up the slag. Some men were laughing, saying she couldn't do that

job. So I went down there, took up a shovel and began to work with her. She didn't know how to take it.

"That job *was* hard. I could hardly do it and I'm one of the strongest guys in the mill. Used to be the only one who could turn an 8½ by 10 billet by myself. After so many years, a younger guy came along who could turn that billet, too. But he did it easy. I tried not to show that it was getting hard for me.

"There was one little problem though. The superintendent saw me with a shovel in my hand, helping the woman at Number 4 grinding machine. He told me that's not my job. I told him I *was* doing my job, showing her the right way to work with the shovel. And that's the God's honest truth. Because what I told her was, 'Look, you can put a little in the shovel or a lot.' Long as you keep the shovel working, you're doing your job.

"The job they put the woman on was too hard for one person. Then some others went down to help. One way or another, the company tried to force the women out. A few months before the plant closed, we had some big layoffs. Most women were low in seniority and were laid off. The kind of union we had, PSWU, not CIO, didn't do much about women getting their rights.

"Like I said in Save Our Jobs. We're all in this fight together. The women have the same rights as the men. Anyone who thinks one should have more rights than the other doesn't belong in our committee."

Lumpkin at CLUW demonstration for family needs, Washington D.C, 1988

However, within the home, the steel workers had conflicting ideas of the role of women.

Ernie Syrek, chainman and yardman:

"My wife never worked. She was always a housewife. My theory was, that's the place for a woman. Housewife, take care of the kids, and that's all. She could have worked. But it wasn't my idea of living. When I come home from the mill I want a meal. I never want to wash clothes. I never want to do nothing. I always told her that's why I got married. That's why I always tease her, 'Lady, we can live on love.' She says, 'Yeah, when you go to the gas station and fill up the gas tank and say, I'm living on love. See what he tells you!'

"Today it's too expensive. Today's cost of living, a husband must have his wife working. Otherwise they couldn't survive. I sympathize with these young kids because no way can they get a down payment on a home. When they do, the tremendous down payment and then 20% interest, it makes no sense.

"These kids have to live with their families, with the in-laws, either way, and they both have to work.

"We say, 'How about children?' 'We can't afford children.'

"That's why the population is going to decrease. That's a shame. They're paying $500 a month rent, then all the food prices and what-not. I know I couldn't bring up three kids today. There has to be a change. I don't know what. But these politicians, they've got to change. Because it makes no sense the way things are going."

Rafael Huerta, a younger pickler in the scarfing dock, has a different view. [He has returned to Mexico since this interview.]

"My wife is from my hometown. Women are stronger than men. They adjust more easily to a strange environment. They say, 'If I can do nothing about it, I might as well enjoy it.' My child was born here, and we're expecting one.

"I have met a lot of women, women friends, relatives, and I know they are more stable. Their minds are more stable than men. In Mexico, we men feel this macho feeling. It's keeping us from becoming better men. "Macho" in Mexico means a man can do anything he wants, and his wife can do nothing. The wife is a child-making machine.

"I think women are equal. Women and men, they are on the same level. This attitude is changing in Mexico because women are liberating themselves. Not that they are slaves, that they are chained—they are in all the colleges; they are getting educated. They are dealing with men in jobs in all fields. Women are lawyers, women are doctors, women are engineers, women are politicians. Women are changing, yes. Only in little villages up in the mountains where they don't have contact with radio or television, they see themselves the wife, the mother, and that's all. The husband gets drunk or whatever and goes to town and comes back without groceries. They are suffering, still suffering."

Political Discrimination

In addition to racism, Frank also had to fight political discrimination.

"Anytime you had pressure of the government on Communist Party people, you really had to organize. Though we were nearly forced underground, we still recruited. They hounded us, but still we played a role. Once you were known, you had to dot every 'i' and cross every 't'. One day I went to get my check and it had a 'brick' [slang for garnishment] on it. I had co-signed for a loan for my friend Chuck. I woke Chuck up and told him they had put a 'brick' on my check 'What are you trying to do, get me fired?' But Chuck had paid the loan. They were just playing games.

"One time I came to work and the foreman said, 'Don't change your clothes. Go to the main office.' At the office they showed me Red Squad reports on me and other Communists who lived on the block. [The Red Squad was a department of the Chicago Police Department engaged in surveillance and harassment of many progressive organizations. The Red Squad was supposed to disband as part of a 1986 settlement in a civil liberties suit in which the City of Chicago paid some who had been harmed by the City's unconstitutional interference with their right of free speech and peaceful assembly.] They asked me, 'What are you going to do?' I said, "I'm going to work." And that's what I did.

"When I got back to my department, the foreman asked what happened.

" They didn't tell you? I replied. 'No,' he answered.

" Maybe they didn't want you to know. "

Community Organizing in the '50s and '60s

"Don't believe them when they say colored people can't stick together."
Katie Dowd, Gary activist

Frank Lumpkin loved grass roots organizing. It gave him the chance to do what he liked most, visit people and talk about what needed to be done. In his Lake Park Avenue neighborhood on Chicago's South Side there were many urgent issues. Discrimination in housing was flagrant. Chicago was known by the dishonorable title, Most Segregated Industrial City of the North. Since that time, racial segregation in Detroit and Gary has become as bad.

Lake Park Avenue was an example of so-called changing neighborhoods. Banks and real estate companies wanted to keep rents artificially high. They did not permit stable, integrated neighborhoods. Real estate companies "changed" neighborhoods by moving out the white tenants. Then they rented to people of color and charged much higher rents. The motivation was greed. Racist lies were used to create "white flight" out of the neighborhood.

There were two steps in "changing" the Lake Park area from white to African American. First landlords rented apartments vacated by white tenants to Japanese American families. The same landlords refused to rent to African American families. Most of the new Japanese American tenants were Nisei, American-born children of Japanese immigrants. They had moved to Chicago to get as far away as they could from the racism and the "concentration camps" in the Western states.

Concentration Camps

During World War II, the U.S. government imprisoned Japanese Americans in concentration camps. The U.S. was also at war against Germany and Italy. But U.S. citizens of German or Italian ancestry were never forced into camps. Fifty years later the U.S. government apologized to Japanese Americans and paid token reparations to survivors of the camps.

The early 1950s saw quick kills by real estate companies in the Lake Park area. The second step of creating a ghetto had begun. Japanese and white tenants left or were evicted. Like sharks in a feeding frenzy, greedy landlords cut up large apartments into several one- or two-room "kitchenettes." The kitchenette apartment was kitchen, dining room, living room and bedroom, all in one room. These were rented to African Americans at triple the previous rent.

In five years, the slumlord had his investment back plus a very fat profit. Nothing was spent to maintain the buildings and they crumbled fast under the pressure of overcrowding. The slumlord then abandoned the building. Racists said "those people" ruined the neighborhood. The tenant victims were blamed instead of the guilty banks and landlords. And the city government found nothing illegal in this profitable destruction of communities.

Grass Roots Politics

The Lake Park Avenue community also introduced Lumpkin to electoral politics. He doesn't know who wrote the graffiti "Lumpkin—Communist Republican" on a boxcar at Wisconsin Steel in 1950. It was not interpreted as a compliment. Frank was helping the Farm Equipment Workers (FE-UE) sign up members at Wisconsin Steel. The press was redbaiting FE-UE and right-wing union leaders were raiding UE locals. Lumpkin's connection to FE-UE probably accounted for the "Communist" label in the graffiti.

But Frank a Republican? Frank supported the election of State Representative William H. Robinson who ran as a Republican. Robinson was an African American social worker who went into politics to help his community. He was not controlled by either the Republican or Democratic machine. At that time, each Illinois legislative district elected three state representatives. A voter could vote for three, or even cast a "bullet" vote for one. State law did not allow all three to be from the same party. Some independent politicians, running as Republicans, were elected under this system. Since then, the system has been changed to single-representative districts "to save money."

In his South Side neighborhood, Frank felt the need to protest against the Democratic Party machine that held African Americans in a choke grip. At that time, Booker Money was the Democratic precinct committeeman. The policeman known as Two-Gun Pete held sway in his Hilltop Lounge at 39th St. and the Outer Drive. Frank was never one who went by labels. He knew that Vito Marcantonio, the pro-labor N.Y. Congressman, was first elected as a Republican. Still it's amusing to think that the boxcar graffiti, "Lumpkin—Communist Republican" may have traveled the rails, spreading Lumpkin's fame and confusing onlookers.

Housing and Health Issues

Five small children died in a flash fire that broke out in a converted garage-apartment a block away from the Lumpkin apartment. Police arrested the two mothers of the children, who were in a nearby grocery store when the fire began. The police blamed the victims instead of those responsible for the dangerous housing conditions. The Lumpkins and their neighbors organized a "Safeguard Our Homes Against Fire" committee. The Committee included Communist, church, and other community activists. They pressed for enforcement of the housing code to stop more fire tragedies.

A tragedy of another kind struck even closer to home. The innocent victim was a child in the Lumpkins' apartment building. Mozella, a neighbor and good friend, had recently come to Chicago from Mississippi. Her 13-year- old son, Sonny, had an appendicitis operation at Cook County Hospital. The emergency surgery saved him. Friends rejoiced and thought he was lucky to be in Chicago where he could get the necessary medical care. About a year later Sonny began to feel pain again. A visit to the doctor found nothing serious, but the pain persisted and got much worse.

"Wait for Frank," Sonny said. "He'll do something." But Frank was working at the mill. By the time he came home it would be too late. Mozella and her sister, Arlene, took Sonny to nearby Michael Reese, a private research hospital. The hospital turned him away. "You'll have to go to Cook County Hospital," they told Mozella. That was seven miles away. When they got to the emergency room at County, the doctor was busy with a severely burned patient.

Sonny sat on the bench, suffering for four hours, and died without receiving medical care. He had an intestinal adhesion, a not uncommon occurrence after abdominal surgery. Emergency surgery could have saved him. But he died from the racist refusal to admit him at the private hospital and the lack of staff at Cook County Hospital. The outcry after Sonny's needless death and similar cases led Dr. Quentin Young to organize the Medical Committee for Human Rights. Woodlawn Hospital retaliated when Dr. Young publicized the death of an infant who had been denied admission to the hospital. The hospital canceled Dr. Young's staff privileges, in fact the same day that he had admitted Beatrice Lumpkin to the hospital for treatment of hepatitis. Dr. Young went on to become a national leader of the fight for universal access to health care, a fight he continues to lead 45 years later.

Ethel and Julius Rosenberg

In the1950s, the Cold War, followed by the hot Korean War, was putting its icy grip on grassroots movements. Activists charged that the real goal of the Cold War was to divide and destroy people's movements everywhere.

Julius and Ethel Rosenberg were on Death Row. The Lumpkins believed that the Rosenbergs were victims of a monstrous frame-up. Despite the fear, millions rallied against the death penalty. In Washington, DC, 15,000 marched for clemency but President Eisenhower turned a deaf ear. People feared a replay of the case of Sacco and Vanzetti, executed in 1927 and later proved innocent. On June 19, 1953, a call came to the Lumpkin's apartment to rush down to the Federal Building. It was feared that the execution of the Rosenbergs would be moved up, instead of delayed, because of the onset of the Jewish Sabbath. Quick calls brought many neighbors over to pile into the Lumpkin's beat-up old car. Perhaps it was the overload that brought the old car to a sudden halt. Two taxis rushed everyone to join other demonstrators who hoped to stop the execution. While the pickets marched, the executioner pulled the switch. Jeanleah, the Lumpkin's seven-year-old daughter, said, "Mommy, the policeman is laughing." The callousness of the police and the cruelty of the executions haunted her for many years.

Tenants Organize

It was hard to force some South Side landlords to supply enough heat to keep temperatures from dropping below the legal limits. Frank used his Merchant Marine engine-room experience to feed the coal-burning furnace himself. The real estate company that operated the building reacted by locking the coal room, forcing the tenants to take collective action. The Lumpkins and two other Communist families organized the other tenants, all Nisei families. The tenants decided on a rent strike, putting their rents in escrow until the landlord agreed to give enough heat. That struggle was won. Later, the Lumpkins and the Brighams, rent strike organizers, were served with eviction notices. The tenants decided to go to court to fight the evictions.

The courtroom was full of reporters because Rent Control had just ended in Chicago. Under Rent Control, landlords could not evict tenants they did not like. The hearing was held at the height of the McCarthy "witch hunts," The real estate company did not accuse the Lumpkins and Brighams of misconduct. The landlord's only complaint was "they're Communists." Although there was no evidence of wrongdoing, the eviction was granted.

The Chicago Tribune carried the story on the front page, perhaps as a guide to other landlords who wanted to evict activists. The article did not go unnoticed at the mill. In the locker room, a worker came up to Frank and asked, "Your name Lumpkin? Do you live at 3650 South Lake Park Avenue?" Then he turned to his buddy and added, "I told you that was him!" That newspaper article was on the desk of the Wisconsin Steel manager when Lumpkin was called in and confronted with the report of the Chicago Police Red Squad on his community activity. However, the company took no action against Lumpkin. He concluded that he got more protection from the union contract in the mill than he got from the U.S. Constitution in the courtroom.

Gary and Septic Tanks

Landlords gave the Lumpkins a hard time. Many would not rent to African Americans. Also, rental ads often said, "No children." In 1954, the Lumpkins moved to a prefab house in a semi-rural Gary neighborhood. There they could not be evicted as long as they made the mortgage payments. Beatrice's hand shook as she signed the $500 check for the down payment. It was by far the largest check the Lumpkins had ever written. The house was on a sand dune with woods across the street, ideal for children. But in a month, neighbors called to ask, "Why is the FBI interested in you? Yes, they were here, asking questions." That was the signal for the Lumpkins to organize the community before the FBI could isolate them. There were plenty of urgent issues.

The semi-rural charm of the Wooded Highlands subdivision had attracted Frank to the Tolleston area on the West Side of Gary. At the time they moved, the Lumpkins were not too concerned that drinking water came from a well and that the sanitary waste went into a septic tank. Afterwards they discovered that the septic tanks were too close to the wells. Beatrice, city-bred, thought if the great city of Gary allowed septic tanks and wells inside city limits, it must be "all right." Frank had lived with wells and septic tanks until he left the orange groves, and he thought wells were "all right." But there was a case of typhoid fever in the Wooded Highlands neighborhood. It was *not* all right.

Quickly, the Lumpkins formed a community organization that took samples of the well water. At least 30% of the wells showed contamination from the septic tanks. Within a month, the Lumpkins and their new neighbors had organized a big demonstration outside

City Hall. At City Hall, demonstrators held up large, single letters that spelled "WE WANT WATER! WE WANT SEWERS!" Eventually, both demands were won, but it took over 10 years. The City of Gary could not act because the water plant was privately owned. Installing pipes to bring out the private water service was very costly. The residents could not afford to pay the full cost. A proposition for public ownership of the water supply was put on the ballot. It was defeated by a massive advertising campaign paid for by the utility company. The company used the cleverly deceptive slogan, "Keep the politicians' hands out of our clean water!"

Katie Dowd, a key supporter of the campaign for water and sewers, had been a youth leader of the cotton sharecroppers' fight of the '30s. "Don't believe them when they say colored people can't stick together," Dowd told the Lumpkins. As a teenager, she had been part of a historic uprising of sharecroppers who had been displaced by mechanical cotton pickers. They decided not to wait to be evicted, one-by-one. Instead, they planned a bold, dramatic move to focus attention on their demands. One night, 5,000 sharecropper families moved all of their possessions—cooking stoves, animals, and all. They camped along Route 66, then the main East-West highway to California where the whole world could see them. The mass move took the authorities completely by surprise. Not one person of the more than 5,000 had leaked their plan.

FBI Harassment - Hattie Tells Off the Un-American Committee

FBI harassment continued through much of the '50s. FBI agents literally jumped out from behind bushes to accost Beatrice on her two-mile walk home from the Pennsylvania Railroad train station. They walked into Frank's back yard to make him an "offer" while he was grinding rust off the heating-oil tank. They left empty-handed because Frank continued to run the grinder. His face did not change its expression except to tell them to "get off of my property." In Buffalo, N.Y., Frank's mother, Hattie, was called in by the House Un-American Committee. That was about the same time that they called in Dr. Benjamin Spock, pediatrician and peace activist. Hattie freely testified about her community and church work to improve the life of workers. The un-Americans didn't want to hear any of it. Hattie was not intimidated and continued her struggle. Nor was Frank intimidated. He did not go underground and did not stop organizing. Other members of his family were also deeply involved in the fight to protect workers' rights to organize.

Hattie Lumpkin, c. 1960

Hattie's courage and wisdom set an example for the large Lumpkin family. A young writer recorded some of Hattie's insights:

> I used to have hard times with reading. I always got headaches reading some of these pamphlets and books on Marxism. I said to myself, You're getting older and never had much education. But you've seen a lot of troubles and had a lot of experience, that should be helping you to understand such matters.
>
> One day I got my first eyeglasses. At last I could see everything sharp and clear. Lots of words are still new and difficult, but I'm learning all the time—about chauvinism, surplus value, imperialism, and all those things. Once in a while I stop and think that not everyone has such glasses and sees things so sharp and clear. The world still looks very

blurry to lots of folks. If I start acting uppity because things seems so clear, and talk to people in a strange or funny way, without even listening to them, or say, Why bother about him? Everything's blurry to him. Then I can't be surprised if they won't listen to me either, with or without the glasses. [68]

Wooded Highlands Democratic Club

Lumpkin did not let FBI harassment stop him from organizing a political action club in Gary. The club was an independent political organization made up of steel workers, auto workers and truck drivers from the community. They named it the "Wooded Highlands Democratic Club," but it was entirely independent of the Democratic Party. Club members made a deal with a homeowner for the upstairs of a two-story house on Chase Street. The only problem was that the second story, which was to be the clubroom, was unfinished and not habitable. The club had no money but lots of skilled members. The carpenters showed others what to do. Electricians completed the wiring. Every skill that was used in the steel mills was represented. Their "sweat equity" paid for the rent, and the club served the community for 5 years.

On the surface the club seemed mostly social. It was a place for couples to go on the weekend and have fun. Drinks and snacks were at cost. A jukebox supplied the music. There were no salaries and expenses were low. Club leaders kept a close watch to prevent offensive behavior. Women in the community appreciated the club because their husbands could go there and not get into "trouble." Through cooperation in making the club work, steel workers learned organizational skills and confidence in their own abilities. Lumpkin made it a center for educational discussions. A core of leaders emerged to make the Wooded Highlands Democratic Club a force in city politics. At Frank's urging, Beatrice produced a community newsletter, *The Wooded Highlands Comet. The Comet* helped bring out people to fight on the issues.

Sometimes the Club's efforts were misunderstood. A member's 13-year old daughter had studied ballet and gave a dance performance at a club event. At one of the small churches that profusely dotted the community, a sermon was preached against the "strip dancing" at the club. Perhaps *ballet* was confused with *belly*? There was also occasional confusion as to what rights the Club would fight for. It did not get involved when a friend was arrested for running a private still. The still was detected from the air in winter because it was in the only house that did not have snow on its roof.

After helping to elect many other candidates, Frank decided to run for Democratic precinct committeeman as an independent. Becoming a Democratic committeeman may seem to contradict political independence. That was not the case. The precinct committeeman in a city like Gary was often the workers' main resource in the community. During strikes or family emergencies, the precinct committeeman was the person to see about getting on welfare. With Frank as committeeman, it was different. There were no kickbacks and people were educated about their rights. Welfare was a right, Lumpkin explained, not a political favor. Often he would have to go into his own pocket when he saw hungry children who could not wait while a check was processed.

Precinct committeeman races in Gary were hotly contested. The machine put up a candidate against him in every election. Frank won by substantial majorities. He loved electoral campaigning because it took him to the home of every one of the over 1,000 voters in the precinct. Even after Lumpkin had left Gary, he returned to help elect Richard Hatcher as the first African American mayor of a large city.

Talking, listening, teaching, learning and joining in struggle with workers helped him survive the McCarthy repression of the '50s. He said that as long as he was among the workers, he felt that he was doing something. Lumpkin also took a lot of political flak because of his interracial marriage. His response to that issue was part of the educational process that Frank conducted in the community. "Race is not the issue," he explained. "Oppression is the issue. Fighting for our rights is the issue."

The Gary police relied on Frank's experience. Sometimes they asked him to investigate reports of domestic violence. Many organizers would not consider such a dangerous assignment part of a community activist's responsibility. But Frank was willing to take the risk in the hope of preventing violence. Often he succeeded. One day he circled a beach parking lot but could find no parking. Then he made a second circle of the lot.

"I have to stop a friend of mine who's about to get into trouble," Frank explained to his friend, Bill. "My friend had a gun in his hand and they were having an argument."

On the second time around the lot, the friend and his gun were gone. "What would you have done if you had found him?" Bill asked. "I would have said, "Give me the gun! And he would have given me the gun." "Have you ever tried that?" Bill asked. "Yes, more than once."

In 1959, Soviet prime minister Nikita Khrushchev became well-known in the United States because of a strongly worded speech at the United Nations in which he used the term "gangsters" to describe the United States government. Based on Lumpkin's experience in Gary, the charge of gangster influence on government didn't seem far-fetched. People in Gary believed that organized crime made payoffs to precinct committeemen, policemen and other officials. In turn, these officials looked the other way, whether it was the numbers racket, drug dealing or prostitution. Even some politicians who cared about their constituents were said to be on the payroll of organized crime. There were some honorable exceptions besides Lumpkin who were not on the take. But there were not many paths to prosperity open to African Americans. Frank's Gary neighborhood had a few prosperous homes that stood in sharp contrast to the small prefab homes of the workers. Two kinds of people lived in the "rich" houses—medical doctors and racketeers. That was surely a confused message going out to the youth of the community.

Wade in the Water

Less than a half-hour's ride from Gary is beautiful Indiana Dunes State Park. The Lake Michigan dunes and beaches attract people from many areas, including Chicago. Although there were not many African American families hiking the State Park trails in the 1950s, Frank Lumpkin was always welcomed by the other hikers. But it was different at some of the Gary beaches. The real-estate companies had started a wave of "white flight" out of many Gary neighborhoods. Miller and Glen Park areas remained "off-limits" to African Americans. The *Gary Post-Dispatch* was full of scary "news" stories about white racist violence against African Americans at the city's Marquette Park Beach in Miller. Frank decided to check it out with his family.

As he drove up to the beach it looked like an all-white enclave. Frank allowed no time for a family discussion because he knew what he had to do. He quickly parked and hopped out of the car in his street clothes—swimming was not one of his things. He grabbed the hands of his two younger sons who were dressed in swimsuits. Frank looked neither to the right nor left, just marched forward to the water. After the boys had a swim, they left without incident. But if looks and glares killed, they would have been dead. On the way out they saw another African American family seated on the sand, a perfectly natural place to be on a sunny summer afternoon. "Those are some brave people," Frank said in admiration.

Joe Norrick

One of Frank's rich experiences in Gary was working with Joe Norrick. A coal miner from Princeton, Indiana, Joe had moved north to become a steel worker. He took his militant brand of unionism to his job as an electrician in Youngstown Sheet and Tube. Along the way, Joe joined the Communist Party and met his second wife, Fanny Hartman. She had been a Communist Party leader for many years in New England. The Norricks helped the Indiana Communists survive the McCarthy period of the 1950s. For years their house was a center for rank and file steel workers. People enjoyed visiting the Norricks for good conversation and to admire the house Joe had built with his own hands. He kept a tractor running to farm the bottomland fields around his Gary house. As a special treat, he let Frank run the tractor. Of Joe and Frank it could be said, "You can take a person off the farm but you can't take the farm out of the person."

After Fanny died, Joe met Ruth. Each was making a rare visit to their hometown of Princeton, Indiana. Ruth had worked with Harry Hopkins to put people to work in the '30s on public works jobs for the WPA (Works Progress Administration), PWA (Public Works Administration) and other New Deal agencies. She was a living witness to the success of public works programs. In just four months of 1935, her agency had put 4,000,000 people to work.[69] The public works jobs ranged from construction and water conservation to writing and live theater.

Over the years, Frank traveled to steel towns in other parts of the country. He found some regional differences. Still the streets in Pueblo, Colorado, looked a lot like the streets in Gary. He saw similarities in all the steel towns. One was the sense of community and solidarity that steel workers share. Perhaps that is what made it so hard for Frank to leave Gary, a decision he reluctantly agreed to in 1960. Layoffs hit U.S. Steel's National Tube plant where Beatrice was working. She went back to electronics work near Chicago's

Loop. Then, in 1959, the electronics company moved 14 miles west to the suburb of Maywood and 50 miles from the Lumpkin house in Gary. Worn down by months of traveling 100 miles a day, her choice was to quit the job or to move. Quitting a job was not an option. So the Lumpkins moved to Broadview, Illinois, a suburb just south of Maywood.

Wooded Highlands Democratic Club farewell party, Gary IN

Broadview and Chicago's Western Suburbs

For the next 18 years, Frank drove 30 miles each way to Wisconsin Steel. He never complained, not even when he drove with his foot fractured in two places. The new house was brick, a big move up from the prefab pressboard house in Gary. Although the five-room Broadview house was small by suburban standards, it had a basement and attic. The back yard, instead of sand as in Gary, had rich black earth that would grow grass and plants,. Streets were paved. All the houses had sidewalks, city sewers and water.

The Broadview political scene was difficult. The village was a low- to middle-income suburb west of Chicago. At that time it was 90% white. African Americans were confined to one corner of the village that bordered on a large African American community in Maywood. Since trustees were elected on a village-wide basis, there was little chance of electing an African American to the Broadview village board. The village-wide method of electing city councils was used in many towns; it denied representation to African Americans and Latinos.

Broadview did not remain untouched by the civil rights movement of the '60s. Julian Smith, a brave African American who lived near the Lumpkins, became a candidate for village trustee. His campaign protested the racist policies of the Broadview village government. The police harassed him, followed him in police cars and stopped him without cause. Nonetheless, the Lumpkins distributed Smith's flyers to all parts of the village. Election returns showed great strength in their own community, as expected. Although Smith's vote was small in the white-only areas, he received some votes in every precinct.

The peaceful appearance of the Broadview streets was deceiving. African American families in Broadview were under intense pressure on housing and school issues. The school district in which the two youngest Lumpkins were enrolled included the towns of Maywood and Melrose Park. Maywood had a majority African American population. Melrose Park was all white. Racists from Melrose Park dominated the school board. They resisted demands for a middle school that would have benefited all of the children, white as well as African American. Melrose Park members of the school board did not want their children attending the same school as African American children.

The Lumpkins attended a school board meeting to support the demand for a middle school. The rumor was that some towns, such as Broadview and Melrose Park, were controlled by the Mafia. The rumor may have started because Melrose Park was home to well-known mob figures. Perhaps it was more than a rumor. At the school board meeting, a Chicago Peace Council leaflet came to the attention of a member of the school board. The flyer advertised a talk by a priest from Sicily who was featured as a "Mafia fighter." The meeting of the school board was thrown into consternation. The board declared a recess and left the room. After a half-hour executive session, board members probably concluded that the flyer was not referring to any local Mafia. The board reconvened the meeting and voted down construction of a middle school.

Everything from zoning practices to school organization in the small towns of Broadview and Melrose Park was affected by racism. The town governments and banks that controlled real estate policies worked together. African American families who wanted to build on vacant land were denied building permits. Instead, real estate speculators were given the green light to build apartment buildings in an area zoned for single-family dwellings. The apartments were rented to whites only, apparently to keep the African American community from growing. The Lumpkin family helped organize massive protests to keep the single-family zoning at the zoning board hearings. The Lumpkins believed that the fight could have been won with more militant tactics of picket lines and sit-ins. But the adults weren't ready to take their protest to the streets.

In contrast, the African American youths of Maywood, Broadview and Aurora were more than ready in 1967-8. Under the dynamic leadership of NAACP youth leader Fred Hampton, the young people were demanding a swimming pool for their Maywood community. The town had a swimming pool in another community but children of color were not welcome. "Go slow," the community elders told the young people. But they didn't listen. Paul and John Lumpkin were at the high school with Fred Hampton, and they wouldn't listen either. The village claimed that there was no money for the pool. Store windows were broken, and it became clear that the anger could not be contained. Then the village "found" the money for a pool.

The fight spilled over to Proviso East High School in Maywood when school officials refused to accept an African American homecoming queen. The Cook County Sheriff's office declared war on the students and moved in like a military occupation. Guns were mounted on the rooftops of homes surrounding the school. Police sprayed mace freely in the school corridors to control the students. That morning, as Frank returned from the night shift, his car was rear-ended by a sheriff's car. The deputy apologized; he was in a hurry to deliver a load of guns to sheriffs at Proviso High School. Two days later, Frank saw his son John with a group of high school students, protesting racism at the school and demanding an end to the sheriff's war against them.

"John," Frank said, "Don't you know that the most important thing for you now is to get your education?"

"You're wrong, Daddy," his son replied. "The most important thing for me is to become a man!"

Sheriff's police spray mace at a crowd of Proviso East High School students.

Duane Hall photo, Oct. 21, 1967 *Sun-Times*. Reprinted with special permission from Chicago Sun-Times, Inc.

Somehow, the 1968-1969 school year was completed without any student being killed at Proviso East High School. But Fred Hampton would not be that fortunate in the following school year. Hampton had become part of the leadership of the new Black Panther Party. The Party was doing such "revolutionary" things as cooking hot breakfasts for little children. John Lumpkin helped cook the Panthers' breakfasts for kids in 1969-70, while a scholarship student at the Massachusetts Institute of Technology (MIT).

Fred Hampton was the type of African American youth leader who posed a great challenge to the system. During summer vacations, Fred worked in the Argo plant where he saw African American, Latino, and white employees working together in the Union.

No doubt, Hampton's labor experience contributed to his broad outlook. His parents, long-time employees at the same cornstarch plant in Argo, Illinois, were stewards, rank and file leaders in their local of the Oil, Chemical and Atomic Workers Union. Fred was an eloquent speaker, and totally devoted to the "people," not only his own African American people, but all people who were exploited. He was on the same high school track team as John and Paul Lumpkin, and later a student at Malcolm X College where Beatrice Lumpkin taught mathematics.

On December 4, 1969, while Fred Hampton, Mark Clark and other Panther Party members were sound asleep in their beds, a squad of Chicago police broke into their apartment. The police were armed with a submachine gun, shotguns and a map of the apartment showing the location of Hampton's bed. State's Attorney for Cook County Edward V. Hanrahan had ordered the murderous raid. The police fired up to 200 rounds into the apartment—enough bullets to kill Hampton and Clark many times over.[70] Twenty-five years later, Paul Engleman in *Chicago* magazine, revealed some of the larger forces responsible for the killings:

> Though he had not yet viewed the apartment, state's attorney Edward V. Hanrahan claimed during a press conference following the raid that his men were victims of a vicious attack and managed to survive "by the grace of God." Hanrahan's account was the first of many falsehoods that would be told, repeated, and revised by law-enforcement personnel during the course of a police inquiry, a coroner's inquest, three grand jury investigations, a criminal trial, and at the time, the longest civil trial in U.S. history. It emerged that Hanrahan and the police were minor

players in a larger production staged by the FBI, a secret counter-intelligence program—COINTELPRO—designed, in the words of J. Edgar Hoover, to "disrupt" and "neutralize" black groups and "prevent the rise of a 'messiah.' " [71]

News of the killings stunned Chicago. Thousands came to the West Side funeral parlor to pay their respects and then went to the apartment to view what was left after the massive firepower. Hampton's blood-soaked mattress and the front door riddled with bullets were nightmarish memories that angered the viewers for years to come. Maywood, Fred Hampton's hometown, was shaken to its roots.

Shortly after the murders, Edward V. Hanrahan, instigator of the raid on the sleeping Panthers, decided to run for Congress in a district that included Maywood. The Hampton family felt somewhat vindicated when Hanrahan lost the election, in part because normally Democratic Maywood voted heavily against him. Hanrahan's Republican opponent, Henry Hyde, became Congressman. Hyde went on to become a leader for everything that Fred Hampton had fought against. Hyde even managed to get district lines redrawn so that most of Maywood was no longer in his district and he didn't have to worry about the Black vote.

With dozens of young Black Panthers killed, Frank feared for his son's safety. But he did not tell him to quit the Panthers. Instead, his advice was to be more effective and to watch out for paid provocateurs. He knew that police agents were trying to destroy the organization from inside by urging terrorist actions. On his own, John decided to move in another direction in 1970. He left MIT to study medicine and prepare to serve people as a medical doctor. Since that time, the government has been forced to establish a breakfast program. Children who otherwise would have had no breakfast have benefited from the Panthers' initiative.

Today there is a new swimming pool in Maywood named for Fred Hampton, but even this recognition involved a sharp battle. Maywood Councilman Tom Strieter, his wife Doris Strieter later elected to the City Council, Joan Elbert and Ted Elbert were among the progressive white residents who tipped the balance in favor of honoring Fred Hampton. Tom Strieter paid a price for standing up for justice—he lost his faculty job at Concordia College. Rev. Strieter is reluctant to assume the role of a hero. Some said that differences in church doctrine were a factor in the loss of his faculty position.

Thomas Strieter became the pastor of a Lutheran church in the suburb of Glen Ellyn, then moved on to a large church in an African American community on Chicago's South Side. In 1995, the Elberts and their friends honored the memory of Fred Hampton by producing a publication that focused on the human qualities of the remarkable young leader: *The Essence of Fred Hampton.*

The families of Mark Clark and Fred Hampton and survivors of the police raid filed suit against Hanrahan and the police in 1970. As Engleman described it, "If the raid demonstrated the power of the police to subdue with deadly force, the civil trial revealed the power of the government to overwhelm through bureaucratic deception."[72] On February 28, 1983, the civil suit against the policemen who had killed Hampton and Clark, and the federal, city and county authorities involved in the assault, was finally settled for $1.85 million. The settlement was paid equally by federal, city and county governments. City and county taxpayers also paid two attorneys $2.2 million to defend Hanrahan and the police.[73]

Stop the War

All the Lumpkin children were swept up into the anti-war movement to get the U.S. out of Vietnam and Cambodia. Jeanleah and her friends at Shimer College joined anti-war picket lines. On a cold day in March, she bicycled 80 miles to join an anti-war march. Carl left graduate school and taught high school to avoid serving in the Vietnam War that he opposed. Some of John's friends were hit in the head when the Chicago police attacked anti-war demonstrators at the 1968 Democratic Party Convention. In 1969, John Lumpkin became an anti-war leader at MIT. He led a demonstration of thousands against the bombing of Cambodia. A member of the university staff, seeing John distributing anti-war flyers to all of the offices warned him, "You better watch out or they'll send you back to India."

"But I'm from Chicago," John retorted.

"Then they'll send you back to Chicago, and that's worse," the staffer persisted.

On May 7, 1970, Frank got a call from Champaign, Illinois, that Paul Lumpkin had been arrested. Paul was a sophomore at the University of Illinois. He was known as a fine athlete and had been a three-varsity athlete in high school. The day before, there had been a campus demonstration against the bombing of Cambodia. Michael Parenti, a visiting professor from Yale and a peace activist, was brutally beaten and severely injured by police. Another teacher may have saved Parenti's life by throwing his own body over Parenti's prone form to absorb some of the blows. Both teachers were arrested and held in $10,000 bail. That bail was double the bail for a policeman charged with "manslaughter" in the death of Edgar Hoult one week earlier. Edgar Hoult was an African American youth who had never been charged with any crime but was killed by Champaign police.

Paul was one of thousands of students who went to the police station to peacefully protest the brutal attack on their teachers. The police charged into the crowd of unprepared students. Students tried to get away, resulting in panic. Several student leaders, including Paul, locked arms in order to hold the crowd back. They were trying to prevent students from falling and being trampled as had tragically occurred at Southern Illinois University. Just then, a man in plain clothes who never identified himself as a policeman said, "Paul Lumpkin!" and grabbed him. Paul broke away and ran for his life. He was intent on avoiding the fate of Edgar Hoult.

But Paul tripped and was arrested. He was held on $1,500 bail and charged with "interfering with an institution of higher learning, disorderly conduct and mob action." Friends brought in the $150 to pay 10% of the $1,500 to a bail bondsman to get Paul out. The next day, the judge raised Paul's bail to $7,500. That was $2,500 higher than the bond placed on the policeman charged with manslaughter in the death of Edgar Hoult. The police appeared to have orders "to throw the book" at Paul. They knew him as a prominent speaker on campus for the anti-war and civil rights movements. The police claimed that Paul had tackled a state trooper who had grabbed another student. Two additional charges of "resisting arrest" and trying to escape were also added. At that point Paul's comrades called Frank because they could not raise the additional $600 needed for bond.

Frank got the call late in the afternoon. He had to move fast to get the money. Tomorrow might be too late. Too many African American teenagers ended up dead after a night in jail. Frank got $600 in cash and left at once for the three-hour drive. It was dark when they reached Champaign. The police officer at the desk took

15 minutes to count twelve $50 bills. Each count was different. Finally he agreed that the amount was correct and they let Paul out. Paul's first thought was how to raise bail for another teenager still being held.

Fortunately, no students were killed at the University of Illinois. Students everywhere mourned the tragic deaths of students at Kent State in Ohio and Jackson State in Mississippi. Most universities ended the year early, giving students a "pass" instead of letter grades. Neither John nor Paul Lumpkin returned to their universities. Paul was suspended for his anti-war activities and decided to go to another school. Then he tried different jobs until he became a railroad engineer on a commuter run. While his train sat in the station, he attended classes at the Chicago campus of the University of Illinois until he finished his degree. John left MIT, giving up the goal of biological research. He enrolled in medical school, eventually becoming an emergency medicine doctor and public health officer. Both Jeanleah and Carl became scientists, she in theoretical computer science and he in biology.

"You have a responsibility to your kids, grandchildren, other people's kids. If you have knowledge, you have responsibility to share that knowledge. You can't take it easy." Frank Lumpkin

8. Meeting Workers Around the World

Frank Lumpkin has learned a lot from workers that he met all over the world as a merchant seaman. In 1965, he got the chance to return to Europe when Beatrice lost her job at Knight Electronics. The president of the company told her, "for the money I'm paying you, I could hire a man." She lost her pension rights but got a lump sum instead—just enough to buy four tickets to Europe.

It was cheaper then to pick up a car in Europe and ship it home later. They chose a Volkswagen "squareback," a car with a square back, a rear cargo gate and a price tag of $1600. Tent, stove, sleeping bags and very few clothes weighed in under the combined airline allowance. Paul and John, the two younger children, came along. In Paris, they camped in the Bois de Boulogne, something like camping in Central Park in New York. In 1965, auto clubs throughout Europe had set up auto camps in the heart of many cities. Camping was $5 a night, and the Lumpkins cooked most meals, especially in France and Germany. That made it possible to live within the $100 a week budget for four people that they had allowed for the eight-week trip across Europe. Gasoline was the biggest expense with the price of gas $3.50 a gallon in Western Europe. In the Soviet Union, the price of gas was cheap, $0.35 a gallon, about the same as in the U.S.

France

With visas for three weeks in the Soviet Union, the Lumpkins drove east across France until they came to Alsace-Lorraine. The countryside was as pretty as a calendar cover. Neat rectangles of yellow and green formed a quiltwork of farmland. In Alsace-

124

Lorraine they knew they were close to the German border because the signs in the villages were in German. They were getting by on Beatrice's basic high school French. In Alsace-Lorraine she switched to basic high school German. But high school language class was not like real life. How do you ask for a mineral oil laxative in basic German without a dictionary? How do you describe its purpose?

Frank had his family splitting their sides with laughter at his graphic enactment of a hen in labor delivering an egg. That's how his Puerto Rican fellow workers showed him how to ask for eggs in a store when you didn't know the language. But a dignified pantomime of the purpose of mineral oil was a challenge. At the Alsatian *drogeria*, cooking oil, kerosene and Mazola corn oil were brought out, one at a time. By now other customers had joined in the fun to help with the translation. "No." Beatrice said. It's not for cooking, not for burning, not for eating; it's like medicine but not medicine. Finally the owner of the *drogeria* got the idea. "Oh, für umkehren." Beatrice agreed. She thought it meant to turn upside down and shake out the contents! The mineral oil was speedily produced.

Germany

The Lumpkins crossed the bridge over the Rhine. After a night in Frankfurt, they pushed eastward towards the city of Nuremberg. It was getting dark and time to find a camp for the night. Finally, a kind German driver led them to a large field where they seemed to be the only campers. When they awoke the next morning the place looked strangely familiar. It was an abandoned stadium, overgrown with grass, with a large reviewing stand and rows of flagless flag stands. It was an eerie feeling when they realized where they were. It had been the stadium home of the Nazi Party, usually shown in World War II newsreels with Hitler at the podium! The decayed condition of the stadium was visual proof that Hitler's "1000 year Reich" lasted less than 12 years. Frank's sense of history told him that capitalism would not last forever. He truly believed that "everything changes."

Czechoslovakia

After camping on ground that reminded them of the war and the concentration camps, the Lumpkins were more than ready to leave Nuremberg. Soon they crossed the border into socialist Czechoslovakia, the first time they had set foot on socialist soil.

They had heard all the scare stories about shortages of food in socialist countries. So before they left Germany, they loaded the front trunk with canned goods (VW motors used to be in the rear.) As it turned out, they never had to open a can in Czechoslovakia. The Czech food was good, tasty, abundant and cheap. In Pilsen the beer was as good as its reputation, and the soft drinks were better. Prague was lovely, its Gothic architecture unharmed by World War II. They did not see any homeless or unemployed. In Prague, there was an air of prosperity and well-being.

Many young women were working in the streets on non-traditional jobs, from electrical maintenance to installation of sewers. In the streets and the cafes, men came over to Frank to shake his hand and express their solidarity. Most were veterans of the anti-fascist struggle. "And are you a comrade, too?" an old timer asked Frank. When Paul's football knee swelled up, they quickly got medical help. Treatment at the emergency clinic was free. The camp was in the outskirts of Prague, along the beautiful Vltava River. They walked on the bridge from which Charles II was thrown to his death. But that summer of 1965, Europe was experiencing a "green winter." It rained almost every day. The river was rising, threatening to flood the camp grounds. The sleeping bags never dried out. Anyhow, it was time to go. They continued to drive east, through Slovakia and towards the Soviet border at Uzhgorod. Slovakia, they had heard, was the less developed part of the bi-national country. They found scenes of great change. The contrast was sharp between old and new. Every region had a medieval-looking castle perched at the edge of sheer cliffs. And every region had a new factory under construction.

The Soviet Union

It was late in the day when they crossed into the Soviet Union, but Lvov seemed pretty close. At least it looked close on the map. Soviet vacationers were camping on the green slopes. The camping looked tempting, but the Soviet visa was very specific. The visa called for staying in Lvov that night, and that's what Frank would do if it was humanly possible. It was slow going because the winding mountain road was narrow. Livestock crossed the road at will. At one turn, a white horse reared up suddenly in the headlights. Frank was enjoying the drive. "Just like Georgia [USA]," he said as livestock crossed the road. This part of the Ukraine became part of Soviet Ukraine only after World War II. The countryside seemed underdeveloped. It was obvious that the Soviets could have invested all of their capital right in their own country, especially in areas devastated in World War II. Soviet aid to the countries of Africa, Asia and Latin America was made at a big sacrifice.

After the anxious night of driving, the rest of the three weeks in the Soviet Union was interesting, pleasant, even restful. Along with the night's camping permit ($5) came time with an Intourist guide. That was surely the world's best bargain. In Kiev the guide was a daring graduate geology student whose name was Igor. Paul and John politely suppressed a laugh when they heard his name. Monster culture was then big in the U.S.; Igor was the name of a character in the Frankenstein movies. But sometimes Igor was too daring. He directed Frank to drive the wrong way down a one-way street near the stadium. The street was closed for a soccer game. The militia man on the street corner turned purple, blowing his whistle in protest. "Keep going," Igor calmly told Frank. "If he stops us, I'll tell him you're a visiting African prince."

But in other ways, Igor was a model Soviet citizen, absolutely incorruptible. He refused to let the Lumpkins buy him lunch. "I am like a camel," he said. "I can go for long periods without food or water." Then he would insist that they see everything, so there was no time for lunch anyway. Since the Lumpkins were not camels, they made Igor stop one day so they could buy some of the famous Soviet ice cream. He insisted on paying for his own ice cream. With one exception, all the other guides during the three-weeks of travel in the Soviet Union were equally sincere and did not appear corrupted by me first-ism or consumerism.

Igor was not religious, but one of the first sights he insisted on visiting was the great cathedrals. Time after time, in the Soviet Union and Poland, the Lumpkins saw great architecture rebuilt after the Nazis had leveled it to the ground. These buildings had no military value but were destroyed in a deliberate attempt to erase people's history. In the Ukraine, the beautiful blue and white Orthodox churches of Kiev were bombed to the ground. These churches had been completely restored by the time the Lumpkins visited Kiev. The Soviet government had rebuilt and reopened the Ukrainian churches as great works of art. The catacomb burial sites for church leaders and princes were also high on Igor's list. Natural conditions had caused corpses buried there to mummify. The preserved bodies were hailed as miraculous many years ago and are now on display in the catacombs. The Lumpkin boys, like many other children, were fascinated by the mummies.

Frank's main problem in the Soviet Union was how to break away from all the bear hugs. So many men insisted that they knew him from service in World War II. Since they were long lost friends, Frank had to accept a drink, and then another. When the Lumpkins admired the socialist construction, saying, "You have quite a few new buildings," Igor corrected them. "Not quite a few," he insisted, "quite a many." In camp at Kiev they played baseball, joined by Japanese tourists. Tourists from other countries thought it was a strange game. It was not yet an international Olympic sport.

In Minsk, capital of Byelorussia, painful signs of World War II were everywhere. The population was still far below pre-war levels despite massive immigration from other Soviet republics and years of natural growth. At the Byelorus Tractor Works, the concern for workers' comfort was apparent. Drinking fountains for the workers offered a choice of cold water or seltzer (carbonated water)! When the Lumpkins arrived, there seemed to be a rest break going on. Nobody was working very hard. That started a debate within the Lumpkin family. Workers deserved to work without being pushed too hard. But it left an uneasy feeling, a feeling that they should have been working harder because they were working for themselves. In the 1990s Frank rethought the issue:

"I went to the Soviet Union and walked through the tractor works. Joe Norrick, my steel worker friend and a former miner, had watched Soviet miners work. I told him the workers weren't working hard enough at the Minsk tractor works. They took too many long breaks. Joe Norrick disagreed. He didn't blame the workers for not working hard. "That's what they fought for," he said. "Workers here [in the U.S.] work too hard. They deserve to take it easy, not to kill themselves."

Later Frank decided, "That's wrong. You have a responsibility to your kids, grandchildren, other people's kids. If you have knowledge, you have responsibility to share that knowledge. You can't take it easy."

The Lumpkins noticed a very positive aspect of the Soviet economy. Many "retirees" were still working and collecting their pensions. The pensioners could work as many hours as they wanted, at regular pay. That seemed an ideal solution to the problem of remaining productive in old age. Walking the streets of Moscow late at night without fear was an exhilarating feeling. It was certainly a contrast to Chicago where Beatrice had had her purse snatched when eight months pregnant, or Gary where she had been knifed in the street. Frank visited the Soviet Union with labor delegations in 1985 and saw how much the economy had developed in 20 years. Workers had many advantages. After the Gorbachev period, Frank spent hours reading and thinking about mistakes the Soviet workers may have made. He thought workers needed to learn from mistakes made by the first socialist societies. More than ever, Frank was convinced that capitalism could not solve the problems workers face: wars, unemployment, homelessness, lack of health care, lack of education, and crime. More than ever, Frank was convinced that socialism was the only answer.

Poland

When the Lumpkins left the Soviet Union and drove west to Poland, their stock of canned food was still in the trunk, unopened. Rumors of shortages and high prices were unfounded. The variety of food was less than at home but often the quality was better. One could live on the Russian bread alone. There were vegetables, especially cabbage, but not the year-round supply of Central American fruit and vegetables that North Americans take for granted. A visible difference between Soviet and Polish cities was the scarcity of children on the streets in the Soviet Union during the summer. Most Soviet children were out of the cities, away in summer camps in the countryside.

The canned food was not needed in Poland, either. The exchange rate of zloty to dollar was so favorable that the Lumpkins were concerned about taking advantage of the Polish people. Tourists like the Polish emigres from London could easily leave Poland with more money than when they had entered the country. Some cheated by exchanging Western currency on the black market, then selling the zloty to unwary tourists (like the Lumpkins) at the border.

Standing on the site of the Warsaw ghetto was a very emotional experience. In a neighborhood of new buildings, Beatrice asked a Polish woman (in German), "Where is the Warsaw Ghetto?" "You're standing right on it," the woman replied, and began to cry. Some bombed-out buildings were left as museums, but the rest of Warsaw had been rebuilt with amazing speed. Historic old Warsaw was rebuilt from the ashes with the aid of old photographs and records. They had defeated the Nazis not only militarily but also spiritually.

With Soviet aid the Poles had restored their history. The respect for history was a contrast to Chicago where historic architecture was destroyed to maximize short-term profit.

In Poland, far fewer people came up spontaneously to shake Frank's hand in solidarity. Perhaps the Poles were just more reserved. Near the Polish-German border, the Lumpkins were stopped for questioning, perhaps because they were driving a German car. In 1965 the pain of World War II was still fresh. In Eastern Europe, brick walls were still pockmarked with bullet holes and many adults had grown up without parents.

In just a few hours on the Autobahn, the Lumpkins had crossed the German Democratic Republic (GDR). Frank could not stop because his leave was ending. Years later, in 1988, he came back and saw a developed GDR, with rich culture, good education, health and job security. An East German economist told him that a huge building program had finally solved the housing shortage. She also said that East German workers were only 75% as productive as West German workers.

Frank understood that lower productivity could result from many causes, other than laziness. Lumpkin also heard complaints from East Germans that they could not afford the luxury goods that they saw displayed in West German television programs. After the socialist German government was overthrown, plenty of luxury goods became available in East German stores. Unfortunately, most people then could not buy luxuries because they had lost jobs, low-rent housing, cheap or free utilities and transportation, health care, low-cost child care and other necessities taken for granted in the socialist GDR.

Italy

From West Germany, the Lumpkins crossed the Swiss Alps and drove to Milan. They made a side trip to Venice. Frank watched the gondolas glide by but resisted renting one because it was not in the budget. When the gondoliers saw Frank, they saw a fellow worker, an oppressed worker of color, not a tourist. They rose in their boats and gave him the clenched fist salute, a gesture of international solidarity. Venice had the glittering facade of San Marcos Plaza, and charming bridges over the canals. Just a couple of blocks away was the other Venice, a city of grinding poverty.

Lumpkin wanted to see Genoa again, a port that his ship visited right after the war. Then he was homeward bound, driving along the beautiful Riviera road. Monaco lay like a sparkling jewel at night, sitting on the Mediterranean between Italy and France. Frank thought of looking at the world-famous casinos but he was dressed for camping, not the glamorous night life.

If Monaco was anything like Las Vegas, the Lumpkins may not have missed much. Las Vegas they saw years later while attending a convention of the Coalition of Labor Union Women. Although Frank enjoyed a good poker game, and most any other game with a chance to win a small pot, the commercial gambling of Las Vegas turned him off. Three days after the Lumpkins left the Riviera, Frank was back at Wisconsin Steel.

Lumpkin arriving in Cleveland from Chicago via motorcycle

Travels and Activism in the 1970s

Looking back, the middle and late '70s seemed to have been a relatively quiet time for Lumpkin, but he never sat still for a minute. He continued to visit Gary to help promote the progressive program of Mayor Richard Hatcher. The Vietnam War did not end until 1973 and Frank never missed an anti-war demonstration unless he had to work. He also attended Communist Party steel workers meetings. He managed to find time to work a second, part-time job in a Harley Davidson motorcycle repair shop and to do some traveling. In his spare time he rebuilt motorcycles.

Chile

Frank's next chance to take a long trip came in 1973, when he got a 13-week vacation. That was a once-in-seven-years benefit that the steel union had won for the more senior half of the workforce. Lumpkin had heard that the Popular Unity government was doing wonderful things in Chile, and he wanted to see for himself. Thirteen weeks would give Beatrice and him enough time to take a bus from the Colombia-Ecuador border all the way to Santiago de Chile. If they drove to Miami and flew to Colombia, the trip would cost only a fraction of a through flight to Santiago. In a white Miami suburb, they left their car with the parents of a friend. Frank thought, "Florida sure had changed, the white neighbors are so friendly." Only years later did Frank learn that a neighbor had complained about the visit of an African American. The friends' father silenced the racist complaint by declaring that Frank was a brain surgeon. That was the highest compliment he could think to use. Frank thought that was very funny since his hands, with calluses and missing finger joints, could not be mistaken for surgeon's hands.

After stops in Bogota, Colombia; Quito, Ecuador; Lima, Peru; and Arica, Chile, Frank and Beatrice eventually reached Santiago, capital of Chile. The bus followed the Pan-American Highway, crossed the mountains between the volcanoes and came down to the Pacific coast. Along the highway, there were many signs of the workers' struggles. In Chile, the workers' struggle was at a fever pitch. The Lumpkins heard President Salvatore Allende speak at huge outdoor rallies of workers. Almost every day workers filled the streets in a show of strength. They made a desperate attempt to stop the rise of fascism that threatened to drown their country in a blood bath. They were also fighting to save the gains that workers had won during the three years of Popular Unity government under Allende.

"If you want to see revolutionary workers," Frank was told, "visit the coal miners of Lota." "I'd like to see the steel mills first," Frank replied.

He was directed to the train for Conçepcion, a large city near a steel mill formerly owned by Bethlehem Steel. The train rolled through a green countryside, very different from the dry desert country of the north where iron and copper were mined. Frank passed many cooperative farms that had been private plantations before the Popular Unity land reform. Stands of pine trees looked like scenes from Wisconsin, but more often the beauty was distinctly Chilean. There were snow-topped mountains, lines of poplar trees and rocky rivers rushing the short distance from the Andes mountains to the Pacific Ocean.

In Conçepcion, the Lumpkins took the bus to Huachipato, a steel-making suburb of Conçepcion. Union leaders greeted Frank and offered him a tour of the mill. They added, "Steel mills are all the same. What you want is to talk to the workers."

Frank agreed. The mill belonged to the people of Chile. It had been nationalized on December 22, 1970, soon after the Popular Unity coalition won the elections. Companies were offered compensation equal to the assessed value of the plants. If that value had been underassessed to avoid their fair share of taxes, that was not the fault of the Popular Unity government. Domingo Palma, a steel worker with 24 years of service, expressed the feelings of the workers:

"Nationalization was the best thing that ever happened to the workers. The profits used to go into just a few pockets. Now the profits go to the State for the benefit of all workers. Now we can work with more security, without the fear that the boss will say, 'I think that this department is not producing enough and it would be better to close it down permanently.'

"Such statements kept us in a state of constant alarm. But that phase is over and I hope to God that it will never return to Chile. I am participating in voluntary labor weekends. I want to help other companeros without expecting any pay other than knowing that I served my country."

The Chilean steel workers were thrilled to meet a real steel worker from the United States. "We've had other delegations," they said to

Frank, "you're the first steel worker. But why don't you talk Spanish?"

Lumpkin had to answer that same question in Wisconsin Steel. He worked in the midst of Spanish-speaking Mexican workers. Learning a second language didn't come easy. When he told the Chilean workers, "I don't speak English that good," they understood. When it came to formal education, most Chilean steel workers had also been short-changed. The Communist steel workers of Huachipato warmed to Frank as one of their own. They would not let him go but took him to their Party headquarters and into their homes. It was dark and time to go but the Chileans insisted on taking the Lumpkins to dinner. By this time the dinner party numbered 20. Lots of the good Chilean wine and delicious seafood were enjoyed as the Chilean workers declared, "Isn't it wonderful? Wherever you go in the world, you have family."

The very next morning, Frank had an appointment to visit the famed Lota miners, who worked far from shore under the ocean floor. The Chilean fascists, whose ties to the Nixon administration were well-documented,[74] decided otherwise. Early on the morning of June 22, 1973, fascist army leaders made their first armed attack on the legally elected Popular Unity government. Workers rushed to their defense posts, and loyal government forces put down the armed uprising. But it was like stamping out some surface sparks while a fire continues to burn underground. Supported by the military might of the United States, the fascist fire broke out again on September 11, 1973. The U.S.-trained military murdered President Allende and thousands of workers. Frank never got to meet the Lota miners, and he doesn't know if his friends in the steel mill in Huachipato survived the massacres by the military. Still Frank was sure that the movement in Chile was too strong to kill. In time, he felt confident, a new Popular Unity coalition would return to power.

Cuba

When large numbers of North Americans went to Cuba to protest the U.S. Blockade, Frank joined them. He became part of the Venceremos Brigade in 1975 to help Cuban workers build apartment buildings. Of all the countries he visited, Cuba was where he felt most at home because it was a working trip. The climate was like Florida, where he grew up, and he enjoyed construction work. Everywhere he visited during two later trips to Cuba, he saw houses that looked like the ones he helped build. The work process itself and the accountability of the workers interested him. Frank admired the ability of the Cuban workers to make the spare parts that they could not import because of the U.S. blockade. "Cuban workers are the most innovative in the world," he concluded. He was also impressed by the Cuban success in providing health care and education for all.

The 1970's were also a decade of continued actions against apartheid in South Africa, a campaign that was very close to Frank's heart. In 1976, the uprising of the children of Soweto helped relight the torch of hope that lit up the world. It created the irresistible force that eventually brought the African National Congress (ANC) leaders out of the jails and into government leadership. In the '70s, representatives of rival South African groups spoke in Chicago. The Freedom Charter of the ANC was closest to Frank's own thinking because he believed in the unity of all working people, regardless of race.

Dr. John for Alderman

Frank never lost his love for electoral campaigning. When the great Olympic medallist, Congressman Ralph Metcalfe, broke with the Chicago Democratic machine over the issue of racism, Lumpkin worked for his reelection. In 1979 there was an electoral campaign that Frank plunged into heart and soul. His youngest son, Dr. John Lumpkin, ran for 7th Ward alderman in Chicago as an independent. The Chicago aldermanic elections were non-partisan but tightly controlled by the Democratic machine. Two years earlier, John had successfully coordinated Harold Washington's 7th Ward primary campaign for Mayor of Chicago. Washington carried the 7th Ward although he did not carry the city in 1977.

Working in the hospital emergency room, Dr. Lumpkin came in daily contact with the tragedies of poverty and racism. The number of knifing and shooting victims was high, directly related to the lack of jobs and hope. Many sick people, who lacked regular access to medical care, came to the emergency room only after their illness had become critical. His experience as an emergency physician led John to make unemployment and jobs the central issue in his campaign for alderman. The campaign united African American, Latino and white workers around issues of jobs, better housing, fairer taxes, public transportation, lower utility rates and adequate funding for education. Although Dr. Lumpkin was not elected in 1979, he did

Volunteers to elect Dr. Lumpkin, l. to r.: Jonnie Ellis, Dave Wood, John Lumpkin, Frank Lumpkin and Sara Reyes.

help defeat the machine in the race for mayor.

The 7th Ward included much of the South Chicago steel district, Frank's familiar stomping grounds. There was a problem—it was hard for Frank to stomp with a plaster cast on the foot that had been fractured in the plant. In the winter of 1979, when it snowed, it never melted. Instead, Frank's cast began to melt. He had to quit stomping in the snow until the fracture healed and the cast could be removed. The snow was also a factor in sweeping out the machine candidate for reelection as mayor, Michael Bilandic.

Michael Bilandic was the standard bearer for the Daley machine. He had been appointed interim mayor after Richard J. Daley died in office. During the record snows of 1979, Mayor Bilandic angered Chicagoans, and especially African Americans, when city snow-removal crews bypassed their neighborhoods. Adding insult to injury, Chicago Transit Authority trains went non-stop from the central Loop to outlying white areas. Trains passed, but did not stop at the inner-city open-air platforms loaded with African American passengers. Disgusted with the blatant racism of the Bilandic-Daley machine, African Americans voted overwhelmingly for Jane Byrne for mayor. (No African American candidate had entered the 1979 mayoral election.) The victory by Byrne, who posed as an independent, showed that the machine could be beaten. But in a matter of days, Byrne made peace with the machine. She joined forces with Edward (Fast Eddie) Vrdolyak and the rest of the "evil cabal," as she had labeled them during her campaign. For Lumpkin, Byrne's betrayal was further proof that workers had little room to maneuver within the Democratic Party. He believed that Chicago needed a genuine labor party to promote workers' issues.

Frank managed to cover a lot of ground before the cast on his foot began to melt in the snow and forced him to quit. The experience he gained was invaluable. One short year later, the mill would close and everything would change. In the next period, Frank would work closely with other independent candidates in Southeast Chicago. Lumpkin, and the movement he led, helped elect Rep. Miriam Balanoff, her son Rep. Clem Balanoff, Congressman Gus Savage, Congressman and later Mayor Harold Washington, Congressman Charles Hayes and State Sen. Alice Palmer. Then Frank would become a candidate himself and mount three hard-fought campaigns for the State Assembly.

Working in Dr. John's campaign for alderman convinced Frank that he needed to move closer to the action in Chicago. With the children working or away at school in the 1970s, Frank and Beatrice had fewer ties to the Broadview community. Bea had lost the electronics job near Broadview and she was teaching mathematics at Malcolm X College. The Lumpkins found a house in the South Shore neighborhood of Chicago, much closer to Wisconsin Steel. The 1979 elections were over but Frank was very, very busy. He wanted to help rebuild the Communist Party and repair the damage caused by years of cold-war McCarthyite persecution. He was also working with the rank-and-file labor newspaper, *Labor Today*, campaigning for a more active, more democratic union movement. Still most of Frank's time was spent at Wisconsin Steel, putting in long work weeks. Long hours at the mill helped pay for tuition costs, family vacations, travel and hobbies. Frank did not know that he would have only a few months to enjoy being close to his job and would soon face the biggest challenge of his life.

By March 28, 1980, Frank's foot was mostly healed but he still had a limp, especially when he was tired. The company offered him only a couple of thousand dollars of compensation, which Frank did not accept. Later a Workmen's Compensation hearing officer awarded Frank $12,000. As late as 1995, the award was still unpaid. The State of Illinois had allowed the Wisconsin Steel Company to be "self-insured." When the company went bankrupt, the fund was estimated to contain only half the amount needed to pay claims. The State of Illinois took over the Wisconsin Steel compensation fund and sat on the money for 15 years. Finally they offered only 20 cents on the dollar as payment of the compensation awards. Adjusted for inflation, that was about 10 cents on the dollar.

Part III

"It was like a nightmare, but you couldn't wake up." Steel worker's wife
"I felt like they had lined me up against the wall and shot me in the head." Blast furnace worker.

9. Don't Come in Tomorrow —Maybe Never!

"The plant's closed. Don't come in tomorrow. Maybe never."

On the phone the foreman's voice sounded strange, as though he was reading a script. Frank Lumpkin didn't know what to believe. Just an hour ago he had finished his shift, two weeks into his 31st year at the mill. He had 13 weeks worth of Wisconsin Steel checks in his pocket, ready to take a long vacation. He had a trip to Africa planned, and now he didn't know what would happen.

On his way home Frank stopped in the union office to talk about his compensation claim for his fractured foot. Although PSWU was a one-company union, their contract followed the USWA contract. Frank thought his rights were protected. But at the PSWU office a message came in suddenly: "The plant is closing!" Nobody believed it, but Frank was not too sure. He knew big companies do anything to make bigger profits. Yet it didn't make sense.

Just the night before the company had an overflow plant-wide meeting to thank the workers for "saving" the mill. Because of the hard work and sacrifice of the employees, company officials said, Wisconsin Steel's financial problems had been solved. There was a book full of customer orders. The federal government had loaned Wisconsin Steel $75 million to completely rebuild a blast furnace that was ready to operate. How could the company be closing?

But it was all too true. On Friday, March 28, 1980, during the second shift, an announcement was made in the mill, "The plant is closing!" The workers didn't believe it and worked the full shift, for which they were never paid. Some even went in and worked the third shift. On the next day, Chase Manhattan Bank put a padlock on the gate. Wisconsin Steel was bankrupt! Meanwhile, Chase Manhattan emptied the payroll account on which paychecks had just been issued. The Wisconsin Steel paychecks bounced in family taverns and in banks all over Chicago.

Living a Nightmare

The full shock and horror of their situation did not hit the 3,500 Wisconsin Steel workers until a few days later. "It was like a nightmare, but you couldn't wake up," a steel worker's wife said. "I felt like they had lined me up against the wall and shot me in the head," was the reaction of a blast furnace worker. Suddenly 3,500 workers were out on the street, left with nothing—no jobs, no pensions, no sick pay, no medical benefits, no SUB (supplementary unemployment benefits), not even pay for the last three weeks they worked. Since their union was a one-company union, they didn't even have the protection of organized labor.

When Frank's 13 paychecks bounced, the bank retrieved its money by emptying out the Lumpkin savings account. The money for a long trip to Africa was gone. Medical insurance was canceled. Many families had been living from paycheck to paycheck. They were left without money for food. Parents were afraid to let their children play outside. In case of injury there would be no medical insurance. Most families, especially in the Mexican community, did not have a working spouse to take up any of the slack. It was hard for steel worker wives to work. Weekly rotation of shifts—mornings, afternoons, nights—complicated child-care arrangements and meal preparation.

It took weeks, even months, to understand that a corporate plot had deprived the workers of their pension and health benefits. For 75 years International Harvester owned Wisconsin Steel and squeezed out big profits. Little was put back to modernize the mill. In 1977, Harvester came up with a scheme to transfer ownership of Wisconsin Steel to avoid paying millions in pensions, severance pay and other benefits. They loaned the sale price to Envirodyne, a very small company with no steel-making experience. Harvester kept the mortgage on the mill and the coal mines at Benham, Kentucky, and partnership in iron ore mines in Upper Michigan. Envirodyne, for its part, used the cash infusion to avoid bankruptcy. Chase Manhattan Bank became part of the deal by loaning $10 million towards the purchase price.[75]

Two and a half years after the sale, Harvester forced the UAW union at its farm equipment and truck plants out on strike. The strike lasted six months. These plants were Wisconsin Steel's principal customers. With the loss of these orders, Wisconsin Steel could not make its mortgage payments to Harvester. Then Harvester made its calculated, and for the Wisconsin Steel workers, fatal move. They called in the mortgage and repossessed the profitable Wisconsin Steel mines. A few minutes later, Chase Manhattan Bank emptied the Wisconsin Steel payroll account. causing paychecks already issued to bounce. Only the workers, small business creditors and local and federal governments lost out.

That's how it all would have ended except for Frank Lumpkin and his co-workers. As attorney Tom Geoghegan told the 1988 workers' meeting, "Harvester never, *ever*, expected to have to pay the Wisconsin Steel workers." The company had not reckoned with the ability of workers to organize, develop their own leadership, and win allies.

Retirement Plans Shattered

Lumpkin, with thirty years in the mill, had been thinking of retiring. The accident to his foot had been a warning. But Frank liked working and enjoyed fixing machinery. Of course, if he retired he could put more time into his hobby, working on cars. His wife wanted him to quit, but that was only one factor. He'd rather stay and fight to make the mill safer. Now he had no choice.

Except for a few skilled craftspeople who found comparable work, the workers' lives changed drastically. The impact of the closing was especially severe for the women of the Wisconsin Steel families. For some it was an immediate question of food. There were families with no reserves. But for most, the sudden loss of medical insurance was the most frightening. "What if we get sick? What if a child is hurt or another baby comes?" [For the following three family situations, names have been changed to protect privacy.]

Esmeralda Ramirez had just got the good news that she was pregnant. Her husband would be so happy when he came back from work! They had two children and wanted a third. On March 27, 1980, the company said its financial problems had been worked out. Employment was assured. Esmeralda's husband was a hard worker. With his wages they could make the payments on the house, put food on the table and keep their car running. His insurance would pay most hospital bills.

The night of March 28, 1980, it seemed that their world came to an end. The job was gone. With thousands laid off, where was the next job? The medical insurance was cut off. It would still pay for the delivery of a child on the way but not for the child's medical bills. Esmeralda had to find a job. She was lucky enough to find work on the night shift at a local hospital. At least there she could get medical care.

Rebecca Brown was already working when Wisconsin Steel closed. She did not work every day because she suffered from crippling headaches. She and Clyde had two daughters but wanted another child, perhaps a boy, but another daughter would be welcome. When she became pregnant she thought of quitting her job to take care of her health and her family. On March 28th, her husband was one of 3,500 suddenly out of work. Now, as the only wage earner, she could not quit. At least her job gave her medical insurance.[76]

The headaches became worse. Rebecca was forced to miss work and faced loss of her job and insurance. Somehow, she forced herself to go in to work, no matter how she felt. Fortunately the child was born healthy, a darling boy. Now there was an additional reason to go back to her job. Clyde had to baby-sit and tensions mounted. "Sometimes he just goes down in the basement and kicks boxes around, he's so frustrated," Rebecca said. "No, he doesn't have a job yet. When he gets one, we'll write it in the sky!"

Many women had to go to work for the first time. That created a sudden reversal of roles, with husbands staying home to care for the children. Strategies that families used to survive are described in the following interview, recorded in February, 1982.

Interview with Pilar Hernandez

What change has there been in your living conditions ?
"Our conditions changed a whole lot. We weren't that well off, but we were making it. Once the job was gone, we had to really struggle. We had help from the church and from our relatives, or we would have starved those three months. We applied for public aid and they wouldn't let us have any. They said we had to sell everything we had worked for.

"It was the worst thing when we had to go on public aid. It was very depressing, to have to make a confession. You had to sit there two or three times all day. It was very depressing. I had to sign papers and name all my children and sign that now they were dependent on public aid. It was very frustrating. I felt that now I was a slave, that we couldn't move or do anything more on our own. There was nothing we could do about it. We had to learn to live with it."

Was that when the unemployment compensation ran out?
"Yes. It was also very hard when the job first closed. We applied for unemployment. I think we waited about a month, a little bit more, before we got an unemployment check. So we weren't eligible for welfare, and we weren't eligible for unemployment right away. That made it hard. And the other part was when the unemployment ran out. We went for three months with no check. It was very hard, real hard.

"OK. Then finally Albert did get a job but it paid real low. We were still struggling, because once he got that job we had to give up public aid and food stamps. I don't even know how we were living on public aid. Except that they did give us food stamps. They gave us about $450 a month, but still with a family as large as ours, it was hard to get by even with $200 in food stamps. Always by the last week, we didn't have food any more. And the money, well we had $200 for rent [mortgage] and we had the light bill and all the expense. Everything we had to pay, we had to pay out of that $450. plus pay for any necessity that came up. And I don't know how we made it but we made it. And now that Albert's working, they take out so much for taxes and insurance."

It's not more than public aid?
"No, it still adds up to the same thing. I was getting $450 in public aid and $200 in food stamps. That's $650. Now Albert brings home $300 - $320 every two weeks. It adds up to the same thing. We really fell back the first time they took out for insurance. They took out for a family policy. It was $200. One pay check was $57 for two weeks. So if we wanted to eat, we couldn't pay the rent. Up to now, we're one month behind. We juggle our bills, and that's the way we survive. They cut off

our phone twice. Then the third time, they wanted a $100 deposit. That's when we had to close down our phone.

"Our car's been sitting there ever since Wisconsin Steel closed. Now it won't start because it's sitting there. We can't afford to run it because of the gas, because of the sticker, the license plate.

"But the main thing is that our household is together. We have had our problems. But it's not as bad as other households. Other households have had divorce, or the husband started drinking or chasing women. Or the wives thought it was the husband's fault that he didn't have a job, that he wasn't looking for a job. But I knew Albert was looking for a job. So we didn't have problems that way.

"Now we did have arguments when we didn't have things. Sometimes he would get very desperate. He has always been the provider. In a way he felt inadequate. Before he felt he had the responsibility. He was the man. 'I'm bringing in the money—I have the say.' I guess it tore him apart. It tore most men apart.

"They look for a job and they can't find one. And they begin to think, 'What's wrong with me? Maybe it's because I'm too old. Or maybe it's because I'm not trained.' Or maybe, when they went for a job, the new place thought the mill would open up again. And they'd ask, 'How many years did you work there?' They thought if they gave him a job, he wouldn't keep it but would go back when the mill reopened. For two years Albert couldn't find a job.

"He got a job through the church. Someone we knew recommended Albert and told them we had kids. And they saw Albert was a hard worker, so they kept him. I went with him to apply for the job. Albert wouldn't go by himself. That's another thing that happened. He didn't feel adequate. With Albert it wasn't drinking or going out every night. With Albert it was, "What am I going to do?" So I went down there with him. Thank God he passed the physical and everything else. In December we had a scare. They talked about layoff. Now he has a week coming. I hope when he goes back he still has the job.

"A lot of the other workers still have no job. They're getting by on public aid. Albert's working, but we're still struggling the same as on public aid. To me it's better to be working. I know a lot of them would rather be working than on public aid. It gets so depressing. You go from place to place and nobody hires you. Then you have no transportation money. How are you going to look for a job?

"We need some new furniture. At least some used furniture that's better than what we have. But we can't afford it so we do with what we have. I've never been very picky, so to me it don't matter. The house—as you see we haven't been able to keep the house up either [pointing to crumbling concrete on the outside steps]. That happened last winter. If Albert had been working [at Wisconsin Steel] we would have fixed it up by now. But we can't afford it.

"You either can't afford to pay the rent, or you can't fix the house. It's really going down. What else can I do? We cut down on food. We don't eat as well as we used to. We cut down on clothes. The only way we got by was my teenager bought his own clothes with his summer job. With the younger children I've been very lucky. Those I can get in a second-hand store. Or I have friends with older children who are just leaving their clothes. You know, every year when school started I bought something new for each child, a blouse or a pair of pants. But this year NOBODY had new clothes, unless they had worked in the summer."

Do the children understand the situation?

"In a way they do. That first Christmas was the first time they didn't get something they wanted. They never got everything they wanted. Sometimes they'd ask, 'Why can't we get things like other kids get.' Or they'd see something on TV, and they'd ask for it. And you know darn well there was no way you could buy it for them."

Do you know couples that have divorced since the plant closed?

"Yes, of course. Maybe they were having problems before. But I have heard a lot of women complain about their husbands' drinking. I would have gotten a divorce, too, if Albert had taken to drinking.

"Another thing I had to do was go out to work. I had worked before, but not out of necessity. I needed something for the house, or the kids needed something, so I would baby-sit to make a little extra. I did it because I wanted to. Not, hey, if you don't go out there, you're not going to make it. So that was a new experience I had to have.

"Albert had the experience of staying home and taking care of the kids. At first we did get hot over that, because I would come home and he would be sitting there watching TV with the kids. After two weeks of this I got quite angry. I told him that's not what I do when I stay home. So after that he has learned. I think that was one of the good parts that he has learned. A lot of fathers have learned to be with their families, to get the children some food. I was just working part-time, leave at 9 in the morning and come back at 2:30. Then it was time to get supper. It was very hard on him to watch the children. He would rather be working. At first he did nothing, but then he learned."

Whose fault was the closing of Wisconsin Steel?

"First of all, International Harvester. Because they knew it was going, and they sold it to a company that wasn't worth it. What hurt me the most was that Harvester loaned them the money to buy it. How you could buy a steel mill without collateral, I don't know. And I blame Envirodyne, the company that bought it because they knew they didn't have the money. Then I blame our union president Tony Roque because he never gave any explanation, before or after. So I think a whole lot of them are to blame.

"Again, I'm quite angry because of the pension fund. Why do all of these workers who worked all their lives have to fight and struggle for their money when all of these years they paid for it? Not to pay the pensions is sickening. You might not be old, but still you can't find a job and you worked for the pensions all of your life. And they're not paying the right amount. The insurance, that worried me a lot. We had no medical coverage. It's a good thing the children didn't get sick. I don't know what I would have done.

"So then I began to think, maybe if women would get involved, women and the kids, maybe things would change. Then the newspapers wouldn't always write about 3,000 Wisconsin Steel men. If it was 3,000 men and 3,000 women plus I don't know how many children, it could have been different. But the newspapers always made it sound like it's just some men, that it wasn't hurting families.

"Another thing I can't understand. The government owns the plant. Why don't they put the workers back to work instead of pushing people on public aid? And it's not only the Wisconsin Steel workers. There are other steel workers who need jobs. And they're cutting down on the summer jobs for the kids. What are the kids going to do? Gang together and get into something they shouldn't?"

The Republican governor of Illinois, James Thompson, visited the emergency public aid office next to Wisconsin Steel. The office had just been opened to process welfare applications filed by unemployed Wisconsin Steel workers. According to the *Chicago Sun-Times*, Thompson told the workers not to "feel demeaned" by accepting public aid. "As he shook hands with the men, he told them they had paid into the system and they should accept aid to 'help their families.' "[77] Just a few years later, Republicans spearheaded a drive to end welfare. Workers on public aid were called "underclass," as though they were to blame for being unemployed. The newspapers made much of the category of the "new unemployed," workers who never expected to have to go on public aid. The Wisconsin Steel workers experience was yet another example of the old saying: Workers are just one paycheck away from having to go on welfare.

Some Wisconsin Steel worker families were relatively better off when the plant closed because they had savings and their children were grown. But they were also older, with less chance of finding another job. Florencio (Floyd) Ortega, one of the most senior

Wisconsin Steel Workers, viewed the workers' tragedy in class terms, of the rich against the poor.

Florencio (Floyd) Ortega, billet dock: [78]

"I heard they were going to have that big meeting with the company. They did that on a Thursday, and everything was all right. Friday at 6 o'clock they said, 'We're shutting down.' If you look at the books, they had a lot of orders for steel.

"I was in the mill Friday, working second turn, when they closed at 6 o'clock. I came in at 3 o'clock, and I didn't know anything. About 5 o'clock the delegate was called to the union office. He came back at 6, said, 'Hey, we're closing down.' That was March 28. So, what the heck, I had only a few hours to go. We stayed there until we finished at 10. The foreman came over and said, 'This is it until further notice.' That was the 28th. Some guys worked 3rd turn yet. Saturday, first turn, nobody came out. They locked the gates. I don't know who gave the orders.

"That last check, they only paid us for 40%. I didn't sign up for compensation until two weeks later. We went to see Roque and he said, 'Don't worry. They'll probably open Friday.'

"But Roque was in there. He knew everything that was going on. I don't think they sold this plant to Envirodyne; it was a front. How come Envirodyne went bankrupt twice in California? Now they come here. They didn't have money. Harvester just turned it over to them.

"Right now, if there was another war, you're going to fight for the rich. The rich don't give a damn about the poor. In my opinion, they want protection. Like Harvester, they've got companies all over the world. They want us to protect them. What they did to us is a sin.

"A company like Harvester never kept up the mill. They used it to save on income tax. Sure they put in 1-mill since I was there, and maybe that blast furnace. But from there on, 5-mill, it's scrap. 3-mill, it's scrapped already. They never kept it up. Like a house—if you don't paint it and fix it, the weather here eats it up. Now if you want your house, it's got to be costing you money every year.

"The 31st of August [1980] I'd have had 40 years. I live about two blocks and a half from the mill. Yes, now the air's cleaner, no smoke from the coke plant. But you can't live on air."

Rafael Huerta, pickler in the scarfing dock: [79]

"I didn't work long enough at Wisconsin Steel to get a pension. Wisconsin Steel let loose handicapped people. People who had only one job, 30 years. People, they never did anything else but steel work. So any job in this mill, or in U.S. Steel or in Republic Steel can only hire so many guys. They are taking those who are young, strong in body, so they can still squeeze their strength out of their hands. They took me. At Wisconsin, I was a pickler. At Republic, I'm a laborer. "How come the government don't do something? They call it a recession. It's a depression. You've seen those jobs for machinists? You have to set the machines, run the machines, and they pay you $4.25 an hour. No insurance, no benefits. "One day I'll go back to Mexico. I'm going to become self-employed. I'm going to—if I have to sell peanuts. Let the work I do be mine. Why make somebody else rich? I wouldn't mind if they would say, 'You stay here 20 years, you stay 25 years,' but you work for them and they lay you off whenever they feel like. They fire you, they ... Yes, I could go into business here if I wanted to stay here all my life. But the weather. I'm from Zacatecas [Mexico]. It really doesn't take that much money to make a living there. All you have to do is work, work maybe longer hours. There are steel mills in Mexico, too, but I heard you have to pay for your jobs. You have to have a connection to get a job in the oil company.

"I was 15 when I came. It was very cold. I hated Chicago when I came here, coming from the sunshine into the cold winter. I hated Chicago so much because we were so poor. We lived at 87th and Buffalo, what they call the ghetto. And everybody around us was poor. My brother and I, we had a real light coat. I remember my father couldn't afford to buy us a good coat and send some money to my mother and other brothers. He used to work for Illinois Central. A short time after we arrived, he got laid off. He was out of work for six or eight months. But I had three older brothers. They were working, making $2.50 an hour 15 years ago. I remember when I came to Chicago. It was real cold then. I was in shock. Coming from the sun, a sunny place where you could speak Spanish and you say hello to everybody and everybody's friendly. Then in Chicago, people are more to themselves, less expressive, more occupied in the daily struggle for a living. They don't talk to their neighbors. They don't say hello, or good morning. They don't even look. They go straight ahead, just go on, take the bus.

"At the J. N. Thorpe School, 88th and Buffalo, they had a program for newly arrived immigrants. But the teachers didn't have the time to really help you adjust to the new environment. They just put you aside like lunch bags. All you could do was listen because the teachers were not bilingual. I went to school just six months.

"I understood nothing. But I always had a great passion for reading. I read every sign in this city. I bought dictionaries. That's how I learned to write and read. I speak only about 40% of what I can read. I read any books that I could get a hold of. I remember reading a book about Booker T. Washington, the early days of the Blacks in America, all their experience. I remember feeling like Booker T. Washington. He had his mind set on something higher than working every day and just making a living. Booker T. Washington went to school to become a teacher, a great one.

The only difference between Booker T. Washington and me is that I was young and lazy. I didn't care too much about working. I only cared about going back to Mexico as soon as I could. I worked three or four weeks and when I had enough to go on a bus I went back. My mother was in Mexico. I didn't like it here.

"Now I'm adjusted to living here. But I always had it on my mind to actually go and try to make a living there. Why do I have to live here? Why can't I make a living there?"

Herman Caldwell, 6-mill: [80]

"With 27 years in, I thought I would be at the steel mill until I took my pension. Since the mill shut down there have been some days I couldn't even afford a 25-cent newspaper. Now I take some of my nieces and sister, my daughter-in-law, I take them shopping. When they shop, they buy some groceries for me. That's how I keep my kitchen stocked.

"My payment on my house is $382 a month. That's one of my wife's checks right there. She gets only two checks a month. So what do you have for food? They charge what they want for gas. My gas bill [heat] went up $700 and over. Then they even turned me down for help on the gas because if somebody in your house is working, they don't care how little they're making. You don't get anything.

"It is a poor system that allows this to happen. And we had a poor, poor union. When the mill closed down, we found out it wasn't like they said. Then Frank Lumpkin formed this Save Our Jobs Committee and that's the only thing keeping people informed about our jobs. If it hadn't been for him and Illinois Congressman Gus Savage taking us to Washington, D.C., we wouldn't have had the 40% pension that we have. If I was getting my full pension, which would be nice, I would be getting $411; 40% of that comes to only $164 a month. It's only a little help I can give my wife. I can probably pay only one bill out of that; it's better than nothing. Now we've got to fight to get the rest of it.

"I'm going to try and get a job meanwhile because, you know, my wife is carrying things on. Since December [when unemployment checks ran out], I haven't made a cent. We can only get the bare necessities. They turn me down on age [47], everything else, you know. Just a year before the mill went down, I had just bought this house. Now the people you owe bills to, they're harassing you. The credit union is harassing all of us. They're calling day and night, writing letters and what not. We don't have anything to give them.

"They're threatening me, stuff like this. There's nothing that I can really do. I've got applications in different places. To really get a job, you have to know somebody. And all I know is steel mill."

After this interview, Caldwell found a part time job as a car-parker, at minimum wage and tips. Finally, in later years he found another factory job that used some of his mechanical skills. It was in a food-processing plant that paid much less than steel.

Raymond Gutierrez

"I worked part time at Jewel—$3.35 an hour. You can't live on that. I know men who work part-time at one McDonalds, then they run to another McDonalds and work part-time there. No benefits.

"At·least my wife found work. She never had to work before. But then Goldblatts laid her off. That was the final blow. I didn't even have health insurance. Sometimes I could just sit down and cry."

Higinio Lopez

"I am supposed to get $352.50 a month plus the supplement, $300 a month. But the PBGC [Pension Benefit Guaranteed Corporation] is paying me $117, which is not what they wrote according to the contract. No, I cannot get welfare because I get $117. It messes you up. We are suffering because of the red tape and the bureaucracy and the system, which is not working too good for the poor people, the working people.

"It is a shame. In the greatest country in the world, the people have to suffer so much. Thanks to the Wisconsin Steel Save Our Jobs Committee, which is doing a great job, better job than the PSWU which didn't do anything—so thanks to them we got part of our pension.

"There's a lot of families too proud to say what is happening to them. It's not only physical, but also psychological. In their minds they feel trapped down. We have some people in the [SOJ] committee who have some trauma. They don't want to speak about it. Some, they are real hurt because they don't have food for their families. They not only lose their possessions but they lose their loved ones. I'm not talking about one or two but hundreds.

"They lose their wives, they lose their sons and daughters. You see, when you can't support your family, your wife doesn't stick around, or your sons or your daughters. Too much pressure in the home. You're not prepared to deal with those problems. You have to be real good to be able to cope. Some separate by the red tape of the federal aid. They have to go out so their family can collect aid or welfare. Some go out on their own. Some think, 'I served my purpose. I worked. I'm not on the job and I have no other income, so I'll go on my own.' You understand? It is a shame, believe me, but it is the truth. Some people can't get on welfare because of some technicality. So they think, well, I'll go out on my own. I think something else. I won't tell you what I think. I blame the system.

"I know one family, they used to be a real nice, happy family. Their daughters, sons, some they grow up, some are teenagers. When we worked, everything was beautiful. His wife loved him and vice versa. When they closed down and he had no income, his wife left him. She said, 'I'm going back to Mexico. The hell with the United States.'

"A lot left, some to Mexico, some to Italy, some to Texas, New York. Some who left came back. I don't know what happened, but I figured it didn't work that good over there so they're back looking for work here. "Who's responsible? The working force? No. It's the duty of the system to look after the people. The system lets American companies go overseas and enslave them, pay them less. They don't want the American people to work. They want more profits overseas. That's the reason we're in this shape. The American companies, they go to Mexico, Taiwan, they enslave the people over there *plus* they want to bring those products back into the United States. Then the big corporations expect the American people to buy the products they're making overseas.

"The government says we'll build each unit [bomb] to get better power. We have enough power to destroy the whole world population. What is the sense to build more and more, instead of to get more food, [or] to build up agriculture? The United States government wants to police the whole world around. So the government should have more food for the whole world instead of selling arms to them. We should produce more food. Actually, the whole world population could live on sea food, out of the sea. But we're destroying the sea food, polluting the Atlantic, the whole water. The money should be used for jobs. It is a shame that the biggest industrial city in the whole world is going down, the worst city in the whole world for unemployment, besides Detroit."

In a *Chicago Tribune* interview, John Nuño said some were driven to suicide. "A man I worked with did away with himself. He was my age [51], a single man, didn't have any family responsibilities. He couldn't handle being out of work. Every time I saw him, he'd say, 'John, I don't know if I can make it.' A jogger in Calumet Park found the body in Lake Michigan."[81]

Some younger workers were also unable to face the prospect of a life of unemployment. No name was given in this newspaper story but some identified the victim as a Wisconsin Steel worker:

Body Found in Wolf Lake[82]

Police yesterday morning recovered the body of an unidentified young man from Wolf Lake, 126th Street and Avenue O.

Area 2 Homicide investigators could not give a cause of death yesterday afternoon for the victim, described as a white male, 21 to 25 years old, wearing black shoes, blue socks, blue pants and a white T-shirt. According to witnesses, a score sheet from a bowling alley in Indiana was found in his possession. A citizen saw the body floating in the water about 10 a.m. and notified the police.

10. Fight or Die—the Save Our Jobs Committee

What would happen next? Nobody knew what to expect. The uncertainty was killing. Would the Bankruptcy Court help the workers win justice? Would the bounced paychecks be made good? Would pension payments start? And foremost of all was the question, "Will the mill reopen?" At the very least, people expected that the bankruptcy court would order the company to pay for the last two weeks worked. Didn't the "mechanics lien" laws passed in the 1800's cover unpaid wages?

What about the government? The U.S. Economic Development Agency (EDA) owned the biggest share of the mill. Taxpayers had spent many millions to modernize Wisconsin Steel. Why didn't the federal government operate the mill until a buyer could be found?

The telephone lines were busy. Workers called each other to try to get information. But from the PSWU there was not a word, not even a postcard for four agonizing weeks.

"We're in a bad fix," one worker said. "I wish we were in the AFL-CIO Steel Workers. Then at least we'd have someone to back us up."

Nobody knew what to do. What could you do without an organization? Frank Lumpkin had read about the "Save Jobs" committees at the Youngstown, Ohio and Detroit Dodge-Main plants in the rank and file paper, *Labor Today*, and in the Communist *Peoples Daily World*. These papers were urging workers to fight plant closings. Frank realized that Wisconsin Steel workers had allies and did not have to fight alone. Fred Gaboury, then editor of *Labor Today* and a trusted friend, encouraged Frank to take the first step: "Get a committee going 'To Save Jobs' and start a petition to

Congress to reopen the plant." Frank thought that was good advice as far as it went. But how could you do that when the in-house union refused to move? He decided to talk it over with some friends from the mill. Frank invited some Wisconsin Steel workers to a meeting in his basement. Some he had met during years of work in African American rank-and-file groups in the mill such as "Self-Help" and "Getting It Together." If ever self-help was needed, that was the time. The meeting was open to any idea for action. The unanimous decision was to organize a "Wisconsin Steel Workers Save Our Jobs Committee." Their first action was to petition the President of the United States, asking him to reopen the mill.

Fight or Die
"Fight or die," was the call Frank sent out to his fellow workers. And for 17 years he led the unemployed Wisconsin Steel workers, working without pay, using his house as the first headquarters and his own money when necessary for organizing expenses. No one who knew him would call him a saint, as R.C. Longworth had suggested in the *Chicago Tribune* financial section.[83] However, it was true that Lumpkin's dedication was based on his love for working people. Lumpkin's staying power was strengthened by the belief that workers could change the system if they organized. He often said, "The system's got to go." He thought it was wrong to allow a few capitalists to close Chicago's steel mills and ruin the lives of 30,000 steel workers' families. His ultimate solution was socialism—production for the good of people, not profits for a few.

Under Lumpkin's leadership, Save Our Jobs became a crusade that never quit. The Wisconsin Steel workers took the Save Our Jobs name because their first goal was to reopen the mill. The second goal, which as the years passed became primary, was to get their unpaid benefits.

The committee went into action immediately. They circulated their petition to the President and Congress asking them to reopen Wisconsin Steel. The petition let the world know that Wisconsin Steel workers *would* fight for their jobs. At churches, taverns, beauty shops and grocery stores, wherever steel workers and their families gathered there was someone collecting signatures to reopen the mill. In a few days, over 4,000 steel workers and friends had signed the petition. With thousands in support, Save Our Jobs (SOJ) planned a mass delegation to take the petitions to the state legislature in Springfield, and to Congress in Washington, D.C.

The idea of mass action began to catch on! The in-house union had not organized a labor action in over 30 years. Inside the mill, the rank and file knew how to slow down or "work to rule" to make the company live up to the contract. But they had never carried picket signs or demonstrated with other steel workers. After the mill closed, Save Our Jobs members became the most experienced demonstrators in the Chicago area.

Wisconsin Steel families rally at closed mill to demand benefits

At the first court hearing on the Wisconsin Steel bankruptcy, the workers were in for another shock. The PSWU and its lawyer, Edward Vrdolyak, were not even present. Workers who went to the hearing could not understand what was going on. A friendly lawyer alerted Lumpkin to the fact that none of the workers' claims had been filed. The PSWU had failed to file a class action suit in bankruptcy court. In the absence of a class action suit, each Wisconsin Steel worker would have to file an individual claim form to claim their back pay and their benefits.

Save Our Jobs Goes Public

Save Our Jobs set up office in Lumpkin's house. Three active members agreed to put their phone numbers in the *Daily Calumet* so workers could call for information. The three contact persons included one African American, one Latino and one of European descent. That principle of unity became the hallmark of the Save Our Jobs Committee, and had a profound effect on the South Chicago and East Side communities. In a few weeks, the Committee showed 2,000 workers, one at a time, how to fill out the legal forms.

On April 16, 1980, some angry rank and file members decided to complain to the NLRB about the PSWU. It was 19 days since the mill closed and PSWU had called no meetings, issued no statements, nor made any move in behalf of the Wisconsin Steel workers.

At the NLRB, workers charged PSWU with failure to represent its members, the Wisconsin Steel workers. There had been no word from Tony Roque, PSWU president or the union attorney, Alderman (Fast Eddie) Vrdolyak. Frank did not oppose going to the NLRB. But he refused to be diverted from the fight against the company. "PSWU didn't close down the plant, the company did," he reminded the Wisconsin Steel workers.

Frank was not surprised that the NLRB gave the workers no satisfaction. Some workers also went to the State Attorney General's office to demand an investigation of the thousands of paychecks that bounced. Wasn't there a law against writing bad checks? But the State Attorney General's staff said there was nothing they could do.

PSWU members also wondered about the union's Goodfellow Fund. It was supposed to help families in need. Wisconsin Steel workers never saw any of that money. Workers were not surprised when writer R.C. Longworth and TV reporter Walter Jacobson came out with an exposé of PSWU finances. Many believed that there was a close link between the 10th Ward Vrdolyak organization, the PSWU and the company.

Vrdolyak's campaign fund had accepted contributions from both the company and the union. Since Vrdolyak was the PSWU lawyer, accepting money from the company appeared to be a conflict of interest, to say the least.

Fear and Intimidation

Wisconsin Steel workers were reluctant to buck the Vrdolyak operation. Fear for personal safety or the safety of family members held many back from activity that could be considered anti-Roque or anti-Vrdolyak. In the *Chicago Tribune*, April 27, 1980, Richard Longworth wrote, "The PSWU has a tradition of violence, and most dissident members are reluctant to speak for quotation. . . . A worker who spoke up at a recent public meeting held at a local church said, 'I was threatened about that later. I was told my head would get busted.' "

This intimidation took its toll at first. There were some who dropped out of Save Our Jobs, expressing fear for the safety of their families. Frank Lumpkin believed that his safety depended on the support of the workers and community. He relied on workers' support more than his own considerable physical strength and skill as a former professional boxer. He refused to be intimidated. By example, he created an atmosphere of optimism, which overcame fear. His confidence in the ultimate victory of the workers' cause was contagious. Still, he did not believe in taking unnecessary risks.

About three weeks after the plant closed, the South Deering Improvement Association called a public meeting at St. Kevin's Church. Roque and Vrdolyak were nowhere in sight, and the crowd was angry. They listened politely as State Representative Miriam Balanoff demanded a federal investigation into the questionable finances of Wisconsin Steel Corp. They listened to Gus Savage, who had won the Democratic primary for Congress as an independent, non-machine candidate. Savage spoke in the spirit of the civil rights movement of the '60s. "We'll pack the workers into buses and go in force to Washington, if that's what it takes." African American workers in the audience applauded, but the majority seemed cool to the African American politician. Many of the workers did not seem ready for the struggle tactics of the civil rights movement.

Then, with dramatic timing, Roque and Vrdolyak entered the church hall. They sported fresh Florida suntans. They could afford a vacation. While the workers were suffering, they were still drawing their pay, $51,000 for Roque and a $32,000 annual retainer for Vrdolyak. But Vrdolyak was not called "Fast Eddie" without reason. In little time he had diffused the anger by promising that the plant would be reopened and workers would have their jobs back. "It's not the back pay you're worried about. What you want is your jobs," he declared demagogically. "And we expect to have good news soon." Questions from the workers were not answered. When Lumpkin raised his hand to speak, the meeting was adjourned.

On April 22, 1980, the bankruptcy court was hearing the Wisconsin Steel case again. Save Our Jobs held its first demonstration. They came with picket signs to make the workers' plight known. But no one made a move to raise a sign and begin the picket. Except for Frank, these workers had never, ever held a picket sign in their hand. Then the news media showed up, including a television crew. Frank knew he had to do something. He picked up a sign and began to walk alone. One or two joined him, while the rest stood and watched. As the television camera began to film, one by one other Wisconsin Steel workers picked up signs. They took their first, hesitant steps and then seemed to gain confidence. All they were asking for was what they had already worked for—payment of wages, supplementary unemployment benefits, medical insurance and pensions. Above all, they called for the reopening of their plant. "For us, this picket line was historic," Frank said later. "We Wisconsin Steel workers are joining with other working people to fight for our rights."

Several weeks later the Wisconsin Steel workers learned the terrible truth about the bankruptcy laws. The unpaid wages would *not* be the first claim to be paid. The first claims paid would be the "secured" claims of the banks. Workers' claims were considered "unsecured." If anything was left over, then perhaps workers would get something. Frank expressed the workers' anger when he said, "Bankruptcy laws are written for the benefit of the banks, not the workers!"

At the end of April 1980, four weeks after the plant had closed, PSWU finally sent out a letter for a membership meeting, The letter opened with:

> To the contrary of the rumors that have been maliciously exploited by radicals for the purpose of recruiting, and newspapers for the purpose of sales, and locker-room lawyers for the purpose of attention, we say they are the ones that are unfortunately weak to prey on those that are in need.

To excuse its long delay in calling a meeting, the PSWU stated, "We have waited for substantial and important information to give to you after the numerous meetings with lawyers, government and local officials and judges." Evidently meeting with the membership was the last priority of the PSWU leadership. To avoid the strong-arm tactics that were expected from the PSWU, SOJ decided not to attempt a leaflet distribution. Over 1,500 workers came. They got no information, just some vague promises. State Representative Miriam Balanoff, opponent of the Vrdolyak machine, bravely deflated the politicians' empty promises and said that workers must rely on their own organized strength. The meeting ended without a plan of action.

Springfield Lobby

The next week, on May 1, 1980, SOJ took their petitions to the State Capitol in Springfield. They planned to lobby for state action to

**Left, Lumpkin and State Representative Miriam Balanoff
Right, State Representative (later Senator) Carol Moseley-Braun**

reopen Wisconsin Steel. Representatives Miriam Balanoff and Carol Moseley-Braun met with the workers. (Later Braun was the first African American woman in the U.S. Senate.) The State Legislature's committee received the petitions and recommended passage of a $15 million aid bill for Wisconsin Steel. But it was too little, too late.

Copies of the petition to reopen Wisconsin Steel were taken to Congress by a busload of Wisconsin Steel workers who joined a May 20th lobby in Washington, D.C., organized by Operation PUSH (People United to Save Humanity). The Wisconsin Steel issue was raised everywhere. Earlier that month, a national march for the Equal Rights Amendment (ERA) took place in Chicago. Hundreds signed a petition to reopen Wisconsin Steel and thousands cheered the sign, "Wisconsin Steel Women for ERA." The Wisconsin Steel workers had become a reliable ally for every progressive cause in Chicago.

It was a different story with Tony Roque. He wanted nothing to do with labor or community organizations.[84] "This is a private affair," he told the press when he rejected help offered by the director of USWA District 31, Jim Balanoff (brother-in-law of State Rep. Miriam Balanoff). In taking this stand, Roque was out of touch with his own members. The Wisconsin Steel workers were already following Lumpkin's lead. They were joining workers from U.S. Steel Southworks and Pullman Standard in demonstrations to keep those plants from closing.

SOJ gave its support to the demand of the Pullman Standard workers for more mass transit. Building trains for mass transit would have created a huge demand for steel and kept the steel mills open.

Other demands were for passage of the Miriam Balanoff bill requiring a year's notice before a plant closing. The bill also called for a company fund to help communities devastated by plant closings. SOJ joined the fight for a moratorium on home foreclosures and repossessions. They testified at public hearings for the steel workers' cause. Facts cited at hearings showed that steel companies were lying when they claimed that their profits were low. U.S. Steel profit rates of 6.7% were much higher than Japan's 1.7%, or West Germany's 2.9%.

Unemployment - a show

A few months later, the Chicago-based Phil Donahue show decided to telecast a program on unemployment. It put the Wisconsin Steel struggle before a national audience. The largest group present in the studio was the Wisconsin Steel workers. U.S. Steel, Pullman Standard and Ford workers were also well represented. The pent-up feelings of these workers, who had worked all their lives and now had little hope of employment, created a tension that was electric. Lumpkin, known as a man of few words up to that time, became eloquent as he exposed Harvester's fraudulent deals. He protested the failure of government agencies to help the workers. "They don't prosecute companies, you know. They prosecute unions," he told Donahue. When Donahue thought he had heard enough and began to back away, Lumpkin grabbed the mike and finished saying his piece. On the way out, Donahue told Lumpkin he could never come back to his show because he had taken the mike away. But later Donahue relented and did invite Lumpkin to another show. Although Frank had broken a rule important to a pro, Donahue knew that this was more than entertainment. Perhaps he was moved by Lumpkin's plea for justice.

Pullman Standard workers in Donahue's audience were faced with the closing of their plant within the year. They charged that Pullman had refused to even bid on contracts for railway cars although it was the only American company still making passenger cars. Donahue read the slogan on their T-shirts aloud, "Keep Mass Transit Rolling." The unemployed also commented on the 1980 presidential campaign, then in full swing. They were unhappy with President Carter but saw nothing to gain from a Reagan presidency.

Don't scrap our mill!

In July 1980, immediate action was needed to save the Wisconsin Steel plant for a future reopening that would provide jobs. A motion to scrap the plant had been filed in bankruptcy court. It was an emergency! Any hope of reopening the plant hinged on canceling plans to dynamite the furnaces. Although SOJ had no lawyer, friends at Lehman and Schub warned Frank of the danger. Frank was desperate to attract public attention to the issue. He asked an attorney, former Chicago Alderman Len Despres for advice.

"Hold a press conference," Despres suggested.

"Where?" Frank asked.

"Why not City Hall?"

Frank set the date for July 30, 1980. At City Hall he saw camera crews assembled from every TV station, radio and written media. So he took a seat quietly in the outer room to see what would happen. He didn't know that he was the "star."

After a while the reporters began to ask, "Where is this Frank Lumpkin?" "That's me," he answered.

"You? Get in there. Everybody's waiting for you!"

Then Frank gave the first of what would be many press conferences. Soon State Rep. Miriam Balanoff, herself the wife of a steel worker, and Chicago Alderman Joseph Bertrand stood at his side. Rep. Carol Moseley-Braun joined in a show of solidarity.

Frank warned that if the plant was not reopened, "South Chicago would make Cabrini Green [a low-income housing project with a high crime rate] look like a Sunday School picnic." He said the situation was explosive, that the unemployed were very angry.

Unfortunately, Lumpkin's prediction came true, but it may not have happened in the way he meant. The South Chicago community had been a hard-working, well-maintained, stable community of small homeowners. Ten years after the mills closed, it had changed to a gang-ridden, high-crime, graffiti-scarred area with many boarded-up homes. Still, most families stayed in the neighborhood and continued to fight to survive. They struggle to keep teenagers in school and to find some hope for the future.

That summer of 1980, over 500 Wisconsin Steel workers took their fight to save the mill to International Harvester's world headquarters on North Michigan Avenue, Chicago's "Magnificent Mile." Media coverage was widespread and favorable. "Wisconsin Steel Workers in Last Chance March," reported the *Chicago Defender*, August 5, 1980. The reporter wrote:

"This may be our last chance to save our jobs," Lumpkin told me as we demonstrated. "The decision the judge makes tomorrow should be based on what's best for the people, to save the people's jobs and save the community." . . . I leave Lumpkin and go in to talk to Harry Connor, press spokesman for IH. Connor says, "It's a damned good work force out there. . . .We hope they get some help. But it's in the hands of the court now."

When I return to the demonstration, Gus Savage, Democratic Party nominee for Congress from the Second Congressional District, has joined the march and together with Lumpkin is leading it down toward the Federal Plaza. . . . Savage urges public officials to "join in struggles of this kind." Says Savage, "Your responsibility doesn't end in the office building. You must be in the streets when agitation on issues is needed. Our country can make bombs, warplanes and missiles but it can't make your last paycheck good."[85]

The day after the march, SOJ won a victory in Bankruptcy Court. Judge Charles McCormick rejected the motion for the immediate scrapping of the mill. The workers gained five additional months to try to save their plant. But the summer was half over, and the paychecks that had bounced after March 28, 1980, had not been paid. The word went out that Chase Manhattan Bank was preparing to seize the steel inventory, worth $30 million, as payment for the $10 million that the mill owed them. A quick picket line showed that workers had the power to prevent removal of the steel.

200 steel workers rally to demand reopening of Wisconsin Steel.
Daily Calumet photo, August 5, 1980

Make the Bounced Paychecks Good!

A couple of weeks later, rumors spread again that Chase Manhattan Bank planned to remove the steel inventory. On August 29, 1980, hundreds of workers marched to the Wisconsin Steel plant to prevent removal of the inventory. At first, management only wanted to talk to a small committee, but the workers would not allow it. So the managers, accompanied by police, went out with bullhorns to give the whole crowd their version of the facts. PSWU, management claimed, was allowing the company to move the steel inventory. There was no word about making good on the bounced paychecks.

The anger of the workers exploded. They spontaneously started a march on the PSWU offices, temporarily housed in a trailer. Frank was not for marching on the PSWU, but he was not given a choice. Some big workers lifted him up and he was carried along physically. The police did not see fit to accompany the workers. Protection for the workers was not their assignment. Like management, Roque did not want to come out to talk to the workers. Since this was their own union office, the workers agreed to send in a committee.

A committee of three SOJ leaders, including Frank, went into the trailer. Frank was certain that the union officers were armed. The atmosphere in the trailer was tense. Outside, the workers' anger mounted. They began to rock the trailer, from side to side. "Don't they know that we're in here, too?" Frank wondered. Fortunately, the local newspaper photographer came to take pictures. Then police cars showed up. Otherwise, Frank was not sure how it would have ended.

Although the workers got little information from the PSWU officers, they learned later that the rumor was true. The steel inventory was going to be moved out with PSWU consent and protection. PSWU had made a deal. Their cronies would get the work to move out the steel. The company agreed to make good the bounced paychecks, already issued for earlier weeks. For the last week worked, for which checks had never been issued, workers would get only 40% of their pay. To add insult to injury, from that puny 40% of the last week's pay, PSWU deducted two months dues.

The demonstrations at the plant and PSWU office were preceded by the largest indoor rally of Chicago steel workers in many years. Over 700 jammed the Local 65 hall in a meeting jointly called by

SOJ and "Trabajadores de Wisconsin Steel." The "Trabajadores" had been formed by UNO (United Neighborhood Organization), a Latino organization with Catholic Church connections. UNO kept in the public eye by organizing actions that would attract the media. Almost all of the "Trabajadores" were also members of SOJ. After some months of cooperation between the two organizations, the "Trabajadores" disbanded. The Spanish-speaking workers decided to remain united in SOJ with the African American workers and workers of European descent. Most were fluent in English. Those who were not fluent in English got help from bilingual friends and were able to follow the discussion. Anyone who wished to speak in Spanish did so, and a translation was provided.

It was a strong point of SOJ, from the day it was organized in Lumpkin's basement, that every committee, and the officers and executive board represented African American, Mexican and other Latinos, and whites in equal numbers. That reflected the composition of the Wisconsin Steel work force, with Latino workers about 40% and African American and white each about 30%. Frank's insistence on maintaining a policy of racial equality was understood and supported by most Wisconsin Steel workers. In the disaster that had befallen them, the Wisconsin Steel workers took some giant steps away from the racist divisions promoted by the company.

No Turkey for Thanksgiving

PSWU leaders and Democratic city officials made a cynical attempt to use the desperation of the Wisconsin Steel workers to advance their own political careers. Their play-acting performance took place in the Auditorium Theater. It was only the second PSWU membership meeting in the six months since the plant closed. Coke ovens at Wisconsin Steel were still being kept warm. Workers' hopes for survival were focused on getting someone, anyone, to reopen the mill. The business page of the *Chicago Sun-Times* of October 12, 1980, described the scene:

> The Auditorium Theater, a Louis Sullivan masterpiece that plays host to entertainers and well-heeled patrons of the arts, last week hosted a somber gathering more interested in bread and butter than merriment.
> A crowd of 1,000 unemployed steel workers viewed what might be called, "The Saving of Wisconsin Steel," a real-life drama with tragic overtones, starring Mayor Byrne and a little-known businessman from Philadelphia, Walter Palmer.

Alderman Edward Vrdolyak, Mayor Byrne and PSWU president Tony Roque
Daily Calumet **photo, October 7, 1980**

On the platform, Fast Eddie was never more dapper as he endorsed the election promises made by Mayor Jane Byrne. The meeting was timed to coincide with President Carter's campaign visit to the Chicago area. When Mayor Byrne promised "Turkey for Thanksgiving," and said "You'll be working by November," the audience broke into wild cheers. Walter Palmer, an entrepreneur with vague financial backing, was introduced as the man who would buy and reopen Wisconsin Steel. There was even an announcement of the sale of Wisconsin Steel to Palmer in a radio news flash a few days later! Wisconsin Steel workers were elated. Unfortunately, it was a false report which United Press "regretted." As long as there is a Wisconsin Steel worker left alive, the mayor's promise of "Turkey for Thanksgiving" will bring out a bitter laugh.

The scam was so outrageous that the *Chicago Sun-Times* editorialized on the subject of Byrne's false election promises:

Why did Byrne mislead those 1,000 steel workers—and 2,500 others laid off when the plant closed in March? . . . Was it a cynical attempt to give despairing workers some good news in an election year, hoping the facts wouldn't emerge until after November 4 [election day]?

Picketing President Carter

Throughout October, 1980, the Wisconsin Steel workers continued to make headlines. Frank asked for and won the support of the Illinois State AFL-CIO convention. That was no easy feat since PSWU had never supported the AFL-CIO. President Carter faced a mass picket line at his election rally in Chicago, demanding the reopening of Wisconsin Steel. Even the policemen at the rally were sympathetic to the demand to reopen the mill.

President Carter had the power to reopen Wisconsin Steel because the feds were the real owners of the mill. Federal ownership became official on January 20, 1981. Bankruptcy Court awarded the mill and its assets to the Economic Development Administration (EDA), the biggest creditor. The October 1980 demonstrations by SOJ won a $1.8 million job-training grant from the Carter administration. But it was jobs, not just job training, that workers needed.

Thanksgiving came and went, and still the Wisconsin Steel workers were unemployed. On Thanksgiving Day, the Trabajadores de Wisconsin Steel picketed Mayor Byrne's apartment on the posh "Gold Coast" of Chicago. They were protesting her false promise of

President Carter's reelection rally picketed (*Chicago Defender*, August 5, 1980)

"turkey on the table". Disappointed by City Hall and facing the end of the unemployment compensation checks, Wisconsin Steel workers felt desperation spread through their ranks.

Winter without paychecks

Mass layoffs were hitting other steel mills and the big auto plants. Frank spoke for SOJ at a forum on unemployment organized by a coalition of unions. The coalition began to plan a March on Washington to demand jobs. When the national AFL-CIO organized the historic Solidarity Day 1981, it was in response to the work of these grassroots coalitions. Save Our Jobs members marched in Solidarity Day I, and ten years later in Solidarity Day II, national marches for jobs organized by the AFL-CIO.

January 1981 in Chicago brought the usual snow, zero and below-zero temperatures. But SOJ continued its demonstrations and mass rallies. There was bad news about the unemployment compensation. The rules had changed. To get on to the compensation rolls in 1981, a sum of over $400 had to be earned that same year. Most unemployed workers had no way to earn $400. Without unemployment compensation, they would have to go on welfare. Illinois State Senator Jeremiah Joyce infuriated the unemployed by proposing a bill to give $5,000 to each unemployed person who would leave the State of Illinois. Frank Lumpkin, in an interview with *All Chicago City News*, said, "Most of the men at Wisconsin Steel have 15 to 30 years in the mill. Now, I have a house and strong roots here. And if someone were to offer me $5,000 to get out of town, I'd think it was silly—$5,000 won't pay for most of the men's cars."

Rule 65

Hundreds of Wisconsin Steel workers qualified for pensions they were not receiving. Rule 65 pensions covered workers with at least 20 but less than 30 years of service, and whose age plus years of service added to 65 or more. In addition to monthly pension payments, Rule 65 was supposed to pay a $300-a-month supplement until a permanent job was found, or until age 62, when Social Security would take over. According to company records, the average Wisconsin Steel worker was 42 years old and had 22 years of service.

Ernie Syrek, a billet-dock loader, was very angry about the government's failure to protect the workers. He was an SOJ officer and one of the large group who had not received their Rule 65 pension checks. In a discussion in the SOJ office, Syrek said:

"About the time you get a good job, the place closed down. That was a pension job, out of the rain, out of the weather. A couple of dollars less, but it was still a good paying job. I figured another five years and I had it made. No way. What happened to us shouldn't happen to a dog.

"Yes, it took me by surprise. When they said that was it, it was a shock. 'The company is bankrupt and all the banks are foreclosing.'

"I figured it would blow over in a couple of weeks with IH [Harvester] backing them up, just a financial error. They'll get everything straightened up and start up again. I figured, no way would they do something like that, plan it.

"Yes, it was planned. In fact I saw where Kaiser Steel in Fontana, California, wanted to file bankruptcy. After investigating they said it was too expensive because of the severance pay, the vacation pay, the hospitalization and pension plans. International Harvester found a fall guy—Envirodyne.

"So they give them all the money and keep going. And when you bankrupt, we'll be clean. That was a dirty trick. We didn't get severance, vacation, nothing, which to me is $8-10,000. That's enough for me to survive maybe a year. But they're putting it in the bank over there.

"I don't know why Uncle Sam won't even back us up, It's wrong. I should be getting $300 a month besides my pension for supplementary until I'm 62. I'm not even getting that. Why they're getting away with it, I have no idea.

"Every person that's employed is nothing but a number to the big shots. They care less about people. The politicians, or whoever, they just take care of themselves. Uncle Sam, the same way. If it was their own, they'd take care of their own, but in general they care less. It's wrong. People are just numbers. If you survive, it's your business. If you don't, who cares? International Harvester is too big. Me and my family don't mean nothing to them."

Again, Save Our Mill

In January 1981, the fight to save the mill became critical again. There was no letup in threats to scrap the mill. Ronald Reagan, not known as a friend of the Economic Development Administration (EDA), was President. The Wisconsin Steel plant was going on the auction block again on January 20, 1981. On January 15th, 500 SOJ supporters rallied indoors to save the mill.

Newly elected Congressman Gus Savage was invited to speak. President Reagan's inaugural ball was held the same night. Savage accepted the workers' invitation and sent his regrets to the President. At the rally, the Congressman supported the workers' demand that EDA take over Wisconsin Steel. To keep the pressure on, that same week over 100 SOJ members marched in the snow around the Federal Court building. Inside, at Bankruptcy Court, EDA was awarded ownership of the mill. Congressman Savage congratulated Save Our Jobs: "Today we have gotten through the first stumbling block on the way to get the laid-off workers at the Wisconsin Steel mill back to work. Tomorrow morning, when Ronald Reagan opens his desk drawer, he will see he now owns a steel mill."

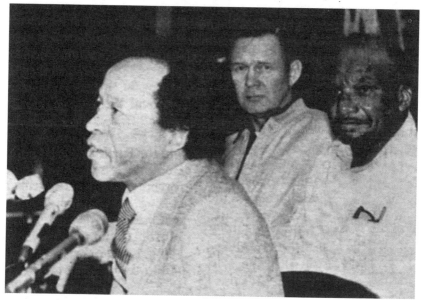

Congressman Gus Savage, Wayne Schwarz and Frank Lumpkin, 1981

As the months rolled by and the mill did not reopen, the demand for payment of pensions and benefits became a matter of survival. February is even colder in Chicago than January. Still, SOJ was on the picket line again. Outside the annual International Harvester stockholders meeting, the steel workers demanded, "Pay us our wages." Leading the picket line, Frank Lumpkin heard a lot of encouraging remarks from passers-by. Save Our Jobs was a cause, which would not give up and would not go away. From 1981 until

Harvester settled the SOJ suit in 1988, every Harvester stockholder meeting was circled by an SOJ picket line.

In March 1981, hundreds of Wisconsin Steel workers marched again in a Chicago labor rally for jobs. The labor rally gave enthusiastic support to the demand for payment of Wisconsin Steel pensions. It was now a year since the mill had closed. In 1975, the federal Pension Benefit Guaranty Corporation (PBGC) had been set up to insure workers' pensions. Those with the longest service were receiving PBGC pension checks. But PBGC had not agreed to pay the largest, hardest-hit group, those under "Rule 65" pensions.

Congressman Savage leads 150 Wisconsin Steel workers to U.S. Capitol

Come to Washington

"Come to Washington," Congressman Savage urged at the Jobs Rally. "Let the Congress, EDA and PBGC learn about your situation and hear your demands."

The idea of a mass lobby in Washington was very appealing. But how could SOJ get the money for buses? It would take three buses. About $6,000 would be needed in a hurry. SOJ appealed to local businesses and banks and raised $4,000 in a few days. Three buses were ordered but SOJ was still $2,000 short. With just a couple of hours to go, Florencio Ortega and Frank Lumpkin loaned SOJ $1,000 each. They were about to make history and would not let money stand in the way. USWA Local 65 members, led by President Alice Peurala, cheered the Wisconsin Steel workers on their way.

They were welcomed at the Capitol by Congressman Savage. Inside the Capitol Building, the Wisconsin Steel workers were given one hour of time on the floor of Congress. *The Congressional Record, House,* April 9, 1981, tells the story: "Wisconsin Steel workers—Save Our Jobs Committee." Members of Congress vied with each other to take the floor to praise Frank Lumpkin and SOJ. Gus Savage led the way, introducing SOJ headed by Frank Lumpkin as "fighting for thousands of deeply patriotic Americans, still mostly unemployed." Illinois Congressmen Frank Annunzio and John G. Fary, Minnesota Congressman James L. Oberstar and Congressman Berkley Bedell of Iowa added their support. Harold Washington, later to become Mayor of Chicago, spoke words of encouragement that SOJ has treasured ever since.

It bothers me deeply that in a crisis situation of high unemployment this administration seems to be turning its back upon that major problem and going out on flights of fancy, talking about a supply side economics. . . . I applaud you, Mr. Savage. I applaud Frank Lumpkin and those fine people who have journeyed here today to make their plight known. It is people like you Congressmen who vivify to the American people every day and also to the administration that their irresponsible fiscal attitude cannot prevail. We will not permit it. [page H1438.]

Lumpkin felt that the official recognition of *their* cause by the U.S. Congress would help workers in other plants, too. The publicity given to the "steelscam" at Wisconsin Steel would stop other employers who were thinking of closing their plants without paying the workers. Still, SOJ needed something more definite to take back to Chicago. Fortunately, there was one more stop to make—at the Pension Benefit Guaranty Corporation. With Congressional support for the SOJ cause, the door was wide open at PBGC.

At PBGC the delegation won an important commitment to pay the Rule 65 pensions. However, PBGC would pay only 40% because Rule 65 had been in effect only 2 ½ years. Pension plans that had been in place 5 years or more were supposedly funded 100%. But a cap on monthly PBGC pension checks reduced the amount due some workers. Special benefits, such as the $300 a month for Rule 65, were not covered by PBGC. Still the workers did not leave Washington empty-handed. Since 1981, over 500 Wisconsin Steel workers have benefited from monthly Rule 65 pension payments!

Wisconsin Steel Women in a National ERA march in Chicago, June, 1980

Women Join the Action

Women of Wisconsin Steel families participated in the SOJ action in Washington. There had been an ongoing effort to bring Wisconsin Steel women into fuller participation. Some steel workers' wives became active in the Save Our Jobs Women's Committee, chaired by Beatrice Lumpkin. Many of these women had never participated in public affairs before and welcomed the chance to develop their leadership potential. Some of the women who had worked in the Wisconsin Steel offices helped SOJ with their specialized knowledge. However, on the whole, there was less participation by women who had worked in Wisconsin Steel than by the steel worker's wives.

Most of the women who had worked in production in the mill had been laid off months before the shutdown. The office workers were caught up in the agony of the sudden closing, but most soon found other jobs. Many lived on Chicago's East Side and in Hegewisch, neighborhoods from which African American workers had long been excluded. Although members of the same PSWU, the office workers had less experience than shop workers with racially integrated organizations. Still Lumpkin was often invited to speak at the office workers' reunions, and the office workers supported Save Our Jobs, but at a distance.

Some changes were made in the SOJ office to make women feel welcome. The calendars on the wall showing scantily clad or unclad women came down. Women research students have been welcomed when they came to conduct interviews. A few women researchers have tried to help with the daily chores to keep the office going. Frank Lumpkin set an example by joining the Coalition of Labor Union Women (CLUW) and inviting CLUW members to the annual workers' rallies. Johnnie Jackson and Katie Jordan brought the support of CLUW to dozens of SOJ actions. Over the years, the number of women attending monthly SOJ membership meetings increased. Many were recently widowed spouses of Wisconsin Steel workers, sad witness to the increase in the death toll after the sudden closing of the mill.

11. SOJ Sues Harvester-Navistar

For many months, SOJ could not get a lawyer to take their case. At first the workers didn't realize that they needed a lawyer. Even experienced activists thought that bankruptcy laws protected workers' wages. It was a shock to learn that employees of a bankrupt company are among the last to be paid, if at all. Meanwhile, Ed Vrdolyak, the PSWU attorney, had failed to file for the workers in Bankruptcy Court. Attorneys Beth Lehman and Zeva Schub, friends of the Lumpkins, told Frank that the workers had not been represented in court and needed to get a lawyer.

Lawyers were afraid of the case. They knew the costs would be great and it would take years. The workers had no money to pay anything up front. But Frank kept trying, talking to one lawyer after another. He got a lot of sympathy but no takers. A year after the mill closed, he made a second attempt to get labor attorney Leon Despres to take the case.

Leon Despres had a reputation for fighting injustice. He was well known for his service as an independent alderman on Chicago's City Council. After the massacre at Republic Steel on Memorial Day 1937, Despres helped organizers for SWOC (Steel Workers Organizing Committee, CIO). But Despres gave Lumpkin the same answer that he had given a year earlier: the Despres firm was small. A case like the Wisconsin Steel workers would bankrupt them.

Enter Tom Geoghegan
Tom Geoghegan, a young lawyer at the Despres firm, heard Frank's appeal. He was so moved that he asked Despres to let him take the case on a contingency basis (no payment of legal fees until, and if, the case was won). "I couldn't say no to Frank Lumpkin," he explained later. He did require Save Our Jobs to raise ten thousand

dollars to cover some of the clerical costs that a huge case incurs. Not until seven years later did Geoghegan and Despres realize any payment for their years of work, charging a minimum for fees and costs, only 7% of the settlement.[*] In contrast, Harvester paid millions of dollars to six top-flight lawyers trying to deny Wisconsin Steel workers their pensions and benefits.

Tom Geoghegan at SOJ rally, March 1983

[*]From transcript of Judge James Moran's comments on Harvester-SOJ settlement, February 1988: I will say the quality of legal work all the way through has been excellent. Then they came in with a request for fees which are about four percent of the fund. I don't know about you, ladies and gentlemen, but I don't see many lawyers come in on a contingent case where the likelihood of any recovery started out to be poor, and years and years and years later are saying we want to recover as our fees a little bit over our normal rate, which amounts to about four percent of the fund. If any of you -- I don't care whether you are talking about a workmen's comp claim or an automobile accident or what have you, that is not the way it usually happens. I must say, I have found their dedication to the interests of the class, and their professionalism, and their modesty in seeking fees all to be very refreshing.

The case was a matter of simple justice. International Harvester had cheated the Wisconsin Steel workers out of $45 million in benefits promised in their union contract. By 1988, with interest added, the amount lost was almost $90 million. The earned benefits included certain pension benefits, severance pay, supplementary unemployment benefits, earned vacation pay and health insurance for retirees. Wages for the last week of work had never been fully paid.

Soon after the case was filed, Frank received the first (but not the last) offer to buy him off. He and the five other Wisconsin Steel workers who filed the class action suit were offered immediate payment of their individual claims. All they had to do was withdraw the suit. The offer caused less of a ripple than a small pebble dropped into the ocean. The Save Our Jobs leaders were not for sale.

Tom Geoghegan took the case against his better business judgment, a heroic move in the opinion of some lawyers. In his award-winning book, *Which Side Are You On?* Geoghegan describes himself as a non-hero who prefers a middle-class life style to living like the workers. But then, if there were a choice, what worker would not prefer a higher standard of living? His description of the human costs of the plant closing reveals his sympathy with the workers.

So not only did the workers lose their jobs; that would have been bad enough. But they also lost the $45 million, which was their "deindustrialization" money. The closing of Wisconsin Steel was, in many ways, like an earthquake. The first shock was that the mill closed. The second shock, like an aftershock, was that they would not get this money either. The money that would have cushioned the blow, that would have given them time to think, figure out what to do next, hold on to the car or the home a little longer: it was not much money, really, but it was enough, just enough, to make people lose their balance. Some of them could never get their balance back.

I spent all the Reagan years on this case. It was endless. I felt like I was in prison. I used to think of that line from *Richard II*: "I wasted time, and now doth time waste me." I came to hate "deindustrialization." The mill had closed, but it seemed as if the litigation would never end, and I might have to clean up after this mill forever. I felt as the men must have felt ... always living in the year 1980. I could not seem to leave 1980. [86]

Tom Geoghegan did what he had to do, just as Frank Lumpkin did what he had to do. Despite his humorous complaints, Geoghegan did not quit in 1988 when Harvester settled. He went on to fight the legal case for another eight years, seeking justice for the workers against

Envirodyne, their last employer. Geoghegan brought more than legal expertise to the cause. He often acknowledged that the case would not have prevailed without SOJ actions that kept the issue alive.

Piercing the Corporate Veil

The legal issues were tangled, to say the least. International Harvester, later known as Navistar, operated Wisconsin Steel for 75 years. In the 1970s they decided to get rid of Wisconsin Steel without paying the pensions and plant-closing benefits provided in the union contract. Detroit's McClouth Steel and others looked, but did not buy. So Harvester made a deal with Envirodyne, a consulting firm with at most 19 or 20 employees. Gordon L. Clark describes the deal:

> Envirodyne had no experience in making steel. Before they "bought" Wisconsin Steel, Envirodyne was losing money and could not pay its bank loan of $2 million. Then, what appears to be a mutually beneficial deal was struck between Harvester and Envirodyne. Harvester would "sell" Wisconsin Steel to Envirodyne. Envirodyne would get a $1 million a year management fee and Envirodyne's loans would be paid off. Envirodoyne would assume the pension liabilities, pay Harvester $15 million in cash to be provided by Chase Manhattan Bank, and Harvester would hold a $50 million mortgage on the mill secured by the profitable mines and railroads that belonged to Wisconsin Steel.
>
> Harvester saved at least $76 million in pension costs, and Envirodyne paid off its debts that were overdue and got out of its cash crunch. At risk were only 3,500 Wisconsin Steel workers and the government's Pension Benefit Guaranty Corporation (PBGC). In the event of bankruptcy, PBGC would be asked to take over payment of the pensions. Business analysts have used words like "sham" and "fraud" to describe the sale of Wisconsin Steel to Envirodyne.[87]

Tom Geoghegan faced three big legal problems.

First, the union contract was signed by PSWU, not Save Our Jobs. The "Lumpkin plaintiffs" had to win recognition by the court to represent the class of Wisconsin Steel workers. SOJ solved this problem in just a few days by collecting signatures from a majority of the workers. It was enough to convince the judge to accept the case as a class action suit. Joining Frank in signing the suit were SOJ officers Florencio Ortega, John Randall, Stephen Jarzyna, Ernie Syrek, and Felix Vasquez: two African Americans, two Latinos, and two of European descent.

The second problem that Geoghegan faced was that he would have to "pierce the corporate veil" in order to sue Harvester. At the time the mill closed, it was operated by "Wisconsin Steel Corp.," a subsidiary of Envirodyne, not Harvester. He needed to expose the "sale" to Envirodyne as a sham, and to show that Harvester continued to control Wisconsin Steel and was responsible for the workers' benefits. This was not easy. Naturally, Harvester and Envirodyne had tried to cover their tracks as much as possible. Geoghegan describes the problem with the aid of a graphic image:

> But Harvester had to have an accomplice. It found one in a small engineering company, Envirodyne, Inc., which knew nothing about steel. Envirodyne was not much of a company, just two yuppies in a garage. But Envirodyne did not want to have to pay the pensions either. So Envirodyne transferred title to a subsidiary it created, EDC Holding Company. Then EDC transferred title to a subsidiary it created, WSC Corporation. One corporate shell came after another. It was like a game of Chinese boxes, and when you got to the last box, nothing was in it. Nobody would be paying the pensions.[88]

There was a court-required "discovery" process which provided some information. But it was expensive. Throughout most of the years in which he filed mountains of legal briefs in various courts, Geoghegan had no money for staff. Sometimes he called on Frank Lumpkin and the steel workers to do some leg-work, or to raise money for duplicating costs. The wives of the steel workers did a mammoth job cooking dinners to raise thousands of dollars for legal expenses such as copying costs. Few workers understood that costs had to be paid even though their lawyers would not be paid until (and if) the workers won.

The third legal problem may have been the most difficult. International Harvester claimed that PSWU had signed a contract, that gave up all the Wisconsin Steel workers' claims on Harvester. PSWU officers had indeed signed a contract with Harvester in August 1977, at the time of the sale to Envirodyne. The contract had a waiver that seemed to release Harvester from any liability for Wisconsin Steel pensions and benefits. Alderman Edward Vrdolyak absented himself from the contract-signing session. At that time, Vrdolyak was on a $32,000 annual retainer from PSWU. PSWU had also been a generous donor to his campaign fund. Yet Vrdolyak let Roque sign a crucial contract without the benefit of legal advice. Surely, any labor lawyer would have advised PSWU not to sign such a contract. Unless, of course, a deal had been struck under the table. And that is what many Wisconsin Steel workers believed. No wonder, as Geoghegan said, "Harvester never, ever, expected to have to pay the Wisconsin Steel workers." Tom Geoghegan gave a kinder interpretation of Tony Roque's actions:

> When the mill went down, ERV [Vrdolyak] closed down the Union and walked away. He's got nothing against labor law. But there's no money in it, see? The money is in worker comp. Poor Roque, the president, was in over his head. He was just a working guy, no genius, trying to figure out a Wall Street deal, with no one to help him, not even his boss, Vrdolyak. Even a good labor lawyer might not have been much help.
>
> When Roque complained [about pensions being endangered by the sale—BL] Harvester handed him a sheet of paper. It said this document was a guarantee of the pensions. Roque signed it. Didn't really grasp it. In fact, the paper guaranteed just a tiny sliver of the pensions. By signing it, Roque unwittingly released Harvester from *everything* else: $65 million in pensions, $20 million in shutdown benefits. [89]

Harvester had no way of knowing that its plot to defraud the workers would be foiled. They did not know that leaders would emerge from the ranks of the workers who could neither be bought nor scared away. And both methods were tried. The PSWU and the Vrdolyak organization had often been accused of strong-arm tactics or worse. In the mill and the surrounding community, it was believed to be dangerous to oppose them. In the 1970s, Luis Guadarrama, Frank's friend and PSWU delegate, survived a brutal beating which left him for dead in an alley. No one was accused and no legal action was taken. There were other examples. Still, Frank Lumpkin and Save Our Jobs went ahead to do what they knew was right.

Geoghegan gives some valuable insight into the emergence of Frank Lumpkin and the Save Our Jobs Committee as leaders of the Wisconsin Steel workers: "He was not an officer, but there was no one else. He said to me, 'I read somewhere, if you can't find a leader, be a leader.' "

> So Frank and a few friends met in someone's house, and they started a committee, the Save Our Jobs Committee. It was a great name. Save Our Jobs. It never saved a single job, I think. But it filed suit, it picketed, it gave food to the hungry. It was like nothing I had ever seen. I used to think I had died and gone to rank-and-file heaven.
>
> Save Our Jobs became the union, not officially, but spiritually. It was "the Union" as it was in the beginning: no buildings, no bureaucracy, just a crowd of people, desperate, broke, their backs against the wall. [90]

From 1981 through 1996, Tom Geoghegan came to the Save Our Jobs rallies, sometimes two or three times a year. To a *Chicago Tribune* reporter who was looking for "reasons" that kept the workers together over the years, Geoghegan said, "When I first got into this in November, 1981, I thought they were just out to get their money back. But now, I think it's something they've come to take pride in. By standing up and staying together, they've done something, and I think they're celebrating that tonight."[91]

As an attorney, Geoghegan came from a strong academic background. As he often said, he was a "double Harvard graduate," having attended Harvard University both as an undergraduate and a law student. He was resourceful and had a fertile legal imagination. In *Which Side Are You On* he wrote, "I tried one legal theory after another, RICO, ERISA, LMRA, and when one claim or theory was knocked out, I tried another one." Finally the judge agreed with one part of Geoghegan's many arguments. Save Our Jobs had a case that could go to trial!

Jobs for Steel workers

If one man can do the work that used to take 10 men, why are we still working eight hours a day? We should work only six hours, four hours, whatever it takes to have jobs for everybody so everyone can make a living.
Frank Lumpkin

The expectation of winning some money from their suit against Harvester kept the SOJ members active and visible. Meanwhile, conditions for most steel worker families worsened. One steel mill after another closed or dwindled to a skeleton crew. About the time Wisconsin Steel closed in March 1980, Pullman Standard announced that it would soon shut down. Pullman was the last plant to make railroad/subway cars in the USA. The Eugene Debs local of the USWA at Pullman had a proud history of struggle. It was the direct descendant of the Great Pullman Strike of 1894, led by Debs himself. An activist modern leadership that included Communists argued that a strong country needed to make its own rail cars. They organized a Pullman Save Our Jobs Committee and formed a coalition with the Wisconsin Steel SOJ.

The last railroad car

Pullman workers took their fight to Congress to demand more mass transit, as shown in the documentary movie, *The Last Railroad Car*. The workers asked for federal aid to build the mass transit systems that were so urgently needed. Improving and expanding mass transit could create a tremendous demand for new subway and

SOJ members with Pullman Standard SOJ picket Sen. Lugar for mass transit

El-line cars. Many more jobs would open up for Pullman workers as well as basic steel workers. When Pullman workers picketed Senator Richard Lugar (R-IN) to demand passage of a mass transit bill, Frank Lumpkin brought a group of SOJ members to join the picket line.

Despite the protests, Congress failed to provide funds to improve mass transit. In the summer of 1981, Pullman Standard workers completed "the last railroad car built in the United States." Pullman shut down. U.S. Steel's Southworks was still working although thousands had been laid off in 1981.

JOIN - Jobs Or Income Now!

Unemployed workers from Pullman Standard, Wisconsin Steel, Southworks, and other plants formed a new organization of the unemployed in 1982. Frank Lumpkin was elected as chairperson. Scott Marshall, from Pullman Standard, was elected the organizer, a position he held until he became the full-time organizer for the Illinois Communist Party. All the officers were volunteers. The unemployed declared that they were willing to work. Many were skilled workers. It was not their fault if the system did not provide them with jobs—their families still had to live. Anyone willing to work had the right to an income. The new organization called itself JOIN, for "Jobs Or Income Now."

JOIN demanded that the government become the employer of last resort. Failing that, government should assure income by extending unemployment compensation for as long as people were unemployed. First-time job seekers who could not find jobs should get unemployment compensation, too. The main demand was for jobs at a living wage. In contrast, company spokespersons and some politicians focused on job training as the solution to the crisis. The unemployed were willing to take job training if it led to a job. But the problem was not the lack of skills among the steel workers. The real issue was lack of jobs at a living wage.

The Wisconsin Steel workers had won a $1.8 million job-training program. It was a Save Our Jobs victory that came out of the October 1980 demonstration in front of President Carter's re-election rally in Chicago. The job-training award was one of the last acts of Jimmy Carter's presidency. Very few, if any, of the graduates of this job-training program found full-time, permanent, good-paying jobs. At least they were paid a subsidy while they trained. (Later job training programs did not pay any subsidy.) After this job-training course was completed, a letter was sent to corporations promoting the qualifications of the students and asking for information on job openings. Not a single call or inquiry resulted.[92]

JOIN, like SOJ, was encouraged by even small victories. For example, they helped win a six-month extension of unemployment compensation. Frank led a delegation of 20 jobless workers to the office of Senator Charles Percy (R) just as the U.S. Senate was acting on extension of unemployment benefits. They feared that Percy would vote against it. "We want to see Senator Percy," the unemployed group demanded. "You can't talk to him. He's on the Senate floor," his aide said. "We've got plenty of time. We're not leaving until we talk to him!" Florencio Ortega told the aide. Ortega, of SOJ, was typical of millions who had worked hard all their lives and just wanted a chance to continue to work.

Faced with this determined group of people, the aide did not want to risk bad publicity by calling security to remove them by force. He quickly located Senator Percy on the Senate floor. Percy took the call and promised to vote to extend unemployment compensation. In a few months, the issue came up again because the extension had expired. Unemployment statistics were not any better. Cutting off unemployment compensation would leave the jobless with few choices. There were some who could apply for welfare. Others could not qualify unless they sold their house or car. JOIN organized another delegation to visit Senator Percy.

This time Senator Percy's aides were ready for the delegation of unemployed workers. Federal security officers were waiting. They rushed in, sat the unemployed workers on wheeled office chairs and rolled them out. Frank was still in the lobby because the group had decided to leave him downstairs as a backup. He was ready to rescue them or at least find legal help in case delegation members were arrested. But there were no arrests. Instead, Frank saw a parade of guards coming out of the elevators, wheeling husky steel workers on office chairs across the tiled floor and out onto the street. The unemployed workers had made their point. (It also gave them something to laugh about for months afterwards.)

Save Our Jobs food line

By 1982, many steel worker families had no food. Save Our Jobs decided to set up a food line. The committee realized that food distributions require a lot of work and money. They did not want to lose sight of Save Our Job's main purpose, to fight for jobs and payment of their benefits. But people were hungry. Food distribution was an emergency. The emergency worsened. One hundred came for the first food distribution. Next time it was 200, then 300 and finally 500. There was not enough food. SOJ called in the press to let Mayor Byrne and the whole city see the people's need for food and jobs, a need government was not meeting. The *Sun-Times* described the scene on July 21, 1982.

First in line was Rebecca Q.[93] "No, I've never stood in a food line before and it's a little embarrassing. You feel like you're asking for charity, and we never lived like this before." She said that her husband had worked for 16 years as a crane operator for Wisconsin Steel. Since the plant closed, he found work, but it lasted only two weeks. The Q.'s, who have five children aged 7 to 16, first lived on unemployment compensation. Then they had to go on welfare. Ms Q. explained, "When the monthly welfare check of $556 comes, the first thing that gets paid is the mortgage payment of $302. . . . Then we pay the utilities, heat, electricity and water. There isn't much left over."

SOJ food line (Suza Matczak Photo. *Daily Calumet*, Oct. 13, 1982)

South Chicago Enterprise Zone

Feeling the pressure of the unemployed, the federal government came up with a plan for "Enterprise Zones." The plan promised jobs, but critics said that Enterprise Zones would do little more than give away money to private business. Mayor Byrne threw her support to the proposal, which named South Chicago as a location for one of the "Enterprise Zones." The plan was to entice companies to move to South Chicago. As a lure, protective regulations would be set aside and government loans would help the businesses get started. Not one new job was guaranteed in the plan. Desperate unemployed workers were ready to grasp at straws. As one Wisconsin Steel worker said, "Hey man, I'm 52 years old. I want to work, and if this means jobs, I'll go for it. It's been too long."[94]

Frank shared the AFL-CIO opposition to this "trickle down" proposal. Throughout the Reagan years, as well as before and after, money was given to big business, but none has "trickled down" to the workers. Frank knew it was hard to oppose any plan that claimed it would bring jobs. So Save Our Jobs staged a debate on the issue to let the members decide for themselves.

The audience was polite but skeptical. Speaking for the Enterprise Zone was Selma Wise, a representative of the South Chicago Development Commission. She argued, "Let the mom and pop stores have a chance to become big businesses and hire people as a result." In opposition to Enterprise Zones was Attorney Joe Welsh, an aide of State Representative Clem Balanoff. Welsh opposed the plan because it failed to guarantee a single job. He asked for written guarantees that the Enterprise Zone would create jobs. "There's plenty of work to do in South Chicago, repairing streets and sidewalks. Why is there no jobs program in the Enterprise Zone bill?" he asked. Welsh described the proposed Zone as "a marriage between Reaganomics and the Byrne-Vrdolyak machine."

Frank did not speak on the issue. He agreed with Joe Welsh that Enterprise Zones were giveaways of government funds to private business with little prospect of creating new jobs. Frank knew that many workers hoped against hope that the Zone would bring some jobs to South Chicago. As Welsh had predicted, no new jobs were created. The Enterprise Zone proved to be just another hope betrayed. Frank's way of handling the issue was typical of his democratic approach. Give the workers the facts, then let them decide for themselves.

Hunger continued to spread in Chicago, increasing the pressure on the Save Our Jobs food line. The *Daily Calumet* described the grim situation on the line.

It was raining. The weather made South Chicago look as gray as it felt. Just a few days before Thanksgiving when every third face you see on Commercial Avenue belongs to the unemployed. . . . The line of the jobless was patient. A young woman held two children in her arms. She rocked the one who was crying. A boy stood next to her and tugged at his father's sleeve. He hummed a song to himself. The rain had matted his hair into three dark yellow clumps.

Whites, Blacks and Hispanics stood huddled together, talking softly among themselves. The line wrapped around the block and those near the end of the line hoped food would be left for them.

After it was over, Frank Lumpkin . . . stood and sighed. It had been his job that morning to tell the crowd that the food had run out. "I feel like hell. I had to tell them that there wasn't any more."

"This is bad," he said afterwards. "I'm thinking of organizing a hunger march of some kind for all of the people around here. It's right before Thanksgiving and people don't have enough to eat."[95]

Hunger March for Christmas

The Hunger March took place just before Christmas 1982. Two hundred Save Our Jobs members joined with another 200 from the Illinois Public Action Council in a march on City and State Office Buildings. People came from the food lines to demand action. They found only stone walls and stone hearts. At City Hall the doors were locked. Police were massed outside of the door to make sure that none of the hunger marchers could enter. At the governor's office an aide took notes and sounded sympathetic. He said all that he could do was to give the information to the governor. There was never a response from the governor. Marches for the unemployed kept the pressure on the politicians to continue the food distributions. Some activists criticized Frank and Save Our Jobs for investing their time in food lines. Frank did not agree. He saw it as a way to keep the protesters alive and to keep the protest alive.

Don't Scab

Another major concern of Save Our Jobs and JOIN was building stronger ties between unemployed workers and organized labor. Unfortunately, many unemployed workers lost their union membership and contact with their union soon after they lost their jobs.   JOIN distributed leaflets at the State Unemployment offices, urging the jobless to refuse to scab. JOIN also took action to stop the State Employment Services from sending unemployed workers to scab at plants on strike. SOJ and JOIN were prominent on the picket line of the striking Greyhound bus drivers. The message of solidarity between employed and unemployed workers was well received. The next year they joined picket lines at USX to help end the lockout.

USX Lockout

U.S. Steel had changed its name to USX. The name change made it crystal clear that the company was interested only in profit, not in producing a vital product that the country needed. U.S. Steel had taken $6 billion of profits, made from the labor of their steel workers, to buy Marathon Oil. In 1983, the USWA contract expired at USX. Oil profits had taken a temporary drop, so USX decided to squeeze extra profit out of the USX steel workers.

Instead of renewing the union contract, the company locked out the workers and shut down the furnaces. SOJ joined the USX picket lines on a daily basis. They believed that their future as workers was tied to the fate of the USX steel workers and workers everywhere. It was the kind of solidarity and class-consciousness that Lumpkin encouraged.

On the whole, the picket lines were a peaceful scene. The company knew better than to try to hire scabs. The company tactic was to try to starve the workers into submission. In some states locked-out steel workers were able to collect unemployment benefits, but not in Illinois. Locked-out USX workers called a demonstration at the State of Illinois building in Chicago to demand unemployment benefits. SOJ members turned out in force, making up half of the demonstrators. Frank's motto was "Always bring a crowd."[96] They did not win unemployment benefits but the company felt their pressure. USX gave in and the workers retained most of their gains.

Crisis March to Springfield—On Foot

Lumpkin was also on the board of Citizen Action, then known in the state as IPAC, the Illinois Public Action Council. IPAC decided on a "Crisis March to Springfield For Jobs and Human Needs." On May 10, 1983, SOJ members led the March on its first leg from Chicago to Springfield. Jan Schakowsky, an IPAC board member who was elected to Congress in 1998, helped lead the March. The marchers demanded that the State of Illinois take emergency action to relieve hunger and homelessness.

Frank decided to walk all the way from Chicago to Springfield. As chairperson of the Save Our Jobs Committee, he enthusiastically supported the goals of the Crisis March. The physical and political challenge appealed to him. On the way to Springfield, thousands of workers would participate in the March, joining local actions held at

Lumpkin (left front) leads Crisis March (Jim Klepitsch photo, May 10, 1983)
Reprinted with special permission from the Chicago Sun-Times, Inc.

towns along the way. All together, they would walk 200 miles in 2 weeks, and hold rallies and press conferences at every stopover. Frank was one of about 20 who walked the whole way, with the exception of a couple of days off for urgent SOJ business. At 66, he was the oldest long distance marcher but none were more vigorous.

Lumpkin (upper left) speaks to thousands in State Capitol

The Crisis marchers were welcomed in all of the small industrial towns hurting from layoffs, shutdowns and an uncertain future. Unions and churches opened their doors to host the marchers overnight. The local press in many towns carried the story. The message went out that there was a way to fight back, that government has the responsibility to create jobs doing useful work at a living wage. The March culminated inside the state capitol building in Springfield with a 5,000-strong lobby for jobs and human needs.

Washington and Byrne—the Contrast

When the preliminary Crisis March picketed the Chicago City Hall, Jane Byrne was still Mayor. She locked the doors to keep the marchers out. On April 15, 1983, Harold Washington was elected mayor. What a change a few months made! Washington did more than invite the marchers into City Hall. He personally awarded Olympic-size medals to each of the long-distance marchers in a ceremony inside his private office. Frank treasures the medal and the memory of Washington hanging the medal around his neck.

By 1983, organizations of the unemployed had formed in many cities, often under Communist leadership. The commercial media fabricated a high-sounding phrase to cover up the ugly reality of unemployment and hunger. Millions of workers who had been dumped in plant closings or mass layoffs were labeled "dislocated workers." "Dislocated" implies a temporary condition, as though unemployed workers would soon be "relocated." The term was a cover-up for increasing profits by closing plants and downsizing jobs that paid a living wage. No organization of the unemployed ever called their members "dislocated." Instead, many took their name from the slogan, "Jobs Or Income Now," or "JOIN."

In Chicago, JOIN took heart from the election of a workers' leader to fill Harold Washington's congressional seat. Charles A. Hayes, a National Vice President of the United Food and Commercial Workers Union, became the only union leader in Congress. The unemployed hoped that Congressman Hayes would introduce a Jobs or Income bill in the House of Representatives.

JOIN organizations were organized in Milwaukee, Rockford, Birmingham, St. Louis, Denver, Houston, Tucson, Cleveland, Buffalo, Detroit, Pontiac, Seattle, Los Angeles, San Diego, Oakland, Richmond, San Francisco, Santa Cruz, San Jose, Pittsburgh and other cities. Some unemployed groups remembered labor history and called themselves, "Unemployed Councils" after the militant organizations of the '30s. Each local unemployed group had its own program and local structure but the problem they all faced was national. National solutions were needed. Bringing together a national movement of unemployed organizations was the next step.

Rudy Lozano Assassinated

A call went out for a Congress of Unemployed Organizations to be held on July 2, 1983, at El Centro de la Causa, in the Pilsen community of Chicago. Arrangements for housing the Congress were made by Rudy Lozano, a grassroots organizer in Chicago's Mexican American community. Save Our Jobs and JOIN officially co-sponsored the Congress.

Rudy Lozano and son José (Pepé), 1983

In addition to Frank Lumpkin and Rudy Lozano, key Chicago organizers for the Congress included Scott Marshall from the closed Pullman Standard plant and a Chicago JOIN organizer, Eloise Webster a union activist laid off from USX Southworks and Humberto Salinas of the ILGWU. Salinas worked closely with Lozano in the community and the union.

Just days before the Congress, Rudy Lozano was assassinated. He was a labor organizer, working for the International Ladies Garment Workers Union (ILGWU). The murder sent a shock wave throughout Chicago and beyond. Lozano was a personal friend of the Lumpkins and founder of Centro Sin Fronteras (Center Without Borders). He had served as a catalyst in uniting the Latino and African American communities during the 1983 mayoralty elections.

Only 31 years old, Lozano gave his life in the struggle. Shortly after the election of Mayor Washington, Rudy was murdered in his home while he held his youngest son in his arms. It was a professional "hit," a political assassination. The triggerman was jailed and convicted but the police never found the murderers who had hired the assassin. Lozano's friends and family charged that the police had not conducted a thorough investigation. After the murder, friends urged Frank to quit jogging along the lakefront. They feared that he, too, could become a gunman's target. Fred Hampton, Rudy Lozano, and later, Chris Hani of South Africa, were leaders who had personally touched Frank's life. They were killed in turn in an attempt to stop their movements. They died but their movements continued.

Unemployed Congress petition

In many ways the spirit of Rudy Lozano guided the sessions of the Unemployed Congress which he had helped plan. The Congress opened with a dedication to his memory. Lumpkin gave the keynote address and was elected chairperson of the Unemployed Congress.[97] The Congress issued a petition for Jobs or Income Now legislation and quickly collected thousands of signatures. The petition campaign was successful. Two years later, the Income and Jobs Action Act of 1985 was introduced in the U.S. House of Representatives.

Keep the wreckers out!

True to its name, the Save Our Jobs Committee fought every inch of the way to save the jobs of the Wisconsin Steel workers. Every delay they won that saved the mill from the wrecking ball kept hope alive. As long as the buildings and furnaces still stood, there was a chance that the mill would reopen and they could go back to work. The blast furnace, in which $75,000 of U.S. taxpayers' money was sunk, was blown up before it was allowed to produce even one load of steel. (See photos.) Through their protests, Save Our Jobs succeeded in keeping the rest of the plant intact for many years. In a press conference on September 22, 1983, Lumpkin charged:

> "Scrapping Wisconsin Steel would be a disgrace - a stupid destruction by the Reagan administration of valuable federal property that would end the hopes of 3,500 Wisconsin Steel workers ever returning to work. The costs in human suffering, and the costs to the government and to the community will continue to multiply."

going—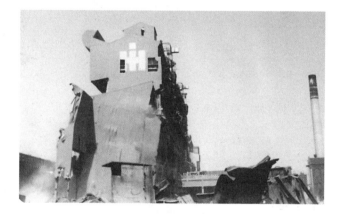

gone!

Newly rebuilt blast furnace blown up

In support of Lumpkin's statement at the press conference, Professor David Ranney, of the Center for Urban Economic Development of the University of Illinois, released the following research done jointly with the Midwest Center for Labor Research. Their study stated:

There are presently 27,600 workers on the Southeast side who are unemployed due to the decline in steel. The loss in income to these workers over the past five years is $1.5 billion, income that could have been spent to bolster the local economy. The cost to government during this period, both in tax losses and increased government expenditures, was estimated to be $607 million.[98]

Public works proposal for Wisconsin Steel

Soon after Wisconsin Steel became federal property, Save Our Jobs proposed a practical jobs plan. The plant was still physically intact thanks to the many SOJ protest rallies against scrapping the mill. SOJ proposed a two-year public works jobs and job training project that would use the Wisconsin Steel machine shop and buildings. Unemployed steel workers would work half of the week and study skilled crafts the other half. They would be paid $12,000 a year plus health benefits, "the wage necessary for the lowest annual family budget for minimum decent standard of living." The suggested work projects would have provided badly needed repairs of the local infrastructure. These included repair or replacement of vaulted sidewalks, streets, bridges, roads, public buildings and parks, as well as maintenance of the Wisconsin Steel structures, railroad and other government-owned property. The study component of the plan included electrical work, machine shop, steam engineer, pipe fitting, welding, pollution control, truck repairs, safety, railroad maintenance and high-school equivalency exam preparation. The plan was practical but never came to fruition. Government would have had to "put people first" instead of its "profits before people" policy.

Frank was proud of the fact that American steel workers were the most productive in the world. He blamed the capitalist system, not the workers, for the disaster that hit steel communities. He was well aware that David M. Roderick, chairman of USX, was boasting that the steel companies were producing the same amount of steel with less than 30% as many workers. Roderick claimed that "USX's steel division is making steel that's of higher quality and relatively lower cost in real dollars than a decade ago. And we are doing it today with

3.8 man-hours per ton as compared to 10.8 man-hours per ton in 1982."[99]

"If one man can do the work that used to take 10 men, why are we still working eight hours a day?" Frank placed this question as a panelist at a discussion of *Coming to Chicago,* a film in which he was interviewed about the African American migration to Chicago. "We should work only six hours, four hours, whatever it takes to have jobs for everybody so everyone can make a living." A shorter work-week with no cut in pay was part of JOIN's solution to the lack of jobs. Lumpkin also called for the public takeover of the closed plants to provide the jobs and make the steel that the country needed. The worst criminals in the country, he said, were the people who closed the plants and left the steel workers' families to starve:

"Crime is a major fact. I think we must change the laws to fit the crime. It is a crime to put people into the street without a penny, children without food or clothing, homes without heat. It is not the unemployed who have committed the crime. Look at South Chicago. When the mill was open, no one lost their home, phone, or had their water shut off. They paid their bills and bought cars and other things that make a community live. Now everything has changed and it is not the fault of the people.

"Let's think a little about what is coming on and see if we can come up with some answers. Take Wisconsin Steel for instance. That mill is owned by the government. In other words, we own that mill and especially the workers who have their lives and their money tied up in the court battle that is going on. We feel that because the workers here have so much of their life tied up in that mill, this government should give them a chance to make a go of that mill. We have worked out a plan by which we believe that can be done. We are willing to go back into that mill as trainers of welders, millwrights, crane operators, steam engineers, electricians, pipe fitters and all types of experience in all kinds of work. We believe that we deserve a chance to make a living. We believe that we should be able to feed our families. We would like to get out of the cheese and butter lines and get in lines where we buy and pay for what we want instead of having to take whatever they give. That's degrading and inhumane."

12. Justice Delayed
—The Case Against Envirodyne

The Wisconsin Steel workers always wanted a jury trial. They felt sure that any jury in Chicago would give them every penny they asked for. Evidently the Navistar lawyers also thought a jury would sympathize with the workers and believe that they had been cheated. To avoid a trial, Harvester-Navistar offered a settlement in 1988. Meanwhile many Wisconsin Steel workers, the number was thought to be 500, had died, including Florencio Ortega and Ernest Syrek, two of the six original signers of the suit. Their heirs would get the deceased workers' share of the award. But for the workers who died before tasting victory, it was truly an instance of "Justice delayed is justice denied."

The settlement of $14.8 million was not that much when divided among 2,700 hourly workers. Those who lost most in the closing got a larger part of the settlement, about $17,000. Frank's share was a little over $4,000, not much for eight years of struggle. Still, to win against such odds was a fantastic victory, and encouraged workers everywhere. The settlement did not go beyond 1977, the date when Envirodyne took over the mill. Workers were not ready to let it go at that. They wanted to be paid for the benefits they earned in the two and a half years that they worked for Envirodyne.

Meanwhile, Envirodyne used the cash from the Wisconsin Steel deal to successfully enter other leveraged buyouts, mergers and all the other financial speculations rampant in the 1980s and 1990s. At one point, Envirodyne made the "Fortune 500" list of wealthiest corporations.

A couple of the original owners of Envirodyne bailed out, selling the company for a very high figure. Naturally, the buyers of Envirodyne didn't use their own money either, but borrowed money

196

at high interest rates (junk bonds). The Envirodyne empire included Vikase, a manufacturer of plastic sausage casings with profitable plants in France and the U.S.

The Case Against Envirodyne

Save Our Jobs was demanding that Envirodyne pay the millions of dollars in pension benefits earned between 1977 and 1980, about $25 million. Lumpkin refused to get tired or old until the case was carried as far as it could go. Geoghegan also could have quit with the Harvester settlement. But justice had not been done. Much as he "wanted to get on with his life," Geoghegan could not walk away from the Wisconsin Steel workers. He optimistically thought that a suit against Envirodyne would be wrapped up in a couple of years since the legal groundwork had been laid in the Harvester suit.

Unfortunately, Envirodyne had been milked almost dry by its first owners and the junk bond companies. Envirodyne filed for, and was allowed to proceed with bankruptcy. SOJ was in Bankruptcy Court again! Then, the Federal District Court dealt another blow to the workers' case. The judge threw out the suit, accepting the company's

Protest at Wisconsin Steel, March 28, 1993

claim that the five-year statute of limitations had expired. Geoghegan went to Appellate Court and successfully argued that a ten-year statute of limitations applied to cases under ERISA, the pension security law. The Appellate Court ruled for the workers and reinstated that part of the case concerned with pensions. The case then bounced back and forth for a few more years between Bankruptcy Court and Federal District Court.

"Little" Ed Sadlowski Joins SOJ

All this time, Frank and the SOJ were picketing, demonstrating, holding forums on unemployment, maintaining a food pantry for the unemployed, signing petitions for public works jobs programs, giving $3-a-plate dinners to raise money and keeping the case and hope alive. Tired SOJ warriors received new energy and ideas from "Little" Ed A. Sadlowski, a young union leader who had joined their staff. Frank called the 6-footer "Little Ed" because he was the son of Edward E. Sadlowski, former director of District 31 of USWA. Little Ed worked for SOJ on a small salary for two years and four more years as a volunteer. He wrote the following account of SOJ actions at Envirodyne for this book:

SOJ vs Envirodyne

To fix the exact amount that Envirodyne owed the workers, SOJ had to hire an actuary. It was decided to issue SOJ membership cards to workers who would contribute $20 for the actuary. I typed mailing labels, begged some stamps from the USWA Subdistrict office and sent out letters explaining the need. Checks for $20 began coming in from all over the country. Lines formed for weeks at the SOJ office as workers brought in their $20 to pay for the cost of an actuary.

We also set up our own picket detail at a plant owned by Envirodyne, located across the street from Chicago's Southeast city line. Rain or shine, hot or cold weather, we marched outside the plant gates and past the administrative offices. The guys had large signs that read, "Envirodyne pays its workers with rubber checks." Some of the men carried placards of their last paychecks, which had bounced when Wisconsin Steel closed. It made a very disturbing visual for those folks who had to cross our picket line each day on their way to their jobs. We also started to have an effect on management at the location. Soon the curtains in the office windows were drawn each time we appeared and a leaflet was sent to employees directing them not to interact with us. The leaflet misinformed the workers, claiming that our struggle was with another party. We knew differently.

Then the Bedford Park police decided to get into the act. First we were warned that we couldn't picket in Bedford Park without first obtaining a permit. We were instructed to get off the sidewalk. If we wanted to picket, we would have to do it across the street, on the Chicago side. We agreed to avoid confrontation at that time, and we moved our line across the street. After a meeting of the Save Our Jobs Committee, and with the advice of counsel, we decided to make a stand with the police.

The next day we were out in full force. We started picketing on the Chicago side. Then about a dozen of us crossed over to the Bedford Park side of the street. The police promptly appeared, and our pickets dispersed back across the street. I refused to move. After a heated debate between myself and one of Bedford Park's finest, I was handcuffed and taken into custody. While sitting in the patrol car, it happened. All of the guys began crossing over to the Bedford Park side of the street. It was a very inspirational experience. The police had now identified Frank as our leader and directed him to order the members of the Save Our Jobs Committee back across the street. Frank bargained for my release, saying that the men would cross back peacefully if I were released. The police refused, saying that a paddy wagon was on its way to take all the pickets into custody. Later, we found out that the Bedford Park Police did not have a paddy wagon.

A few moments later, the Bedford Park chief of police arrived and I was taken to the police station. By the time Frank arrived at the police station, the police had released me without charges being filed. Their lawyer must have told them that they were violating our constitutional right to picket. We returned to picket and had no more trouble with the police.

We also decided that we would start to "bird dog" Maxine and Robert Lynde, then the owners of Envirodyne. In later years they sold off the company for junk bonds, setting the stage for Envirodyne's bankruptcy. We began leafleting Envirodyne's corporate headquarters located along Chicago's "Magnificent Mile." That was real enjoyable picket duty. There we were, outside this luxurious high-rise, mostly older blue-collar types, handing out leaflets to people getting in and out of chauffeured limos, wearing fur coats or $1,500 suits. People walking by or going into the building were visibly shaken by the experience. We were having the time of our lives. That strategy came to an end after we pulled off a Worker's Memorial Service on Memorial Day. We loaded a school bus—Frank always travels with a loaded school bus. On the sidewalk in front of the building, we held a candlelight vigil to remember the Wisconsin Steel workers who had died since the mills closed on March 28, 1980.

"Frank always travels with a loaded school bus"

We had public officials, a Catholic priest, labor speeches on top of a soap box, a folk singer and a gospel singer. It was a very successful event. We returned for our regular handbilling on the following Friday, just four days later, to learn that Envirodyne had moved its entire corporate headquarters 45 miles, out to the northwestern Chicago suburbs. We took a car caravan to the new location, a 1½ hour's drive from the Save Our Jobs office in South Chicago. We had changed the placards to read, "Envirodyne, you can run but you can't hide," and, "We're back!" We felt that we were very effective at what we were doing. We were really enjoying ourselves and proud of what we were accomplishing.—Ed Sadlowski

Envirodyne Bankrupt

Meanwhile, according to *Crain's Chicago Business*, the Envirodyne lawyers were taking millions of dollars out of the bankrupt company, draining away money that should have gone to the workers. The Corporation lawyers charged $400 an hour. At that rate it did not take long to make a million dollars. Finally, Envirodyne settled with its corporate creditors in Bankruptcy Court by giving them shares of company stock. That left only the Wisconsin Steel worker claims, typically the last to be considered.

The Envirodyne suit was even more complicated than the case against Harvester-Navistar. The advice of bankruptcy lawyers was needed. Actuaries were hired at the prevailing fee of $400 an hour to calculate the damages sought. Geoghegan brought in additional legal help from the law firm of Leslie and Tom Jones.

Attorney (and Mother) Leslie Jones

Attorney Leslie Jones showed a degree of dedication that amazed the women at a Save Our Jobs rally. Since Tom Geoghegan was out of town, she filled in for him at an important Wisconsin Steel workers meeting. Frank expected 300 workers, and some of them had not yet arrived. He hoped Jones could wait. But she had come to the rally on her way to the delivery room at the hospital. Her "water bag" had already broken! Jones' son was born two hours after she calmly gave a report on the legal status of the workers' case. Geoghegan went all out to praise her legal contribution, saying, "God sent me a brilliant lawyer, Leslie Jones, to help the Wisconsin Steel workers win their case."

Just before Christmas 1995, a settlement was finally reached. Another year of hard work remained before the checks were finally issued. Ironically, the settlement was in the form of stock. For a few short months, the Wisconsin Steel workers were major Envirodyne stockholders.

Envirodyne refused to administer the settlement and the messy job of selling the stock at the right time and finding all the claimants or their heirs was dumped on the workers' lawyers. The Save Our Jobs Committee continued to keep people together until every cent of the settlement was paid out.

**Attorneys Tom Geoghegan and Leslie Jones report on suit against Envirodyne.
Art Vassey photo. *Daily Southtown*, March 29, 1995**

The settlement brought a sense of completion; a long, long struggle carried through to a final victory. But it did not bring as much joy as the first settlement with Harvester-Navistar. Hundreds of workers had died in the eight years since the 1988 settlement. The case against Envirodyne was signed in 1988 by Frank Lumpkin, Wayne Schwartz, Augustus Delbertson, Rafael Alvarez, John Randall and Felix Vasquez. Delbertson did not live to see the victory. Frank was 80 years old and Tom Geoghegan, the young lawyer Frank met in 1981, had some gray hairs.

As Much Justice as Workers Could Win

At last, justice would be done. Or at least as much justice as workers could win when a company is in Bankruptcy Court. The settlement realized only $4,000,000; it would have been five or six times larger had the company not been allowed to file bankruptcy.

Even Lumpkin was surprised when 500 workers and heirs of deceased workers crowded the union hall at the Save Our Jobs meeting on January 2, 1996. Geoghegan congratulated the workers and their heirs, "If people hadn't worked as a group, if Frank Lumpkin hadn't kept this incredible group together, we would not get anything—nada."

Little Ed drove in from Madison, Wisconsin to participate in the historic meeting. He reported Frank's comments for *Union Labor News*, monthly publication of Wisconsin's South Central Federation of Labor:

The dollar amount that we're going to get on the settlement doesn't move me. What moves me is that these sons of a gun tried to get away with it and we stopped them. The lawyer stopped them, and more importantly, the people stopped them. Envirodyne doesn't give a damn about people. We know that; we worked for them. That's what made me so mad. Before the plant shut down, these guys wouldn't even talk to the workers. I think this is a real victory. They didn't just walk over us and do what they wanted to do. The people stopped them, and I feel very good about what we have accomplished together. [100]

Little Ed also recorded Tom Geoghegan's thoughts "as to what this case represents to the average worker."

This is a story to pass down, from one generation to the next. It's part of a bigger hidden story in this country, one that you won't find in the mainstream media. That people have to band together, hang together, and sometimes invent a union as these workers have done here, when a nominal one collapsed. Even more important is that people refused to be whipped and did create a union and come together. That is the most exciting and important thing about the Wisconsin Steel and the Save Our Jobs Committee story. [101]

Frank Lumpkin agreed with this evaluation, but he called Save Our Jobs a "movement," not a union. He shared Geoghegan's sense of history and hoped that the case sent a warning to other companies thinking about cheating workers out of their pensions.

Rank and File Heroes

Save Our Jobs officers had worked in their office without pay for many years. Robert Thompson of the blooming mill was in there every day. Unlike Lumpkin and many other workers, Thompson was good at keeping records. He was one of many whose names seldom appeared in the newspapers but who kept the Wisconsin Steel battle alive for 17 years.

As the "Lumpkin case" against Envirodyne dragged on over the years, the Save Our Jobs bank account got thinner and thinner. Monthly donations by Wisconsin Steel workers were not enough to

"Little Ed" Sadlowski and Lumpkin (top); with USWA strikers at Acme Steel (bottom)

pay the office rent. The committee reached an understanding with subdistrict director Edward Sadlowski ("Big Ed"). Sadlowski had been district director before he made a historic run for International President on a union democracy program.) The agreement with the steel union allowed Wisconsin Steel workers to work around the union hall as payment for their rent. When Sadlowski retired in 1994, the Save Our Jobs Committee stayed put in its office. As Frank explained:

> "The new subdistrict director of USWA knows what we're trying to do. He [Sadlowski, Sr.] told them, 'These guys [SOJ] will be the backbone of the union. They will go on your picket lines, come to your mass meetings, help you keep the hall. I don't want you to charge them a penny [for rent].' "

For years, Frank, Benny Muñoz, and other workers paid the office rent in kind by doing work on the union grounds, seven days a week. Whatever the weather, they were there in the morning to clean up the parking lots and grassy areas. Depending on the season, they would shovel the snow or cut the grass, trim the trees and pick up large amounts of debris. Frank was never afraid of making a seven-day a week commitment, whether it was maintaining the steel union grounds, or bringing his blind neighbor a hamburger every day.

Lumpkin and the News Media

Frank Lumpkin developed a personal relationship with the working press. Newspeople recognized him as a genuine workers' spokesperson. He had come a long way since the City Hall press conference in which he had kept photographers and reporters waiting because he didn't know he was the "star" of the show.

Dick Longworth, a *Chicago Tribune* writer, was one of the first to recognize the fightback as historic, calling it, "The Wisconsin Steel Workers Saga." Longworth called Lumpkin a "saint, if there's such a thing in Chicago."[102] Shortly after these words of praise, the *Tribune* transferred Longworth to Europe. Perhaps Lumpkin did satisfy some requirements for Chicago "sainthood." He stood his ground in the face of physical threats and never surrendered his principles. He worked for the Wisconsin Steel workers full time, without pay, for 17 years. But the truth is that he was having a wonderful time because he was making a difference. Saint may not be the right word because there is little that is other-worldly about Lumpkin. Nor were the victories won by the Wisconsin Steel workers "miracles."

Cindy Richards in the *Sun-Times* covered the workers' victory in her "Commentary" column. In the last years of the case, Kathy Orr gave Save Our Jobs extensive coverage in the *Southtown Economist* (successor of the *Daily Calumet*). Lumpkin's picture, as "South Chicago's Man of Steel," graced many a front page of the *Southtown Economist* and *The Times* of Hammond, IN. Mike Giocondo and Herb Kransdorf, of the CPUSA's *People's Weekly World*, brought the Wisconsin Steel workers' story to thousands around the country. *The Los Angeles Times, The Progressive, the Atlantic Monthly, The Christian Science Monitor* and *the Chicago Magazine* were among the publications that featured Lumpkin and SOJ.

In Mexico, people read about the case in *Excelsior* and in France it was covered in *Le Monde*. The Wisconsin Steel workers' struggle appeared on Moscow TV. Newspapers in Mozambique, Africa and the People's Republic of Korea interviewed Lumpkin. Extensive television coverage, especially in the '80s, probably reached even larger audiences than the printed media. Street action by SOJ helped keep the public interested. Otherwise the case could have appeared to be an uninteresting, drawn-out legal issue.

Some authors let Lumpkin speak for himself and were rewarded with some of the best pieces in their books. In *Which Side Are You On?* Tom Geoghegan credits Lumpkin with the motto, "Always Bring a Crowd."[103] As a leader, Lumpkin never separated himself from other workers, physically or spiritually. He knew his strength came from the people who supported their cause, more than the force of his individual personality. In an interview for Studs Terkel's book, *Race,* Frank gave a clear explanation of who gains and who loses from racism. *The Nation* reprinted the interview under the title "I'm Saying Racism Is Unnatural."[104]

Lumpkin got another chance to speak for himself in *Ten Good Lives*, a prize-winning TV documentary produced by Jay Shefsky for WTTW, "Chicago's Window to the World." Lumpkin took viewers for a walk through the closed mill while he told the story of the steel workers' fight to survive. The documentary was based on a sculpture exhibit, on permanent display at DePaul University's Monsignor Egan Center. The exhibit includes a bronze bust of Frank in hard hat and working clothes. Margot MacMahon, the sculptor, titled the collection, "Plain hard working,"[105] an apt description of Lumpkin. However, his love of useful work is just a part of his love and confidence in working people. That may be the magnet that attracts working people to him, the confidence that together they can win.

Frank's promotion of *Labor Today* in the '80s and the *Peoples Weekly World* helped link Wisconsin Steel workers with the larger labor movement. For several years, Save Our Jobs also published its own quarterly newspaper, the *Wisconsin Steel Workers Save Our Jobs News* to bring its news to the steel workers community. Lumpkin never underestimated the power of the grassroots press, whether it was just the mimeographed *Wooded Highlands Comet* he edited in Gary, or the nationally circulated *Peoples Weekly World.*

Above all, Frank understood the power of organized workers. And people all over the city were encouraged by his example. Frank responded to the call by Congressmen Bobby Rush, Danny Davis and Jesse Jackson to demonstrate for the Public Works Jobs Bill in 1997. Young people were brought over to meet him, "the man who won justice for the Wisconsin Steel workers." They asked him how he did it. "Unity—workers cooperated; we fought together," he replied." At a Labor Day Rally at Chicago's Navy Pier, Frank took a seat that had been reserved for members of the Food and Commercial Workers Union. Frank offered to return the seat to the ticket holder who showed up late. "No," Frank was told, "If you're who I think you are, you can have my seat, any day." One worker even stopped his car in mid-traffic, flung the door open and ran up to the train platform where Frank was standing, to yell, "Lumpkin, remember me? I worked in 6-Mill."

It was an even exchange. Workers and Frank Lumpkin gained strength from each other.

Part IV

"When I see you, I know things are in good hands."
Mayor Harold Washington to Frank Lumpkin.

13. Political Action and Mayor Washington

Although Save Our Jobs was strictly non-partisan, the Wisconsin Steel workers were always in the middle of the political storms. Alderman Vrdolyak, PSWU attorney, was a close associate of Mayor Byrne. More than one Wisconsin Steel worker was on the payroll of the Vrdolyak machine. When Wisconsin Steel closed, PSWU President Tony Roque was rewarded with a city job. Whenever Frank visited City Hall or Park Department facilities, he would be hailed by former Wisconsin Steel workers who had city jobs. Some Wisconsin Steel workers worked the precincts for Vrdolyak. After the mill closed and it became known that the PSWU contract gave up pension rights, pro-Vrdolyak sentiment began to evaporate.

Save Our Jobs had both friends and enemies among public office holders. Soon after a Jimmy Carter reelection rally, Byrne, Vrdolyak and Roque made their infamous promise of "turkey on the table for Thanksgiving." In contrast to machine politicians, progressive public officials gave crucial support to SOJ. State Rep. Miriam Balanoff donated office space. State Rep. Carol Moseley-Braun and State Sen. Richard Newhouse always responded to Frank's call.

They opened the right doors for the steel workers when SOJ delegations visited the State Legislature. Congressman Gus Savage invited SOJ to put their case before Congress in a special order of business. As Congressman, Harold Washington was also an early supporter of Save Our Jobs. In turn many Wisconsin Steel workers followed Frank's lead and actively campaigned to elect these progressive candidates. SOJ, as a committee, remained non-partisan.

Jesse Jackson and Frank Lumpkin at press conference announcing Harold Washington's candidacy for mayor (Scott Marshall photo, 1982)

Harold Washington for Mayor

The Lumpkins were part of the political explosion that elected Harold Washington Mayor of Chicago in 1983. The Washington campaign was historic for the way it mobilized people. People called it a movement more than a campaign. The bright flame of hope flared up in all of the depressed areas of the city. When Washington was the speaker at Save Our Jobs meetings, the hall was packed, whatever the weather. Coalition building reached a new level with labor and Communists playing a significant role. Progressives of the Mexican, Puerto Rican and other Latino, and white communities joined hands with African Americans to elect Washington.

African American civic organizations, churches, volunteer voter registrars and other groups of activists gave crucial support. They registered, brought to the polls and safeguarded the ballots of the 98% turnout achieved in many Black districts.

Young People Made the Difference

Frank was thrilled by the participation of young people in the Washington campaign. Young people, formerly alienated from electoral politics, came forward to lead voter registration drives. Young, keen-eyed watchers guarded the count and fought for every vote. Youths poured out into the streets to help in any way they could. Frank thought he was seeing the future, the movements to come that would force people's needs to the top of the national agenda. Young people had built and led the CIO in the '30s and they made the difference in Chicago in 1983.

A lot of credit was due to the candidate himself. As a thoroughgoing progressive, Washington presented a unifying program, sensitive to the needs of women, labor and the racially oppressed. Long before he ran for Mayor, he put himself on the line for the causes he believed in. Years before it was popular, he spoke at antiwar rallies, for peace and for nuclear disarmament. As soon as the Wisconsin Steel plant closed, he was ready to help the workers' cause. Washington, first as Congressman and then as Mayor, always honored an invitation to speak at Save Our Jobs rallies. His election lifted the spirits of the Wisconsin Steel workers.

The Council Wars

The struggle to elect Washington did not end when he won the three-way Democratic primary in 1983 with 36% of the vote. Suddenly, his token Republican opponent, Bernard Epton, became the darling of all of the racist forces. Washington had to win a hard-fought two-way election in April, when he gained 52% of the vote. Then a new stage of struggle, called "the Council Wars," began. "Fast Eddie" Vrdolyak and Edward Burke lined up 29 of the old guard aldermen against the Washington coalition of 21 aldermen. The Burke-Vrdolyak "evil cabal" tried to block every move made by the city's first African American mayor. The racist war against Mayor Washington and the people of Chicago became so ugly that the national press began to refer to the city as "Beirut on the Lake." At that time, civil war and foreign invasions were ravaging Beirut, Lebanon.

Three years of Reaganomics had deepened the economic crisis facing working people. U.S. Steel, Republic Steel (now LTV), Inland Steel, General Motors and Ford plants had laid off thousands of workers in the Chicago area. Some of the Wisconsin Steel workers who had found other jobs were laid off again. By this time, Save Our Jobs had become a resource for many organizations. Frank was on more leadership boards than he could keep up with. These included UNO (United Neighborhood Organization), IPAC (Illinois Public Action Council), JOIN (Jobs Or Income Now), the South Chicago Unemployed Center, CUED (Center for Urban Economic Development) of the University of Illinois, as well as the Communist Party USA.

Frank and SOJ were recognized as a resource by the media, TV newscasters, radio news, and the newspapers. A TV newsman asked Frank to find a family being evicted from their home so that they could film the tragedy. He told the newsmen that all they had to do was drive up and down the streets of South Chicago and they would see more than one eviction. The next family Lumpkin saw being evicted had two small children. He called the TV reporter. The reporter and the camera crew hurried to the eviction scene. After they asked a few questions, they left without filming the scene. To Frank's questions, they replied, "We can't show this example. Those children are illegitimate. The woman isn't even married!" Frank was angry and disgusted. How could children be "illegitimate?"

Lumpkin on the Mayor's Task Forces

After the 1983 election, Harold Washington appointed Frank to two of the Mayor's Task Forces: On Hunger and On Dislocated Workers. He also served as an advisor for the Mayor's Steel Task Force. That was part of his work for SOJ. He seldom allowed himself a day off. Frank admitted, that for years he "got up with SOJ in the morning and went to bed with it at night."

Although Mayor Washington's Task Forces were strictly advisory, they served to put the spotlight on workers' issues, including the need for a moratorium on evictions and shutoffs of utilities. In the *Report of the Mayor's Task Force on Hunger*, October 1984, Frank said, "The Federal Government has plenty of money. They're just spending it for the wrong things, for nuclear bombs that must never be used. Freeze the bomb; feed the people."

Lumpkin made the following proposals to the Task Force:

1. The only real solution for the steel workers is jobs.
2. Establish a national policy to rebuild the cities' infrastructure.
3. Do not destroy Wisconsin Steel and U.S. Steel.
4. Unemployment insurance for the duration of unemployment.
5. Provide unemployment compensation to young people looking for their first job.
6. Establish more food distribution centers.

Mayor Washington must have agreed with the spirit of Lumpkin's report to the Task Force on Hunger. He was the featured speaker at the March 29, 1985 Save Our Jobs Rally. Mayor Washington told the steel workers and their friends that Congress was talking about spending $40 billion on MX missiles. "There's your money, sinking into the ground," Washington said. "This is crazy. This is madder than mad. This is insane. The money for one missile could put you all back to work."[106]

1987 Mayoralty Elections

By the 1987 mayoralty elections, support for the progressive coalition around Mayor Washington had increased. The Democratic primary was a two-way race with Harold Washington winning with 53% of the votes to Jane Byrne's 47%. The opposition had agreed not to split the "white vote" and had rallied around Byrne.

Although the primary was over, it looked as though Washington would face two white Democratic candidates in the general election. They were Tom Hynes, county assessor and a Daley ally who was willing to carry the racist flag as "the great white hope," and "Fast Eddie Vrdolyak." During the "Council Wars," the Vrdolyak name had come to stand for the white racist assault against Mayor Washington. Both Hynes and Vrdolyak were running on "third party" tickets. A split of the racist, anti-Washington vote seemed assured. Two days before the election, Hynes withdrew. When Congressman William Lipinski (D) heard that Hynes had withdrawn, he proclaimed him as one of America's greatest heroes. "They'll have to add another chapter to *Profiles in Courage*," Lipinski said.[107] Observers less blinded by racism thought that Hynes withdrew to avoid making a poor showing on Election Day.

Hundreds of Wisconsin Steel workers march to Mayor Washington's community forum.
Daily Calumet Photo, Sept. 23, 1983

Despite the frantic maneuvers of the machine, the Washington coalition gained ground in the 1987 mayoralty elections. In the Latino communities the Washington vote increased 400%, reflecting the strengthened coalition of African American and Latino voters. The Chicago Federation of Labor (CFL) endorsed Washington at a tense, packed meeting in 1987. Over 1,000 delegates crowded the hall instead of the usual 150 who attended the monthly meetings. In 1983 the CFL had endorsed Byrne against Washington. South Chicago steel union locals played a key role in the CFL endorsement of Washington. Steel locals and auto locals paid up their back dues so they could vote.

In the two-way general election, Washington won with 53% to Vrdolyak's 42%. The Washington percentage of the vote made a gain of only 1% over the 1983 election, and the total vote had dropped over 13%.[108] One explanation for the drop in turnout, especially in predominantly African American wards, was the belief that the re-election of Washington was a sure thing.

At that time, Washington and Lumpkin had a special relationship, but it was not a personal relationship. It was deeper than a personal relationship. Washington seemed to draw strength from Lumpkin's participation. At meetings, rallies, street encounters, whatever, Washington would call Frank over and say, "When I see you, I know things are in good hands." At a groundbreaking for the South Chicago Learning Center, a reporter asked Mayor Washington, "What are you doing about jobs?" Washington turned to Frank and replied, "I'm working with Lumpkin." That answer was profoundly true, not just an evasion of a reporter's question.

Washington was Mayor, but the city's economy was still controlled by the LaSalle Street bankers and the transnational companies. The basic, economic injustices remained in place – unemployment, lack of housing, low wages, under-funded schools and lack of health care. In Mayor Washington's five years in office, he extended collective bargaining for city employees and brought street services to communities that had never been served. The biggest change was that people began to believe that they had the power to win better living conditions. Had he lived to serve out his second term, Chicago history could have taken a different turn.

On the Mayor's Task Forces, Frank promoted changes in national priorities. He called for cuts in funding of the high-profit military contracts and increased funding to rebuild the cities and to create jobs. Frank believed that public works jobs programs could turn Chicago's economy around. Wisconsin Steel, publicly owned since 1981, could have been a model for government action to revive steel production in Chicago. Unfortunately, time ran out before the movement could consolidate and build for the future. Washington suffered a massive heart attack in 1987. His death closed a window of opportunity for people's organizations, leaving them to carry on their struggles without the leader they loved.

Many believed that he died prematurely, a victim of the constant pressure of racist attacks. The attacks even included a barrage of stones thrown at him when he and a white priest were attending a meeting to overcome racial division. In the 1983 campaign, Washington appeared trim and fit. He put it like this: "I'm 60, I look 50, and I feel 40. Everything works and nothing hurts." After over four years of "Council Wars," Washington had become 100 pounds overweight with an enlarged heart and blocked arteries.

Vrdolyak never ran for office again after his loss to Washington in 1987. Some weeks after that election, Vrdolyak made a quick trip to Washington, D.C., presumably to Republican national headquarters. He bolted the Democratic Party for the Republicans but failed to drag the East Side with him. He became the host of a radio talk show and is believed to retain considerable political power.

Mayor Harold Washington, Congressman Gus Savage, Frank Lumpkin and Willie Ross, president of USWA Local 65

"I'd be honest if I said I was led as much as I led. It didn't go just the way I thought. Sometimes the workers led me." Lumpkin

14. Send a Steel worker to Springfield

After Wisconsin Steel workers won their $14.8 million settlement from Harvester-Navistar, the whole neighborhood applauded the great victory. Lumpkin never took the applause, or the attacks, personally. His style of combining optimism and reality had a lot to do with the broad support he attracted. Looking back on his experience of struggle, he said:

> "I know one thing. Things continue to go forward. How do I know? I read a little Marxism and I've got some experience. It doesn't mean it's going straight forward. You have to take one step forward and two steps sideward and one step backward and three steps forward. I'd be honest if I said I was led, as much as I led. It didn't go just the way I thought. Sometimes the workers led me.
>
> After the plant closed, the workers demanded that we go to Roque. I said, no way. I'm not fighting the union. I have no intention of fighting the union. It was a foolish thing. They had guns. We're lucky that the press came or a couple of guys could have been killed. Roque told us, 'Lumpkin's doing what he has to do and I'm doing what I have to do.' I knew he was taking orders. I take mine from the workers."

In the summer of 1988, Lumpkin entered politics in a big way. The *People's Weekly World* newspaper threw a big dinner to honor Frank Lumpkin and the Save Our Jobs Committee. Bouquets of roses were presented to Juanita Andrade and Beatrice Lumpkin. They accepted the honor for the SOJ Women's Committee which included Mattie Dixon, Olga Sabola, Rhoda Thompson, Anne O'Neill, Cruz Torres, Martha Cervantes, Delois Randall and Marta Castaneda. They were glad they did not have to collect, cook and serve the meal.

Four hundred labor leaders, politicians and rank and file workers came to the dinner. The dinner attracted a group of *Chicago Tribune* strikers, whose strike had dragged on for years even after some of the craft unions had gone back to work. Frank Lumpkin and the Wisconsin Steel workers gave *the Tribune* strikers renewed hope. The strikers were also grateful for the support that Save Our Jobs had given them on the picket line over the years. At the dinner, people began to ask, "Well, when is he running for political office?"

Lumpkin for State Representative

The steel workers had learned the hard way that many of the laws favored the big companies. Workers said to Frank, "Why not run for office?" Frank had said all along that laws are made for the benefit of the rich. Wasn't it time for a workers' spokesperson to go to the state legislature and fight for laws to benefit workers? So Frank decided to run for state representative in the 25th district, a seat being vacated by the independent Democrat, Carol Moseley-Braun.

Should Frank run in the Democratic Party primary? Perhaps he would have had a better chance of being elected had he taken that route. But it was more than his own election that he had in mind. His goal was to build an independent political base for labor, to build a movement for a labor-based people's party. He decided not to go the Democratic Party route.

The machine saw Moseley-Braun's leaving as an opportunity to bring the district back into the Daley fold. They nominated Donne E. Trotter as their candidate, considered a close associate of John Stroger, a prominent leader of the South Side Democratic machine. The successful 1983 campaign of Harold Washington for mayor had to overcome the opposition of Stroger and other machine politicians.

The district included a middle class area in Hyde Park near the University of Chicago, and the mostly working-class, African American communities of South Shore and Avalon. It did not include a large concentration of steel workers. Still, Lumpkin's work with the steel workers was widely known.

With the call, "Send a Steel Worker to Springfield," Lumpkin's campaign literature advanced national and local action issues. His campaign folder called Lumpkin , "the exceptional candidate," who led a winning steel workers' struggle. Quotations from leading Chicago newspapers were featured:

218

Lumpkin, campaign manager Al Ellis (rear center) and supporters at closed USX Southworks
Scott Marshall Photo

His Georgia drawl and gentle ways can fool you. He used to be a prizefighter... and spent 30 years wrestling hot metal for Wisconsin Steel—M. W. Newman, *The Chicago Sun-Times.*

An amazing man ... Lumpkin, who is probably as close to a saint as Chicago has these days, rallied the workers, kept them together, labored to keep their spirits up.— R. C. Longworth, The *Chicago Tribune.*

He's a hero in our book—*Daily Calumet*[109]

Health Care For All

Among the campaign issues, the first was access to health care, including a trauma center for the South Side. Two big, private, teaching hospitals on the South Side had been allowed to remove themselves from the trauma network that had served the South Side. Steel workers who lost their jobs in plant closings or downsizings felt the loss of health care immediately. Most could not qualify for Medicaid and had no way to pay for doctors or hospital care. Even the better-paid skilled workers felt the issue of medical care keenly. In a short time after the plant closing, their reserves were gone and conditions became desperate in cases of serious illness.

Loss of plant-covered medical insurance was a devastating blow to the Wisconsin Steel workers, including Wayne Schwartz and Carl Fitko.[110] Schwartz's wife was receiving cancer treatments when Wisconsin Steel closed. Wayne had 28 years at Wisconsin Steel as an electrician. These excerpts are from a discussion recorded in the SOJ Office in 1982.

Wayne Schwartz, electrician:

"I never expected this. And it still doesn't seem like they have done it except there are no paydays. It doesn't seem real. You go by there and you still expect it to come to life. But as the days go by, you begin to wonder. The chances are slimmer and slimmer.

"Unemployment compensation helped. When that ran out, I got a few side jobs. Then the hospitalization started increasing. On the conversion plan it jumped from $500 something every three months to $971 every three months. It'll be increased on my next premium. It increases every birthday. They send you a notice and say, "Due to the rising costs of hospital expenses, your premium is being increased. I'll be paying over $1,000 quarterly. And my pension is $400 a month. Right now that averages out to $82 a week for hospitalization."

Bea Lumpkin:
"Isn't there some other way to get medical care?"

Schwartz:
"If there is I haven't found it. The medical insurance is just for my wife and myself, and it's $300 deductible. There's nothing you can do but pay it. My savings are going fast. Everything keeps rising. Your taxes go up. The food prices go up and nothing's coming down. The pension stays the same. When you see kids 25 or 20 can't get a job, how's a guy of 56 going to find a job?

"We thought we had protection through PSWU, but when the mill closed and the days went by, we found that no one was on our side. We had to form the Save Our Jobs Committee to get the little information we did get to try to do something.

"There are a lot of people worse off than us. We feel sorry for ourselves until we talk to somebody else, healthwise, financial. There's one fellow in the billet dock—he's lost legs from diabetes since the place has shut down. You feel sorry for yourself until you see a case like that. I've got my health.

"I'm pretty well off. That guy, what chance has he got? He's got small kids and he's lost a foot. Then little by little, they worked up to his knee. What the heck can he do? His savings are gone. Financially, he's shot. Physically, he's shot.

"When I got my last hospitalization bill, I lost faith in everything. I lost faith in government, the system, everything. I figure I put six years in the service and they could pull that on me.

"I think we'd be further ahead with socialized medicine. They have that in Canada. I have a relation in Canada, and they've told me about socialized medicine. I think it would be a darn good thing if they had it here. I may be wrong, but from what I've read about it, I think that's what they need here. We could take a few lessons from England, from those European countries. But this country would never admit it. We're the best in everything. They pay compensation [in England] until you find a job. I think the American Medical Association will fight to keep the socialized medicine out. So I don't think we'll see that for a long time.

"Yes, I voted for Reagan. I did. I figured, give him a chance. What he promised and what he's done are two different things altogether. When he ran for election he promised a lot of things. Just say he talks with a forked tongue. We lost our jobs under Carter but we can't find a job under Reagan."

Fitko, another Wisconsin Steel electrician:
"I know Wayne ain't against this country. He's just bitter because he ain't got a job."

Schwartz:

"Sure I'm bitter. That's right. Bills come up the way they are. I think labor should get a heck of a lot more consideration. It seems to be a lopsided deal right now. I'm bitter about a lot of things, ha. I'm going to be a heck of a lot more bitter when I get my next premium notice."

Bea Lumpkin:

"That's hard to understand, how a country as rich as this can't take care of the health of its people."

Schwartz:

"Yeah, I can't figure it out. And it's the same way with the old people. When a person gets to be 70 in this country, you'd be better off taking him out, shooting him. I mean, I've seen some of these nursing homes. They're not free. They're over $1,000 a month. But I've also seen some of these other countries that take care of their old people. They put them up on a pedestal and take care of them."

Fitko:

"I got no money to pay for nothing. I got out of the hospital and they handed me a bill for $5,400. I almost had to laugh. I told them I've got no 5,400 bucks. She said, 'Someone's got to pay for it.'

"I had a hernia. I got it in the mill. When I got out it broke open. There's no mill left. So I went down to 88th and Cottage for aid. I couldn't get nothing from them. So I went down to see my doctor. He said, 'Go in the hospital.' So I went in the hospital like a regular patient. Signed all the papers like I had a job and everything. I went in on the 29th, got operated on the 30th of April. Got out on the 4th of May. They handed me the bill. I says I've got no 5,400 bucks. I've got nothing to pay it with. So they kept sending me all kinds of letters. I've got no money. It's just like the credit union. I owe them $4,000. I've got no money to pay them either. But I'm still smiling. There's no sense crying."

Schwartz:

"If you want to cry, I'll cry with you."

Fitko:

"Things are bad. Like Wayne says, there are others worse off. My pension is $400 a month. They can't take any of that. I'm 54. It's a long time to 65. They're going to change it to 68. All that's Reagan's work."

Schwartz:

"If I had a job that was nice and easy and didn't have to go to work until 9 o'clock, I'd like to work until I'm 90. I'd never want to stay home. I don't think any guy wants to stay home who's worked all his life. I enjoy working. When you get up in the morning and you go to work, you enjoy it. Somebody to talk to. Meet different people every day. Better than staying home like I'm doing now, doing nothing. Can't find a job. There are no jobs. Period."

How to Win an Election

The Committee to Elect Frank Lumpkin got advice from Leon Despres. Despres had many years of experience in independent politics as alderman for the 5th Ward, and as parliamentarian for Mayor Washington. Despres had good advice: Raise a minimum of $30,000 and get a committee of 1,000 volunteers. That was how he won his election campaigns.

Probably it would have worked for Lumpkin too. But the workers and students who backed Lumpkin did not have deep pockets, and little over a third of $30,000 was raised. The campaign managers, Al Ellis, retired auto worker, and Katie Jordan, a leader of the Amalgamated Clothing and Textile Workers Union (ACTWU) and of the Coalition of Labor Union Women (CLUW), did not know any rich donors. They had as many as 200 volunteers who rang doorbells and distributed literature. The University of Chicago Student Committee to Elect Frank Lumpkin worked enthusiastically, carrying one student precinct and helping to win more than 20% of the vote in the other Hyde Park precincts. South Shore precincts brought in 17% of the vote for a district total of about 18% of the vote.

This was an unprecedented showing by an independent candidate. In earlier years, before the 3-representative districts were changed to single-member districts, 18% of the vote could have elected a representative. The Lumpkin campaign achieved ballot status for the Independent Progressive Party. The campaign made a contribution to the 1988 presidential election campaign by raising issues of national importance, especially national health care and jobs.

Two years later, with the Independent Progressives on the ballot, Lumpkin ran again and won the support of locals of the United Steel Workers Union for that campaign. The issues for 1990 remained health care, jobs, housing, lower utility rates, affirmative action, and the peace dividend. Innovative proposals included exemption from state income tax for incomes below $20,000 a year and abolition of the sales tax on food and medicine. In this campaign, Lumpkin was going up against an incumbent and won about 15% of the vote.

Lumpkin Campaigns in Vrdolyak Territory

The third Lumpkin campaign (1992) was the most interesting in some respects. Redistricting gave him a choice of two districts in which to run. He chose the district that included parts of the 10th Ward's East Side, Vrdolyak's home ground. That was the district with many steel workers. In some ways it was also Lumpkin's home ground, even those areas that were exclusively white. Whenever steel workers saw Frank on the East Side, they would rush over to shake his hand and ask him what was new in the Wisconsin Steel struggle. This was in the same area where an African American family had rented a house in 1984, only to be forced to leave after their garage was set on fire.

In 1987, many East Side precincts reported as few as five votes for Mayor Harold Washington. In 1992, Lumpkin averaged 60 votes per precinct with his highest vote 109 compared with 363 for his opponent. A significant number voted like steel workers and broke with the machine. The campaign achieved these results despite a break-in at the campaign headquarters. The office was ransacked; all equipment was stolen.

The 1992 campaign used a studio-type picture of the candidate on flyers and posters. In contrast, the picture used in the earlier campaigns showed Lumpkin in his trademark fedora hat, work shirt and rough jacket. The earlier picture looked like Frank. The 1992 campaign staff decided that their candidate should be shown in a more standard pose. He put on a suit, shirt and tie. The campaign found a gifted photographer who could do wonders with lights. The photographer's lights painted out hard-earned wrinkles to show a smooth, much younger face with hair on top of the head. The studio picture still looked like Frank, but a dressed-up Frank, not the Frank you'd find on the picket line or in the union hall.

In 1996 Lumpkin attended the founding convention of the Labor Party as an elected delegate of the Chicago Chapter of Labor Party Advocates. He supported the leadership of Frank Rosen of Chicago, a UE leader. The Convention voted to form a Labor Party and won considerable union support. When the new Labor Party chose to stay out of the crucial 1996 national elections, Lumpkin thought they made a serious mistake. Still he remains hopeful for the future of the Party.

Front of Lumpkin's 1990 and 1992 campaign folders

"Let the steel giant awake, make it happen and win this job program."
Lumpkin

15. Rebuild our Cities
—Create Jobs

After the Wisconsin Steel workers' cases ended victoriously, the biggest problem remained. Steel workers needed living-wage jobs that paid enough to support their families. The government owned Wisconsin Steel but President Reagan had refused to reopen the mill. SOJ had called on the federal government to start public works jobs projects and to start rebuilding the cities.[111]

Back in 1985, Lumpkin presented a petition for a jobs bill with thousands of signatures collected by SOJ and the National Congress of Unemployed Organizations. In response to this grass roots campaign, Congressman Charles Hayes introduced HR 1398, the Income and Jobs Action Act of 1985. Hayes was a long-time leader of the Packinghouse Workers Union, which merged with the Food and Commercial Workers Union. The Hayes Bill required the President to submit a plan to Congress for federally-funded public works jobs. The effect of the bill was to make the federal government the employer of last resort. Failing that, the bill provided an equivalent income for unemployed workers. The Hayes bill implemented the demand raised in the '60s by Rev. Martin Luther King, Jr. King's demand became the slogan of JOIN, "Jobs Or Income Now."

Hearings on the Income and Jobs Action Act of 1985
Fifty-five members of Congress became co-sponsors of HR 1398. Congressman Hayes invited Lumpkin, as chairperson of the National Unemployed Congress, to testify at a public hearing on the bill. Lumpkin appeared before the Subcommittee on Employment Opportunities, a subcommittee of the Committee on Education and Labor of the House of Representatives. His testimony was backed by

the thick stack of signed petitions he held in his hand—over 10,000 signatures supporting HR 1398. The following excerpt reflects the terrible impact of unemployment on workers' families.

How can one describe the agony of a family head, wife and mother, husband and father, after working over 20 years in a plant or a factory, doing what is legal and right, a worker who believes in the country's laws, because he or she thinks laws are made to protect human rights, and then finds out there are no such laws that protect jobs and income. Well, there should be such laws. And that is why HR 1398 must pass, because jobs or income is the basic human right, the right to survive.

And what we are talking about is the few days' notice you get to pay up or move out. For people in this predicament, it is the last stage in their lives. A man has to watch his wife cry and wonder what his kids think, as they look at him hungry and soon to be homeless. When they cannot pay their mortgage note or rent, they count the days before eviction. The law will come and throw their belongings into the streets. There is no answer to give the kids except that is the law.

And sometimes the kids ask their parents a good question. Who makes the law? Should we tell them, not the people, but Congress? How can Congress make such a law, your children ask. Why, after you put everything you have into your house for years, 10 minutes after you are evicted, the police will put you in jail if you so much as stand on the steps of your house.

Passage of HR 1398 will help people keep their home when they are unemployed through no fault of their own. That is a law that we can explain to our children with pride.[112]

Infrastructure and Job Creation Act of 1995

As eloquently as Lumpkin spoke in 1985, the cries of the unemployed were not loud enough to move a Congress made up mostly of millionaires. Hayes re-introduced the jobs bill in the next sessions of Congress; each time it died in committee. In 1992, Charles A. Hayes, chief sponsor of HR 1398, lost his re-election bid. But the jobs issue did not die. In Chicago, Frank Lumpkin and Scott Marshall led another massive petition drive in support of a California labor initiative. The California Labor Coalition for Public Works Jobs, supported by the State Federation of Labor and affiliates, convinced Congressman Matthew G. Martinez to introduce the "Infrastructure and Job Creation Act of 1995." Congressman

Martinez had chaired the Chicago hearing on the earlier Hayes Bill. No doubt he remembered the testimony for public works jobs at a living wage. The Martinez Bill went further than the Hayes Income and Jobs Act. Instead of relying on presidential action to initiate the jobs program, the "Infrastructure and Job Creation Act" provided $250 billion over a five-year period to create jobs and repair the nation's infrastructure. Communities hardest hit by unemployment would get first preference.

USX Southworks Closes.

From 10,000 workers in the 1970's, the huge Southworks steel mills of USX were down to 1,100 in 1992. Although the mill was operating at a profit, USX shut Southworks down completely in 1992. This company action put the last 1,100 workers out on the street. For the thousands already laid off, closing the mill ended hope of ever being recalled.

The plant, one of the giants of U.S. industry, stands rusting in an area that cries out for structural repairs. Some of the drawbridges over the Little Calumet River that snakes around the steel communities are in such dangerous condition of disrepair that they have been closed to traffic for years.[113] Vaulted sidewalks are collapsing and schools are overcrowded. If the needed repairs were made, they would require all the steel the South Chicago and Northern Indiana mills could make.

One by one, the great mills of South Chicago have shut down. In 1996, just a few hundred workers were left at LTV (Republic) and several hundred at Acme (Interlake). These were all USWA union plants. When they closed, workers received their full benefits: Supplementary Unemployment Benefits, severance pay, pensions including a monthly supplement for Rule 65 workers (age + years of service = 65 or over), and of course, their full pay for hours worked. In that respect, laid-off USWA members were better off than the Wisconsin Steel workers. They did receive benefits that were supposed to cushion the plant closing. But those benefits were soon used up and unemployment compensation lasted only six months.

A study by Julie S. Putterman, sponsored by Southworks Local 65 of the USWA and Hull House Association, showed that unemployed USX workers were going through much the same agony suffered by the Wisconsin Steel workers a few years earlier. In response to a survey, one laid-off worker reported that he had to remove his son's cast himself. Others expressed sentiments such as, "I'll never trust another company again as long as I live[114].

Living-Wage Jobs Needed

In the long years between the Wisconsin Steel workers' February 1988 settlement with Harvester-Navistar and the December 1995 settlement with Envirodyne, Lumpkin kept Save Our Jobs in motion on the jobs issue. On March 1, 1994, SOJ sponsored a community forum "to question candidates for city office about jobs for the unemployed, jobs for young people, and health care for all." The SOJ flyer said, "There is plenty of work that needs to be done. Southeastern Chicago has a massive problem of polluted land. We have a massive army of the unemployed who need jobs." They demanded that first choice for pollution cleanup jobs should go to unemployed steel worker families and community residents.

A few months later, in September 10, 1994, SOJ organized a leadership meeting to promote the public works jobs issue. Several USWA locals participated. Lumpkin opened the meeting with these remarks:

"We, most of us here, have worked a lifetime and would like to see our children have the same right—that is, to be able to work for a living. And earn a living wage.

"You have to answer a machine, and that's what it boils down to. You see some of us were there before the machines so we taught the machine. Like everything else, the people began to teach the teacher. In order to learn you have to be able to teach and learn at the same time. That means we must listen and speak. We have to know each other. We have a similar cause. Together we can solve the problem. We need jobs that will feed, clothe and house our families. Nothing else is sufficient."

By 1994, long-term unemployment had spread like a plague. South Chicago, and Broadway, the "main drag" in Gary, looked like ghost towns. Gangs roamed the streets at will, and dropout rates at the high schools were enormous. Classes at South Chicago's Bowen High School could not use the computer room one semester because someone had broken in during the summer and shot 20 computers through their mother-board hearts. It is impossible to imagine what twisted thoughts may have passed through the vandal(s)' mind(s). Perhaps this senseless act was connected to the hopelessness and despair that spread after the jobs were gone.

Clem Balanoff campaigning on jobs issue at Wisconsin Steel site, 1997

Wives of Steel workers check job creation at trash-to-fuel plant, 1988

Lumpkin insisted that there was no answer to the escalating problems except to create jobs at wages that could support families. Large-scale unemployment and plant closings had spread far beyond the steel mills and auto plants. In steel and auto, joblessness was politely called "structural unemployment." Frank put it more bluntly: "American workers are working themselves out of a job with greater productivity, longer work weeks, and lower take-home pay."

Many unemployed workers were forced to take minimum wage jobs without benefits. One Wisconsin Steel worker reported that he was working at two McDonalds. He worked 20 hours at each, the maximum allowed for "part-time workers." His two small paychecks were not enough to live on and he had no medical coverage.

Referendum on Public Works Jobs

To focus support for public works job projects, SOJ sponsored a petition to put a referendum on the November 8, 1994 ballot in Chicago. Many union members, including steel workers, auto workers and public workers, collected thousands of signatures. Community activists, including neighborhood clubs of the Communist Party, set up petition tables on busy streets. People stood on line to sign the petition. The referendum read:

> Should the Federal Government fund a massive Public Works Jobs Program, including affirmative action, no discrimination against immigrants, that would train and put to work millions of Americans to construct schools, low cost housing, hospital and health clinics, and repair streets, bridges, sewers, and other public systems?

Over 70% of those who voted on the referendum voted "Yes" for public works jobs. The overwhelming approval helped fuel a prairie fire that spread the demand "to bring back the WPA." Although the referendum was only advisory, it provided a strong mandate for federal action to create jobs. Wherever Lumpkin could introduce the question, he raised the issue of jobs. "Public works jobs would bring hope back to South Chicago and Gary," was Lumpkin's argument.

He has no illusions that this program would be easy to win. As former Congressman Hayes had warned the steel workers, many members of Congress are working against jobs bills because they don't want anything that "will prevent them from becoming millionaires." Hayes referred to the perverse reaction of Wall Street to rising unemployment. Stocks go up when unemployment rates rise. Workers' misery spells profits for big corporations.

At this writing in 1999, many labor bodies and municipal bodies have endorsed the Martinez bill. Among political parties, the Communist Party USA has promoted the fight for jobs as a key issue. With few exceptions, there has been no construction of affordable housing for many decades. Public works job projects hold out hope for building affordable housing and reducing homelessness. Frank often reminds people that the homeless were not born homeless. Most became homeless because they were evicted. Many of the homeless are working but cannot pay high rents.

SOJ has campaigned for a jobs bill for many years. As Lumpkin put it, it is "time for the steel giant to awake, to make it happen and win this job program." When the Jobs Bill becomes law, Save Our Jobs will count it as another victory that they helped win.

Labor activists Helen Sutton and Larry McGurty at jobs rally at Wisconsin Steel

"The fight isn't just for money. It's for justice for working people. We have to change the system." Frank Lumpkin

16. The Way it Could Be

Frank's belief in socialism, that there could be a better future for workers, sustained him for the many years he worked in Wisconsin Steel. He was convinced that workers, united, had the power to end exploitation. Service in World War II and trips abroad showed him that the workers' struggle was worldwide. In Cuba he saw a different system working, socialism just a few miles from Florida.

When Wisconsin Steel suddenly closed on March 28, 1980, Frank considered canceling the trip he had planned to Africa. But he reconsidered. He knew that the steel workers' struggle was a long, long commitment. In May 1980 he went to Africa, confident that the Wisconsin Steel struggle would still be there on his return.

Southern Africa

Beatrice's son Carl, whom Frank had helped raise, was teaching in Mozambique. In 1980, Frank visited and found that Mozambicans had a lot of hope for a better future. That was before warfare and drought devastated the country. Lumpkin met rank and file workers and leaders in the Mozambican wire mill and on cooperative farms. The best food was on a cooperative farm where farmers had retained the traditional African diet. In the cities the African diet had been replaced by expensive Portuguese food, much of it imported.

The revolutionary FRELIMO government of Mozambique had adopted socialism as its goal. After gaining freedom from Portugal, FRELIMO did not want their people to continue to be exploited by capitalists, European or African. If Mozambique had been an island, like Cuba, perhaps they could have carried out their goals. Instead, Mozambique bordered on Rhodesia and apartheid South Africa.

Years of destructive warfare, paid for by the apartheid governments, tore Mozambique apart. The newly independent government faced a tremendous task of rebuilding and education. With the end of apartheid in South Africa, peace has returned to Mozambique. FRELIMO won the elections in 1995 and plans to rebuild. Without Soviet aid, there are fewer choices for development. Still, as the Mozambicans say, "a luta continua." (The struggle continues).

Chris Hani

Many of the South African refugees that Frank met in Mozambique have returned home, some to leading posts in the Mandela government and the African National Congress (ANC). One of Lumpkin's proudest moments was the chance to host Chris Hani when he came to Chicago to speak at a *Peoples Weekly World* luncheon. Lumpkin told Hani that Wisconsin Steel workers, after picketing Harvester's World Headquarters on Michigan Avenue, always crossed the street to picket the apartheid South African Consulate. SOJ demanded that Harvester pull out of apartheid South Africa. Steel from South Africa was used to build the new Illinois State Office building while Illinois steel workers lost their jobs.

SOJ demands, "Out of South Africa," at Harvester- Navistar headquarters

Chris Hani may have been second only to Nelson Mandela in popularity in South Africa, especially among young people. He and Frank went jogging together early in the morning along the shore of Lake Michigan. As the military leader of the underground ANC armed forces, Hani kept in good shape. On his return to South Africa, Chris Hani was elected to lead the South African Communist Party. His assassination Easter Sunday morning in 1993 left a terrible void, not only in South Africa but in Chicago as well. Frank felt he had lost a friend as well as a fighter for freedom and socialism.

Cuba in the "Special Period"

Frank celebrated Thanksgiving of 1995 by visiting Cuba, again, with the U.S./Cuba Labor Exchange. He saw African-Cubans in leadership everywhere he went. That represented a victory against racism, one of the most important achievements of the Cuban Revolution. During the long years of U.S. domination of Cuba, racial discrimination had affected schools, jobs, and the professions. The Revolutionary government's fight against racism seemed highly successful, contributing to the unity that has helped Cuba survive.

Cuba was overcoming the hard problems of the "special period" by finding innovative solutions. The "special period" in Cuba resulted from tightening the U.S. blockade at the same time that Cuba lost its main trading partner, the Soviet Union. The blockade was a catastrophe that would have toppled a less stable system. Lumpkin visited the largest Cuban oil refinery and learned that oil imports had dropped from 30 million to 4 million units. Ordinarily, modern economies grind to a standstill without fuel. Somehow, Cuba kept going, partly by burning sugar cane bagasse (waste) instead of oil. The human cost was high, with the whole population on restricted diets and imported medicines in short supply. However, the Cubans proudly told Lumpkin, not one school had closed and not one person had to go without medical care.

The high level of Cuban education was also paying off. Frank visited the new Cuban Biotechnology Institute, which develops vaccines for Cuba and the world market. Their technical level seemed to be far out front compared to other Latin American and African countries and even some European countries. The people are similar in these countries—it's the systems that are different. Frank credited the Cuban achievements in education and health to their socialist system.

Chris Hani, martyred leader of the ANC and the SACP

US-Cuba Labor Exchange visits oil refinery workers, Havana, 1995

Senegal

Early in 1997, after the Wisconsin Steel workers received their settlement checks from Envirodyne, Frank agreed to accompany his wife on a week-long educational trip to West Africa. In Senegal, he saw the beauty of the people and the luxuries available to tourists. He also saw the desperation of the street vendors who must sell their small wares or starve. The police were African, and the government officials were African. Still, he asked a penetrating question: "Do Africans own the country? Who are the controlling interests?"

It did not take him long to find out that the World Bank was in control of the country even though the government officials were Senegalese. Just two years earlier, the World Bank had ordered Senegal and all of French-speaking West Africa to devalue their currency by half. Overnight, the purchasing power of wages was cut in half. The high point of the visit was a meeting with Senegalese trade unionists. They were quick to understand the importance of Frank's fight to save the steel workers' pensions. Senegalese trade unionists have a proud history. They are struggling to safeguard the rights they had won, including government workers' pensions.

Frank and museum curator at infamous "Slave House," Goree Island, 1977.

After Wisconsin Steel

When the Save Our Jobs Committee could finally say, "We've won as much justice as we can get in court," it was a relief. Lumpkin wanted to move on to broader issues. He did not see the Wisconsin Steel struggle as his life's work. Rather it was preparation for a broader struggle to end exploitation, to build a better society and a future for all the nation's children. After 17 years of the Wisconsin Steel struggle, and 81 years old, he knew he could use a long vacation. But he wasn't sure that he could spare the time. There was so much to do and so much to learn.

Frank never thought that he had all the answers. He said that, "History is interesting. But I want to know, 'What sparked these changes?' " His confidence in the future was based on his belief that there are answers, and that people could find the answers working together. One of his favorite sayings is, "The solution to a problem is inside the problem."

In Moscow with international labor representatives

From his visits to socialist countries, especially the Soviet Union and the German Democratic Republic, he saw that those workers had found some of the answers. There was no unemployment. There was very little crime. There was no institutionalized racism. The people were educated and they had health care. When the socialist governments lost power, the people lost all of these achievements. Were there lessons to learn from those experiences?

In the Soviet factories that Frank visited, he thought people were not working hard enough. He said, "If they're working for themselves, they should work harder." At Wisconsin Steel, the foreman did not have to constantly stand over the workers to make them work hard. The Wisconsin Steel workers knew that if they didn't work hard, they would be out on the street with nothing to eat. Frank's scarfing department was on a departmental bonus paid for tonnage above the quota. The bonus was divided equally among the workers. Because steel varies in the difficulty or ease of scarfing, the bonus was based on total tonnage finished by the whole department. There was almost no need for a foreman to hold a whip. Workers watched each other to make sure the bonus would be as high as possible. Was there a lesson in that? "Wisconsin Steel workers worked hard but ended up out on the street anyway," Frank said bitterly.

Frank's serious reading has become even more serious after the dissolution of the Soviet Union. The setback for socialism never shook his confidence in working people. The world seemed to turn upside down, but it made no visible impact on him. He felt he had to dig deeper to try to find more answers and regards the setback to socialism as temporary. He is too immersed in the day-to-day struggles in South Chicago, in the here and now, to be thrown off balance.

Lumpkin's support of the Communist Party has been based on their program of struggle to improve conditions of working people in the United States. He told an interviewer, "My whole life has been around the Communist Party. Everything good that has happened to me has been through the Party. Nothing can make me deny it."

Marxism a Science

For years Frank read everything he could find about the Soviet economy, its strengths and weaknesses. He knew there were "answers" and he wanted to understand them. Frank has a lot of respect for science and mathematics. He considered Marxism to be a science. It had to be studied, as he explained:

"To study Marxism is like studying mathematics. If you put down the right figures, you get the right answer. Which means that you have to add, subtract, multiply and divide. It has to be done to get the answer. You must use the best methods to get the right answer, to make things come out the best way. We will learn from all our experience and study. We will find many answers by putting numbers and things together and watching things happen."

High Tech Not the Enemy

Advances in technology were used as an excuse to layoff 40,000 workers at ATT in 1996. But Lumpkin never thought of technology as the enemy. He admired, even loved technology. It was never his wish to go back to a simpler past. He firmly believes that technology could and should be used to create a better life for workers. Under capitalism, high tech inflated corporation profits at the expense of working people. For Frank that was another reason to get rid of capitalism and replace it with socialism. Socialism, as he saw it, would mean more than public ownership of major industries, services and financial institutions. Under socialism, industries and services must be democratically operated by working people.

The Way It Could Be

Frank and his brother-in-law Al Ellis, a retired auto worker and the husband of his sister Jonnie, have often discussed how it "could be," the future of workers under socialism. Here is one exchange:

Al: "When I came to Borg Warner, they had 29 punch presses making clutch parts, with a worker on each press. When I left they had just 3 punch presses doing as much work as 29 used to, working side by side, with automatic feed. It took just one man to watch the presses. At first I thought it was good. But 65-70 men were laid off."

Frank. "That's productivity, eliminating labor. With a mule you can plow a row so wide. [Frank opened his arms.] With a tractor you can plow a row as big as this kitchen. They say Alabama used to breed the best mules. Maybe they're not breeding any more mules. You used to plow with one mule pulling one plow. Now you plow with one tractor pulling 10 plows. John Henry was a steel-making man. But John Henry couldn't beat the machine."

Al. "I can remember driving through Texas in 1963, going to Mexico. You saw about 300 pickers in this cotton field. I went back the same way in 1966. There was hardly anyone in the fields.

There was one man in a tractor pulling a trailer with a cotton picker machine. The cotton was flowing like a stream of water."
Frank. "Back up, give credit to the man who thought of it. Some of these changes in the steel mills, they're good. In fact they're inevitable. We used to chip steel with a hammer, work bent over all day. At the end of the shift you could hardly straighten your back. Then they brought in a machine, you don't even have to mark the cracks. A magnetic powder does that. You just sit down and operate the machine.

"You can't imagine how dangerous some of those jobs were. You'd have to move an eight-foot billet with a wrench. Sometimes, the wrench would slip and it could be a bad accident. To make a billet into a round, you'd have to move it with a wrench so it would go into the roll at an angle. Then the catcher would have to catch it and turn it around so it would hit another roll at the opposite angle. By the time you finished, the eight-foot billet would become a 50-foot long round. Now a machine turns the billet. It eliminates the catcher. What we need is four six-hour shifts instead of three eight-hour shifts at the same pay. That would put more people to work. Steel workers now are working 12 hours a day, getting overtime. That's going backwards. "

Al: "You think you could get the 6-hour day under capitalism?"
Frank: "Yes, I think so. It will be a struggle, but we will get it. We need a committee. A lot of guys have ideas but don't know how to put it in words. Unity. That's the main lesson I hope the Wisconsin Steel workers learned from Save Our Jobs. When workers unite they can win.

"I told Geoghegan, I'm as interested in the struggle as in winning the money. I'm interested in workers learning their strength, not just someone being a 'smart Alec.' The money ain't the whole thing. The fight isn't just for money. It's for justice for working people. It's not simple to separate the two.

"There is a solution to the problems and together we can find it. It is not always easy, but it is possible. We can do it. I have proof because we have done it. We have just won a settlement with Envirodyne, a real tough company with a lot of money but not willing to pay workers what they know they owe them. They made us suffer for 17 long hard years, and you can't imagine what a time we had just surviving this ordeal. We did not all survive.

But the ones who did came out with a feeling of victory which can raise the hopes and courage to fight on, and help people in need like we were, and give hope to the many who have lost it. We have always said that we can win and we proved it."

Al: "As long as you have capitalism, they can take away anything you win. The eight-hour day, the six-hour day. Capitalism wants maximum profits. Socialism means maximum satisfaction for working people. Take the yoke off the workers' neck. Let them earn a living—maintain a decent standard of living. There's plenty of work that needs doing. Clean up the lake. Clean up the streets and the alleys. Fix the bridges. Shovel the snow off the tracks. Grow all the food you can. There's plenty of hungry people here, and all over the world. But what about you Frank? Do you ever get tired and feel like quitting?"

Frank: "I joined the Young Communist League because they were helping people get back in their house after evictions. Study Marxism and you will understand that there's no way out under capitalism. A mother has to give birth to a child. The Communists must make it easier to happen. The first thing workers have to do is unite. We can't let racism, or sexism divide us. We learned that at Wisconsin Steel.

"Capitalism cannot solve the problem. It's going to get worse as production changes with the new science and technology. A road to South Chicago can be made by one guy in half a day. It used to take a gang of men a week. There is no future for the kids under this system.

"We are fighting for socialism, a system that the workers control. Then we can use high tech to help people instead of laying them off. With high tech we can cut the hours and raise the pay. There are many workers seeking a program for action. They are ready to fight back. Every time they win, they learn their strength. When you go on strike everything stops. Nothing can run without the workers. Once we unite, we can get rid of capitalism.

"Back to your question, Why didn't I get tired and quit fighting? I'll give some credit to people you don't know. My mother and father could have quit. They could have said we can't feed 10 children. But they didn't quit. Paul Robeson didn't quit at Peekskill. There is no other way. It's fight or die! It takes a fight to win!"

NOTES

1. Geoghegan, Thomas. 1991. *Which Side Are You On? Trying to be for labor when it's flat on its back.* New York: Farrar, Straus & Giroux, 84.
2. Bensman, David and Roberta Lynch. 1987. *Rusted Dreams.* New York: McGraw Hill, 192.
3. John F. Wasik. 1984. " Waiting for the Brimstone." *The Progressive.* March, 1984, 28-30.
4. Lumpkin, Katharine Du Pre. 1991, 1946. *The Making of a Southerner.* Athens, GA: University of Georgia.
5. Debo, Angie. 1970, 1989. *A History of the Indians of the United States.* Norman OK: University of Oklahoma Press, 88.
6. Randall, Jo Rider. 1980. Washington, *Georgia after 200 years.* Washington, GA: Wilkes Publishing.
7. Ibid. From a poem by Robert S. Armour, fly leaf.
8. Foner, Eric. 1988. *Reconstruction.* New York: Harper & Row, 70, 71. Promise attributed to General William T. Sherman. His Field Order No. 15 settled 40,000 freedmen on coastal land and the Sea Islands. Each family received 40 acres; mules were provided by the army.
9. Shields, Art. 1927. "Fight to Free Negroes Held as Peons in South." *Daily Worker,* June 4, 1927.
10. Gannon, Michael. 1993. *Florida, a Short History.* Gainesville, FL: University of Florida Press, 85-86.
11. Howard, Walter T. 1995. *Lynchings, Extralegal Violence in Florida during the 1930's.* Selingsgrove, PA: Susquehanna Univ. Press, 15, 18.
12. White, Walter. 1921. "Election Day in Florida." *The Crisis* 21 (3): January, 1921, 106-109.
13. Ibid.
14. Gannon, Michael. 1993. 87-88.
15. Jahoda, Gloria. 1976. *Florida, A Bicentennial History.* New York: Norton, 107.
16. "America Still Home of Child Labor." *Daily Worker,* May 15, 1927.
17. Perkins, Frances. 1946. *The Roosevelt I Knew.* New York: Viking Press, 250.
18. Ibid., 255.
19. Buhite, Russell D. & David W. Levey, eds. 1992. *FDR's Fireside Chats.* Norman, OK: University of Oklahoma Press, 120.
20. Lumpkin, Frank. 1992. Interview recorded by Studs Terkel in *Race.* New York: New Press, 88-92. Reprinted in *the Nation,* April 6, 1992.
21. Jones, Maxine D. 1995. "No Longer Denied: Black Women in Florida, 1920-1950." in *The African American Heritage of Florida.* Ed. David R. Colburn and James L. Landers. Gainesville, FL: University Press of Florida, 248.

22. Tebeau, Charlton W. 1971. *A History of Florida*. Coral Gables, FL: University of Miami, 402-403.

23. Ibid. 403.

24. Gannon, Michael. 1993. 97.

25. Ingalls, Robert P. 1988. *Urban Vigilantes in the New South*. University Of Tennessee, 150.

26. Ibid. 182-183.

27. Ibid. 200-201.

28. Argrett, Leroy. 1991. *History of Black Orlando*. Orlando, FL: 46.

29. White, Morgan, Jr. 1985. *The Black Heritage Book of Trivia*. Boston: Quinlan Press, 67, 159. Jackie Robinson signed with a major league farm team, The Montreal Royals in 1945. From the Royals, Robinson moved up to the Brooklyn Dodgers.

30. *Sentinel Star*. March 18, 1973. Orlando, FL, 7-F.

31. Davis, Benjamin J. 1942. "The Communist Party on Black Liberation and the War." Originally "Letter to the Editor" *New York Age*, July 11, 1942. Reprinted in *Highlights of a Fighting History, 60 Years of the Communist Party USA.*, Philip Bart ed. New York: International Publishers, 201, 202.

32. Ibid. Quotation from: Douglass, Frederick. 1941 reprint. *Life and Times of Frederick Douglass:* An Autobiography. New York: Pathway Press, 1941, 374.

33. Fred Briehl operated a popular farm-resort in the Berkshire Mountains, north of New York City. The Briehls made frequent contributions to progressive causes.

34. E-mail to author, January 24, 1998.

35. MacDougall, Curtis D. 1965. *Gideon's Army*. New York: Marzani & Munsell, 25. MacDougall quotes from article by Robert R. Young in the *Saturday Review of Literature*, March 4, 1947.

36. Larrowe, Charles P. 1972. *Harry Bridges, The Rise and Fall of Radical Labor*. New York: Lawrence Hill, 291.

37. Ibid.

38. Smith, Ferdinand C. 1947. "Report of the National Secretary to the Sixth Convention of the National Maritime Union, September, 1947." Reprinted in *Highlights of a Fighting History, 60 Years of the Communist Party USA.*, 249-253.

39. Boyer, Richard O. and Herbert M. Morais. 1965. *Labor's Untold Story*. Pittsburgh: United Electrical, Radio and Machine Workers, 344.

40. Ibid. 364.

41. Ibid. 347.

42. Brown, Lloyd L. 1997. *The Young Robeson, On my journey now*. Boulder, CO: Westview Press, 3. "Tallest tree in the forest," an

expression widely used in the African American Community to describe Paul Robeson, has been credited to Mary McLeod Bethune, the noted scholar.

43. *Daily Worker*, November 4, 1948. Reprinted 1979 in *Highlights of a Fighting History, 60 Years of the Communist Party USA*. Philip Bart ed. New York: International Publishers, 260-261.

44. *The Worker*. August 7, 1949. Upstate edition, page 2.

45. Hine, Darlene Clark. 1998, orig. 1965. In *Paul Robeson, the Great Forerunner*. Editors of *Freedomways*. New York: International Publishers, 143.

46. Grossman, Victor. *Weg über die Grenze*. Published in the German Democratic Republic 3 editions. English translation by Grossman, publication pending.

47. Perlo, Victor. 1988. *Super Profits and Crises*. New York: International Publishers, 75.

48. *Highlights of a Fighting History, 60 Years of the Communist Party USA*. 1979. Philip Bart ed. New York: International Publishers, 282. Also, Boyer, Richard O. & Herbert M. Morais. 1955. Labor's Untold Story. Pittsburgh: United Electrical, Radio and Machine Workers, 367-368.

49. McIntyre, James R. 1950. *The History of Wisconsin Steel Works of the International Harvester Company*. Introduction by R. A. Lindgren, general superintendent Wisconsin Steel Works, International Harvester Co. Chicago: International Harvester.

50. Ibid. 8.

51. Ibid. 11.

52. Foster, William Z. 1947, 1970. *American Trade Unionism*. New York: International Publishers, 43.

53. Ozanne, Robert. 1967. *A Century of Labor-Management Relations at McCormick and International Harvester*. Madison: University of Wisconsin, 133-134.

54. Hoffman, Abraham. 1974. *Unwanted Mexican Americans in the Great Depression*. Tucson: University of Arizona Press, 120. "The Taylor study revealed that a total of over 32,000 Mexicans departed from Illinois, Michigan, Indiana and Ohio, between 1930 and 1932."

55. McIntyre. *History of Wisconsin Steel*. 62.

56. Matles, James J. & James Higgins. 1974. *Them and Us*. Englewood Cliffs, NJ: Prentice Hall, 196-199.

57. The Taft-Hartley law required non-Communist affidavits of local union officers but the law did not extend to stewards and delegates.

58. Fitch, John A. 1989 1910. *The Steel Workers.* Originally published by Russell Sage Foundation, 1910. Reprint Pittsburgh: University of Pittsburgh Press, 3.

59. Farr, Trudy Pax. 1988. In *Hard-Hatted Women.* Ed. Molly Martin. Seattle: Seal Press, 55-56. The following description by Farr also applies to chippers and scarfers at Wisconsin Steel: "Sparks, (in fact small droplets of hot steel) ... shower down when oxygen, flame and air meet molten steel. Still those sparks find their way down my shirt front, into my gloves. At first I stop to inspect each small burn, but before long I do as the seasoned burners do: simply shake the spark out of my glove the best I can, hold my shirt away from my body and let it tumble down, and continue on the job."

60. Foster, William Z. 1954. *The Negro People in American History.* New York: International Publishers, 439.

61. Davis, Horace B. 1933. *Labor and Steel.* New York: International Publishers, 33.

62. Hoffman, Abraham. 1974. *Unwanted Mexican Americans in the Great Depression.* Tucson: University of Arizona Press, 120. "The Taylor study revealed that a total of over 32,000 Mexicans departed from Illinois, Michigan, Indiana and Ohio, between 1930 and 1932."

63. Videotaped interview of Martinez daughters by South Chicago Historical Commission. Commission is located in Field House, Calumet Park, Chicago. Open Thursday afternoons.

64. Brown, Frank London. 1959. *Trumbull Park* .Chicago: Regnery. Brown dedicates his book to the tenants of Trumbull Park.

65. Strickland, Arvarh and Reich, Jerome. 1974. *The Black American Experience.* New York: Harcourt, Brace and Jovanovich, p 133.

66. Kornblum, William. 1974. *Blue Collar Community.* Chicago: University of Chicago Press, 82.

67. Terkel, Studs. 1992, *Race.* New York: New Press, 88-92. Reprinted as "I'm Saying Racism is Unnatural," *the Nation,* April 6, 1992, 103.

68. Grossman, Victor. See note 46.

69. Ruth Norrick, *Labor Today.* Jan. 1983. Also see Hopkins, Harry. 1936. *Spending to Save – the Complete Story of Relief.* New York: Norton, and Perkins, Frances. 1946. *The Roosevelt I Knew.* New York: Viking.

70. Zinn, Howard. *Peoples History of the United States.* New York: Harper Perennial, 1990, 455.

71. Engleman, Paul. *"Night of the Hunters."* Chicago, November 1994, 101.

72. Ibid. 141.

73. Ibid. 143.

74. Sampson, Anthony. 1974. *The Sovereign State of ITT.* Greenwich, CT: Fawcett, 279-282.
75. Geoghegan. *Which Side Are You On?* 93-94. Also see *Chicago Sun-Times,* March 29, 1980, 58.
76. *Save the Wisconsin Steel Workers!* 1981. Chicago: Wisconsin Steel workers Save Our Jobs Committee.
77. Constantine, Peggy. 1981. "Steel workers get a Thompson visit." *Chicago Sun-Times,* January 28, 1981, 24.
78. Recorded discussion in the Save Our Jobs office, 1981.
79. Recorded in Save Our Jobs office, 1981. Name changed for privacy.
80. Discussion in the Lumpkin home, 1981.
81. Gleason, Bill. 1982. "Steelyard Blues." *Chicago Tribune.* June 13, 1982, Magazine section, 21.
82. *Daily Calumet,* August 29, 1980.
83. Longworth, Richard C. 1995. "Man of Steel." *Chicago Tribune.* May 31, 1995, Tempo section, 1,2.
84. *Daily Calumet.* April 24, 1980, 1
85. La Botz, Dan. 1980. "Wisconsin Steel workers in Last Chance March." In the *Chicago Defender,* August 5, 1980, 1.
86. Geoghegan. *Which Side Are You On?* 92.
87. Clark, Gordon L. 1990. "Piercing the Corporate Veil: The Closure of Wisconsin Steel in South Chicago." In Regional Studies, 24, 410. Originally presented to the Conference on Industrial Restructuring, University of Melbourne, Parkville, Australia, November 17-18, 1989.
88. Geoghegan. Which Side Are You On? 93.
89. Ibid. 96.
90. Ibid. 99.
91. Hardy, Thomas. 1983. "Hanging tough in tough times." *Chicago Tribune,* April 10, 1983.
92. *Chicago Defender,* Oct. 20, 1982.
93. Although the newspaper gave the complete name, the name is abbreviated here to spare the feelings of the family.
94. *Daily Calumet.* Sept. 2, 1982.
95. *Daily Calumet.* November 25, 1982.
96. Frank Lumpkin's motto, "Always Bring a Crowd," was first recorded by Thomas Geoghegan in *Which Side Are You On?* 99.
97. *Le Monde.* July 7, 1983. "Congres des chomeurs americans a Chicago," le Soleil, 14.
98. Ranney, David C., Joe Persky and Susan Rosenblum. August 10, 1983. Chicago: Center for Urban Economic Development, University of Illinois at Chicago. *Unemployed Steel Workers in Chicago: A Cost*

Analysis, 2. Study made for SOJ. These costs for 1979-1983 include: $105 million for unemployment compensation to steel workers and $25 million for other area workers, $33 million food stamps, tax loss $444 million, for a total of $607 million. Cost to government for welfare and Medicaid for 27,600 laid off in steel and allied industry not included.

99. Roderick, David M. "Two Thirds Are Always Awake," speech at the Chicago Committee of the Chicago Council on Foreign Relations, February 15, 1989. Pittsburgh, PA: USX Corporation Public Affairs Department, 5.

100. Sadlowski, Edward A. 1997. *Union Labor News.* January. Madison: South Central Federation of Labor.

101. Ibid.

102. Longworth, Richard C. 1995. "Man of Steel." *Chicago Tribune.* May 31, 1995, Tempo section, 1,2.

103. Geoghegan. *Which Side Are You On?* 84.

104. Terkel, Studs. 1992. *Race.* New York: the New Press, 88-92. Also see 1988. *Great Divide, Second Thoughts on the American Dream.* New York: Pantheon, 185-189.

105. McMahon, Margot. 1988. *Just Plain Hard Working.* Published for the sculpture exhibit by Margot McMahon which includes a bust of Frank Lumpkin. In 1992, the documentary inspired by the exhibit won a National Media Owl Award in the Television Non-Fiction category.

106. Penn, Mary Sue. March 31, 1985. "Washington blasts Reagan budget." *The Times,* formerly *the Hammond Times.*

107. Fremon, David K. 1988. *Chicago Politics, Ward by Ward.* Bloomington, IN: Indiana University Press, 19.

108. Ibid. 20.

109. Citizens Committee to Elect Frank Lumpkin. 1988. *Elect Frank Lumpkin State Rep. 25th District Independent Progressive.*

110. Several years later Fitko died; Schwartz found work at reduced pay.

111. Newman, M. W. 1986. "Broken Hearts of Steel." *Chicago,* September 1986, 189.

112. Hearing Before the Subcommittee on Employment Opportunities of the Committee on Education and Labor House of Representatives Ninety-Ninth Congress First Session on H.R. 1398. 1985. Washington: U. S. Government Printing Office Serial 99-26, 94-6.

113. "The Department of Transportation estimates that 40 percent of these highways and half the nation's 578,000 bridges are in need of repair or improvement. *The Universal Almanac.* 1993. Kansas City, MO: Andrews and McKeel, 269.

114. Putterman, Julie S. *1985. Chicago Steel Workers: The Cost of Unemployment.* Chicago: Steel Workers Research Project, 60-64.

Index